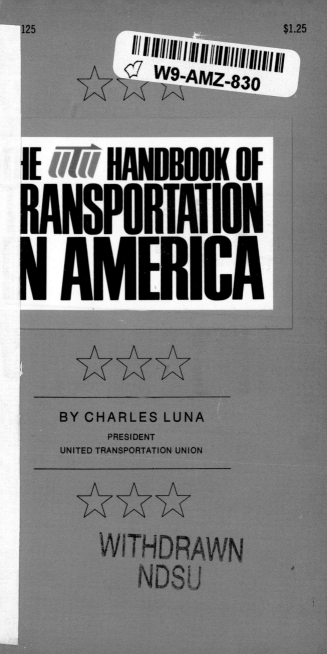

THE *UTU* HANDBOOK OF TRANSPORTATION IN AMERICA

☆☆☆

BY CHARLES LUNA

PRESIDENT
UNITED TRANSPORTATION UNION

☆☆☆

THE *UTU* HANDBOOK OF TRANSPORTATION IN AMERICA

BY CHARLES LUNA

PRESIDENT OF
UNITED TRANSPORTATION UNION

POPULAR LIBRARY • NEW YORK

CONTENTS

GENERAL TRANSPORTATION STUDY

GOVERNMENT ROLE IN TRANSPORTATION

GENERAL
TRANSPORTATION
STUDY

INTRODUCTION

Transportation has always been the lifeline of our nation. Fixed-line transportation, such as rail and water, spurred the development of great urban centers. Later, automobiles added the flexibility that helped transform the old city into today's sprawling metropolis.

Ironically, the progress and growth engendered by improved transportation have created vast problems for current and future transportation. Employment opportunities are now scattered over the entire metropolitan area so that work-oriented travel no longer fits a neat pattern to and from the central business district. The automobile has permitted a diffusion of metropolitan populations which defies the capabilities of traditional mass-transit facilities. Suburban trips unrelated to work are even more diverse in origin and destination. Mass transit, in its present state, cannot feasibly move the tremendous and ever-increasing metropolitan population.

Thus, the urban/suburban traveler has become a slave to the only available mode suitable to his demands—the automobile. The burgeoning congestion of highway traffic compounds safety menaces beyond imagination. Providing adequate highways now would not only involve staggering outlays of funds, but would actually jeopardize urban land they are meant to serve.

We must, therefore, seek new solutions and implement available ones as soon as possible. Planners speak of a "balanced system" as the practical alternative, an arrangement combining aspects of both public mass transportation and private automotive travel. Public mass transit, they hold, can still serve the needs of many who now ride autos to and from the central business district—commuters who must be attracted to mass transit if present congestion is to be eliminated.

Yet, to entice a significant number of riders from their autos, mass transit must quickly reverse its present deterioration. New systems using parking facilities, bus-feeder routes, and rail rapid-transit might provide the integrated network capable of efficiently serving large areas. Creative technological improvements are already available, but only by implementing them can mass transit assume a substantial burden of metropolitan travel.

Intercity transportation also has changed drastically since the end of World War II. Air transport has become the largest common carrier of passengers. Rail travel, once the top common passenger-carrier, is now third, behind both air and bus travel, with only water travel beneath it. Here again, the automobile dominates, accounting for the largest portion of all intercity movement.

Recently, the role of railroads in the intercity passenger field has attracted considerable attention. National policymakers and the public as a whole seem unwilling to let railroads simply abandon passenger service. But the railroads continue to liquidate passenger runs, and service on many surviving lines is generally deplorable. Even so, the prospects for improvement are encouraging since the need increases for high-speed ground transportation as a contributing component of a coordinated system. Congress expressed a recognition of this need when in 1970 it created the National Railroad Passenger Corporation (Railpax), a semipublic corporation which will organize and operate what it considers an essential intercity rail passenger network.

CHAPTER 1

A HISTORICAL OVERVIEW

The continental United States, large and diversified, stretches 3,000 miles from the Atlantic to the Pacific and 1,500 miles from the Gulf of Mexico to the Canadian border, a total of three million square miles. Within that area, a depth and variety of natural resources, and many different climates and land features came to bear on the development of the nation's transportation.

Technology also played a key role, determining not only the types of goods to be transported, but also the means by which they could be moved. The pioneers of American transportation applied their skills to unifying the vast and varied terrain of the new nation. Transportation habits changed with changing periods in the nation's growth and advancing technology. The military's need for fast, efficient transport of goods also spurred development of certain transport alternatives which some believed were in the best interests of national defense. Commercial advertising also has significantly influenced the type of transport service which the public has demanded. One after another, modes have dominated periods in transportation history, each ultimately giving way to something faster, cheaper, or more glamorous. The federal government and several state governments sometimes entered the transportation scene both to support old modes and encourage new ones.

The relationship between investment by the public sector and investment by the private sector has varied throughout our history. In the early days, many facilities (port improvements, canals, and post roads) were provided directly by the government. There were later instances (such as the introduction of railroads) when private investors took the initial step. Only after this initial commitment had been made did the government step in to aid the growth and development of the project.

Water Transportation

Water was the primary avenue of travel in the Colonial and early national periods. Colonies on the Atlantic Seaboard owned many natural harbors, bays, and river inlets. While land transportation was expensive and time-consuming, the problems of moving goods and people by water were relatively simple. Shipbuilding was a traditional and honored craft, and raw material was abundant in the sprawling woodlands of the New World. Furthermore, the mercantilist system of Great Britain encouraged both shipbuilding and ocean commerce; the British Navigation Acts forced the Colonies to channel their raw materials back to the mother country and to transport English-manufactured goods back home.

Although limited almost wholly to the Atlantic seacoast and to the navigable bays and inlets, early water transport was paramount in the development of commerce in the Colonies and the expansion of both commerce and manufacturing in the national period. Passengers traveled primarily by water at this time, although freight was by far the more important cargo. (Often a traveler would board a ship without any idea of how long his journey would last, since the sea merchants made random stops along the way, buying and selling freight.)

Before 1800, sailing vessels, flatboats, and barges were the major vehicles for water transportation. The development of the steamship represented the first great technological breakthrough. In 1786, John Fitch successfully operated a steamship on the Delaware River. By 1790, Fitch was able to provide service regularly between Philadelphia and Trenton on the Delaware. A more efficient service was provided in 1807 when Robert Fulton sailed his steamship from New York to Albany, a 150-mile journey up the Hudson River, in 32 ½ hours.[1]

This first practical application of steam power to water transportation sparked the rapid development of inland steamboat travel. So great was the impact of this advance that steamboat travel became the leading mode of transportation in the United States and maintained its hegemony until after the Civil War.[2]

Another technological development swelled the importance of water transportation in the early nineteenth century—the construction of an extensive system of canals. New York's Governor, DeWitt Clinton, initiated the trend with the completion of the Erie Canal in 1825, connecting Lake Erie with the Hudson River at Albany. The project's success spurred construction of a vast canal system in Pennsylvania, Massachusetts, Maryland, Virginia, Ohio, Indiana, and Michigan. By 1850, this system covered some 4,460 miles and provided relatively fast transportation at far lower cost than that of most land carriers.[3]

Railroad Transportation

When the state of Maryland chartered the Baltimore and Ohio Railroad in 1827, the United States entered an era of feverish railroad construction. The B&O began making regular runs in 1830, the year traditionally assigned as the beginning of America's railroad era.

During the first decade of rail development, workers laid more than 2,800 miles of track[4] primarily in experimental patterns and routes.[5] The earliest lines were built to serve as feeders to waterways and radiated outward from important centers of water transportation. From 1850 to 1900, railroads in the United States expanded and improved tremendously. From approximately 9,000 miles of track in 1850, the railroads built up to 30,600 in the decade that followed. So well developed were the northeastern routes in 1860 that their basic pattern remains unchanged.[6]

In 1869, Omaha, Nebraska, was linked by rail with the cities of Sacramento and San Francisco, California. The completion of this 1,800-mile link made possible the first U.S. transcontinental railroad service. Between 1870 and 1890, track mileage more than tripled to 163,000. The interlacing of routes was so complete that a national-rail map of 1890 shows little divergence from today's pattern of railroad lines.[7]

Crucial to this rapid development were land grants given the railroads by the federal government. Illinois Senator Stephen Douglas initiated this policy to attract private capital into railroad construction in his home state, and to increase the value of land owned by the government. In 1850, Congress granted more than 2½ million acres of land to the state of Illinois, which then granted the land to the Illinois Central Railroad.[8] Federal policy changed in 1862. The new policy reflected a change in the attitude of the government. Instead of providing land for a specific rail development in one state, it decided to tie together the whole nation with a transcontinental network.

To this end, the federal government gave away 131 million acres of the public domain. Each parcel consisted of a strip of right-of-way, plus alternating six-mile sections of land on each side. In return, the railroads gave the government a 20 percent rate-reduction on mail delivery and a 50 percent rate-reduction on all other freight and passenger services.[9]

Many other factors contributed to the tremendous railroad expansion during this period. Local and state governments provided benefits to lure railroad construction into their territories. Free land, tax exemptions, guarantee of bonds, and public subscription of securities were important incentives.

Foreign investment also helped stimulate the American rail boom. Rail securities raised more than $2 billion in Europe in the 1800s, and the total European investment in American railroad stocks and bonds amounted to more than $3 billion by the end of the century.[10] All of these factors contributed to an unprecedented speculative fever, uninhibited by business scruples or public control.

A final contributor to the great railroad expansion was a series of federal government loans to six western railroads, capitalized by more than $64 million in bonds. These loans were repaid with a 6 percent annual assessment, and by 1899, nearly $168 million was returned to the government.[11]

The railroad added great new dimensions to American life. Their far-reaching tracks opened uncharted areas to settlement, as well as lines of communication essential to political unity. New rail routes conquered climate and terrain which had limited the expansion of water transportation. Finally, railroad patterns drew clusters of population into certain areas, and this, in turn, led to the growth of large and important cities.

Road Transportation

Road development in the United States began slowly. Colonial roads were little more than extensions of primitive Indian trails. The need for mail delivery brought about the first major development of roads, especially in areas where water transportation was not readily available. But the "pot roads" of the 1700s were limited to the Eastern Seaboard, where they connected the major cities.

In the 1790s, private enterprises began to construct improved roadways. In 1794, the Philadelphia and Lancaster Company built the first and most famous of these "turnpikes," so-called because of a system of access and exit whereby private owners controlled traffic and collected tolls. The 62-mile road between Philadelphia and Lancaster cost $500,000[12] and signaled the beginning of the construction of a turnpike network east of the Mississippi with considerable assistance from state and local governments.

Pressure for more roadway improvements came from three major groups. The railroads wanted more land transportation to move goods locally from production points to the railroad depots. Farmers needed improved mobility and access to markets and railheads. Cyclists saw the condition of the nation's roads as a barrier to their increasingly popular sport; they were joined in their desire for better roads by the cycle equipment manufacturers.

The demand for new and improved roads swelled in the 1890s and early 1900s with the advent of the internal combustion engine and the birth of an automobile industry. After World War I, the automobile became especially significant in the nation's transportation system; the Ford Motor Company produced more than a million cars in 1920.[13]

The desires of the road lobbyists were soon realized. By 1915, forty-five states had highway aid laws, forty had established state highway departments, and twenty-four had state highway systems.[14] But the ownership, maintenance, and administration of the vast majority of highway miles were still primarily in local hands. The resulting development was chaotic.

Federal grants-in-aid for road development started with the Federal Aid Road Act of 1916. Each state seeking a grant was required to establish a state highway department, as well as meet federal standards for road construction and management. Federal support was limited to the improvement of rural post roads and had to be matched, dollar for dollar, by state funds. In addition, a state could receive no federal funds for the cost of bridges more than twenty feet in length, and could receive only $10,000 in federal funds per mile of new construction.

The federal government then continued to expand its commitments to improve and enlarge the nation's road facilities. Congress passed a series of acts that provided varying types and degrees of federal aid, primarily for new highway construction but not for highway maintenance. For example, in 1921, Congress authorized the use of federal funds for rural highways within a designated Federal-Aid Primary System. States were free to designate their portion of the Primary System, but could not designate any more than 7 percent of the total mileage of rural roads which then existed in their states.

Although the 7 percent ceiling was eventually raised, an even more significant milestone was the passage of the 1944 Federal Aid Highway Act. This marked the first significant federal aid for urban highways. The Federal-Aid Primary System was extended to include the portions of its roads which passed through urban communities. The legislation also created another system of highways called the Federal-Aid Secondary System consisting of "principal secondary and feeder roads, including farm-to-market roads, rural free delivery mail, and public-school bus routes." The legislation also authorized federal funds for selected highways in urban areas which had populations of over five thousand. The Bureau of Public Roads, in cooperation with state highway officials, was directed by the legislation to designate a "National System of Interstate Highways" which would not exceed a total of forty thousand miles. The Interstate Highway System was to be so "located as to connect by routes, as direct as practicable, the principal metropolitan areas, cities, and industrial centers to serve the national defense and to connect at suitable border points with routes of continental importance in the Dominion of Canada and the Republic of Mexico." Almost all of the routes designated as part of the Interstate Highway System were already part of either the Federal-Aid Primary System or the Federal-Aid Secondary System.[15]

An accelerated policy of federal aid emerged with the Federal Highway Act of 1956, when the government assumed 90 percent of highway construction costs for any portion of the Interstate Highway System. This legislation authorized the expenditure of $46 billion for a period of thirteen years, more than half designated for construction of the Interstate Highway System. By December 1969, 29,640 miles of the Interstate Highway System had been opened to the public; 4,782 miles were still under construction; and 6,299 miles of right-of-way were in the process of being purchased.

The boom in road building reflected the increasing dominance of motor travel. Between 1920 and 1930, Americans took to the highways with a vengeance. Of the nearly 200 billion intercity passenger miles logged during that period, private autos and buses accounted for 85 percent.[16]

Air Transportation

The military aircraft industry of World War I proved to be the cradle of commercial aviation in many countries. The infant American commercial airlines bought surplus government-developed airplanes and hired government-trained pilots at the end of the war to launch the nation's newest mode of transportation.[17]

The Kelly Act of 1925 aided the development of the airline industry by authorizing the U.S. Post Office to contract with private air-transport companies for mail service. The Kelly Act also stimulated air-passenger service by requiring that companies entering these contracts also provide passenger facilities.

Just one year after the passage of the Kelly Act, Congress again recognized the growing needs of the airlines and passed the Air Commerce Act of 1926, which empowered the Secretary of Commerce to develop airway facilities for general use. Specifically, the Secretary would designate and establish civil airways and all auxiliary navigation facilities, except airports themselves. This airport restriction was eventually removed by the Civil Aeronautics Act of 1938, which paved the way for the Federal Airport Act of 1946. The $520 million authorized in the 1946 legislation was allocated to the nation's largest airports for improved facilities. To qualify for this aid, which could total half of all costs, an airport had to be included in the national airport plan of the Civil Aeronautics Administration, predecessor of the Federal Aviation Agency.[18]

The military requirements of World War II called for improved airplane designs, and private industry again reaped the benefits of government-financed technological development. More pilots were trained than in any previous year. But perhaps most important was the wide exposure of civilian and military personnel to air travel, which set the stage for a booming postwar air-passenger market. New airline carriers emerged to satisfy the demand. Air transportation grew from relative obscurity to the nation's leading common intercity passenger-carrier by the late 1950s, and the addition of jet propulsion strengthened its predominance. The amount of traffic in air freight has also grown with new technological developments in airplane design and propulsion, although planes still carry relatively little freight.

The beginning of the twentieth century saw renewed attention focused on the nation's waterways. This was partly a result of increasing public concern with the conservation of natural resources and dissatisfaction with many railroad practices. Even nostalgia for the "good old days" of the Mississippi steamboat attracted support for improved water transportation.

The Great Lakes region reaped important benefits. A series of canals and locks had been constructed by 1835 to join the five lakes into an all-water route, with the opening of the locks at Sault Sainte Marie in 1855 as the final act in the construction of the inland waterway. The opening of the Saint Lawrence Seaway, completed in 1959, and the concomitant deepening of the lake channels increased opportunities for lake traffic. All in all, the Great Lakes became an integral part of the Atlantic shipping area, and began to receive oceangoing vessels that had been forced to end their voyages at the Atlantic Coast.

Other inland waterways were improved over the same period. The conversion of the old Erie Canal into the New York Barge Canal in the early 1900s was a $100-million project. The federal government's role swelled even more in 1907, when President Theodore Roosevelt appointed the Inland Waterways Commission to prepare a series of plans and proposals for the improvement of inland water transportation. The extent of such federal aid shows up in the Hoover Commission's estimate that the government spent more than $1.5 billion in inland water transportation between 1824 and 1954.[19]

Unfortunately, projects such as the Saint Lawrence Seaway have not been as effective as anticipated, primarily because of the new containerization method of moving goods. This process entails the shipment of products in uniformed, sealed, and reliable containers which are attached to trucking cabins or placed on flatbed railroad cars and carried to port. Once on a dock, the containers are lifted by modern equipment, positioned in specially designed hulls of ships, and transported to the countries of their destination.

The problem is that the containership is often so massive that inland water channels like the Saint Lawrence Seaway, which were built for smaller vessels, cannot handle them efficiently. Midwest shippers, therefore, find it cheaper to transport goods by rail or truck to the East Coast and, from there, to their European destination, rather than to use the Saint Lawrence Seaway.

The Seaway has thus sunk deep into debt. In its first ten years of operation, the 345.1 million tons actually handled was 58.1 million tons below the projected volume of 403 million.[20] In the end, financial help from the federal government may serve as the Seaway's last hope.

Despite problems, the growth of water transportation has continued. In 1968, various types of water transport carried 15 percent of the nation's freight on 25,260 miles of usable inland channels, about 287 billion ton-miles.[21] With a cost advantage over railroads and trucks, barges are carrying more and more material ordered by oil and chemical companies.

Improvements in America's inland waterways have also led to greater domestic utilization of seacoast water facilities. The waterways and seacoast water facilities have together formed a primary means of American transportation.

Pipeline Transportation

The first major transport-pipeline in the United States was constructed in 1879 from oil fields in Titusville, Pennsylvania, to the Reading Railroad lines 110 miles away. Today, the petroleum pipeline complex consists of 210,000 miles of trunk and gathering lines. No point in the United States is ever more than two hundred miles from a pipeline route.

Pipelines are a highly specialized form of transportation consisting of one-way carriage, primarily of products which can move in liquid form. The discovery of substantial petroleum fields in the United States established a need for such service, and the demand for it has increased greatly throughout the twentieth century. Since 1958, pipelines have ranked third behind railroads and motor carriers in the movement of domestic freight. Pipelines have carried as much as 21 percent of the total U.S. freight traffic in one year.

Certain technological advances may result in the increased importance of pipeline transportation. Pipeline capacity has been greatly enhanced by the construction of lines with a diameter of

13

up to forty inches—more than six to eight times larger than the standard size. During the past few years, there has been a shift from construction of pipelines which move crude oil to lines which are capable of moving refined petroleum products. Experiments are also being conducted to perfect the technique of slurry pipelining, i.e., the movement in a pipeline of a mixture of insoluble substances along with a liquid. Thus far, gilsonite, limestone, and sulphur have been moved by this technique.

Finally, research work is now in progress to develop methods of moving solid- or dry-bulk commodities in containers through pipelines. Various shapes and sizes for the containers have been tested. Soft plastic bags, hollow-steel or aluminum cylinders, and canisters have all been tested as possible containers. One pipeline association is proceeding with a five-year, $4.75-million program to discover commercial methods of moving containers in pipelines.[22]

Urban Transportation

When the first horse-drawn omnibus began operations in New York City in 1830, the United States entered its era of urban transportation. By 1835, more than a hundred such vehicles wove their way through the streets of New York and, within two decades, New Yorkers were suffering the earliest forms of modern traffic congestion. Established routes had grown out of the increased popularity of the omnibus and, by 1885, nearly six hundred vehicles were licensed to operate over twenty-seven different routes in New York City.[23]

The omnibus led to the development of the horsecar, the first urban-transit vehicle to make a major impact on American cities.[24] Whereas the omnibus rode directly over the cobblestone roads, the horsecar used flanged wheels operating on steel rails laid in the street.

The horsecar yielded immediate benefits. Passengers got a more comfortable ride on the smoother track surfaces, and reduced friction allowed fixed amounts of horsepower to pull larger cars with more passengers at greater speeds. Encouraged by these improvements, all major cities in the United States developed horsecar systems.[25]

The logical terminal points for horsecar lines were the business districts, thus not only stimulating the formation of core areas, but also assisting outward expansion. People working downtown now could live farther from where they worked.

Horsecars were most popular in the early 1890s when the number of miles of track in operation exceeded six thousand, about 70 percent of the total street railway-trackage in the United States. (The other 30 percent were mostly electric railways that were introduced for a few years before 1890.) A cable-car system constructed in San Francisco in the early 1870s marked the first departure from horse-drawn vehicles in urban passenger transportation.[26] Between 1877 and 1890, forty-eight cable railways were put into operation throughout the United States. The cable-car system reached its zenith in 1890, when 375 million passengers rode 5,000 cars.[27]

Cleveland became the site of the first commercially operated electric railway in the United States. Although technical difficulties forced the abandonment of that line only a year or two after its appearance in 1884, other lines soon began operating in major cities throughout the nation. In 1890, only 1,200 miles of track were run by electric power, compared with 6,800 miles by animal, cable, or steam. But by 1902, electric-power railways accounted for nearly 23,000 miles of track, while all other types of motive power dropped to fewer than 700 miles.[28]

The development of the motor bus in the early 1900s marked the introduction of the automotive vehicle into urban transportation. Used first by the Fifth Avenue Coach Company of New York, the early buses were crude, uncomfortable, and unreliable. These factors accounted for the small number of buses in operation—only sixty in the whole country in 1920.[29] However, the redesigning of buses for comfort and the introduction of rear engines led to a growing popularity for this means of transport.

The first trolley coaches also appeared in the early 1900s. These rubber-tired vehicles were first used in Laurel Canyon, California. They operated on electric power received through sliding contacts on overhead wires. The vehicles were flexible in traffic and free from noxious exhaust. However, the difficulty and expense of maintaining the overhead power supply and the superior flexibility of the motor bus led to the decline of the trolley car.[30]

Because of the tremendous costs involved in the construction of facilities and the purchase of rights-of-way, rapid transit systems are economically feasible only in areas of relatively high population density. Some elevated railways were built in major United States cities as early as 1868, but never gained popularity, both because of high construction costs and general unsightliness.[31]

Subways usually replaced the elevated railways and also appeared in a few of the nation's largest cities which did not originally have elevated trains. The first subway line was opened in Boston in 1897.

The development of commuter railroads in the mid 19th century was of utmost importance to the growth of several major American metropolitan areas. Boston, Chicago, New York, and Philadelphia all relied heavily on the commuter rails, as did Baltimore, Pittsburgh, San Francisco, and Washington. As a by-product of regular intercity passenger service, steam-powered railroads initially offered commuter service from outlying communities to urban centers. These trains simply made a few extra stops at the outskirts of the city along their established routes.' This service brought the smaller communities along the railroad routes into effective range of the major city. The radial pattern of the tracks emanating from the central city also contributed to the starfish-like distribution pattern of cities as new centers of population sprang up along the commuter routes.[32]

But the most influential development in urban transportation was (and is) the automobile. Many feel that the car can eliminate public dependence on mass transportation since it does not restrict the traveler's route or time of departure and arrival. Despite these advantages, however, many planners fear that total reliance on the car might invite catastrophe. The public transportation system is therefore challenged to compete effectively with the auto, not only to further its own cause, but to prevent the mammoth social and economic problems which an overdose of the auto can inflict on our urban areas.

CHAPTER 2

URBAN METROPOLITAN TRANSPORTATION

Improved transportation increased mobility of both goods and people and encouraged population to settle in metropolitan areas. Fixed-route travel modes and, later, the widespread use of cars spurred this trend. Good supply lines from rural areas, as well as metropolitan regions, assured the newly developing communities food and other necessities not produced within their own boundaries. As the cities developed, two distinct areas arose with the availability of transportation: the central city and the suburbs. The city-suburb configuration constitutes the basic metropolitan area of today. But, ironically, the very urban growth that transportation made possible has created monumental transportation problems. How did this come about?

Before the turn of the century, more than half of all Americans lived in rural areas. Not until 1920 did urban residents outnumber their country cousins. As in later periods, the mushrooming of metropolitan areas during the first twenty years of this century was largely determined by available transportation. For the most part, waterways, railroads, and electric streetcars helped compress the urban centers into tightly packed clusters. Subway and elevated transit systems added to this clustering in four large cities: New York, Chicago, Philadelphia, and Boston. Because these transport modes had fixed routes, people and commerce automatically gathered at the terminals. After 1920, however, rising personal incomes and popular pricing of automobiles increased the ownership of private cars and motor trucks. This tendency grew, and the restraints which the fixed-route modes of transportation imposed upon city development began to weaken. Thus, American urbanization expanded. The trend continued unabated after 1900 and even accelerated in recent times. Whereas our population was only half urbanized in 1920, today two persons out of every three live in metropolitan areas.[1]

The vast expansion of urban America results in the annual addition of a million acres for metropolitan land use, an area equivalent to all of Rhode Island. And in the fifteen-year period between 1950 and 1965, urban complexes have added enough new residents to duplicate the combined metropolitan populations of New York City, Detroit, Los Angeles, Chicago, and Philadelphia.[2]

These tendencies seem certain to continue for some time. Estimates indicate that by 2000, urban residents will account for 70 percent of the nation's population.[3] In fact, between 1960 and 1970, the metropolitan areas of the nation accounted for 85 percent of the national population increase.[4]

The proportion of our national area to be urbanized will double approximately every twenty years. By the year 1985, the population of the United States is expected to be between 240 and 250 million persons.[5] Although the existing metropolitan areas will account for much of this expansion, new metropolitan areas are almost sure to develop. The trend of recent years provides a solid clue: the 212 metropolitan areas in 1960 increased to a 1970 total of 230.

The 1970 census found that 54.3 percent of America's metropolitan population were suburban residents. Between 1960 and 1970, the suburban rings of the nation's 230 metropolitan areas increased by 25.6 percent, while the central cities increased by only 4.7 percent. In the fourteen largest metropolitan areas, population in the central cities showed an absolute total decline of 700,000, or 3.1 percent. Many of the nation's larger cities suffered net losses in residents: Chicago lost 225,000; Detroit, 180,000; St. Louis, 140,000; Cleveland, 140,000; Pittsburgh, 91,000; Boston, 70,000; Baltimore, 35,000; and Milwaukee, 30,000.[6]

The trend of increasing metropolitan areas with swelling suburban populations and declining central cities is expected to continue through the century at an even quicker pace. By 1985, it is expected that nearly 50 percent of the nation's population will be residents of suburban communities.

New York City is a convincing illustration. During the past decade, the population of central city Manhattan decreased almost 190,000—an 11 percent decline. The loss, however, was offset by increases in Queens and Staten Island, so New York City's population as a whole remained stable, declining only one tenth of 1 percent. But in the same ten years, the populations of the four suburban upstate and Long Island counties (Nassau, Suffolk, Rockland, and Westchester) rose by 720,000—a 19 percent increase. The most spectacular growth occurred in Suffolk County, which encompasses the eastern half of Long Island. Suffolk —huge, sprawling, and almost rural in parts—swallowed up over half of the suburban growth, with a 67 percent population increase between 1960 and 1970.[7]

Housing construction reflects the ever-increasing lure of suburban life. Since World War II, more than two thirds of the new, single-family homes constructed in the United States have been built in the suburbs. During the same period, more than five thousand new shopping centers arose to serve the suburbanites. Of these, many were huge, regional centers resting on tracts of land equal to those of the central-city retail areas and providing all the services and conveniences available downtown.[8]

Along with the population distribution, the suburbs increasingly offer new employment opportunities, often at the expense of the central city. A recent study of the thirty-nine largest metropolitan areas in the United States (excluding New York) concluded that, in a few years, the suburb will have surpassed the central city not only in total employment in wholesaling, retailing, and selected services, but also in manufacturing.[9] For example, in the metropolitan area of Detroit between 1958 and 1967, manufacturing employment increased by 117,000. While 40,000 new jobs became available in Wayne County, the city of Detroit suffered a decline of 4,000 in manufacturing employment.

Although 70 percent of the nation's population now live on 2 percent of the land,[10] during the last two decades our metropolitan areas have undergone a decline in overall population density. A study of major urbanized areas (100,000 or more) from 1920 to 1960 discovered the following: population per square mile in these urban areas declined from 6,580 in 1920 to 4,230 in 1960. By the year 2000, the population per square mile in these urban areas is expected to decline to 3,732.[11] Thus, people are moving further and further from the original city areas.

While urban populations soar, the mass of land covered by urban development expands even faster. This population dispersal, occurring without direction or effective planning, has caused an urban sprawl in both central city and suburb and a full catalog of chaotic conditions for transportation planners.

For approximately two hours each morning and two hours each afternoon, the traffic arteries of the city are at flood stage; outside of these peak-hour periods, traffic moving via public and private transportation is at a relative ebb. This is, of course, primarily due to the institutionalizing of work hours. Most places of employment open between 7:30 and 9:30 A.M and close between 4:30 and 6:30 P.M.[12] Nearly half of all mass transit trips occur in these four busy hours.[13]

In the few large metropolitan areas, mass transit provides important peak-hour service to the central business district. A twenty-four-hour survey of passengers entering downtown Manhattan on a typical business day revealed that mass transportation accommodated 70 percent of the riders, while only 26 percent moved by automobile.[14] In Chicago, the Transit Authority carries 50 percent of all the rush-hour traffic.[15] Therefore, besides providing transportation for persons to whom automobiles are not available, mass transit has the strenuous task of moving large numbers of persons during the peak hours to and from the central business district.

But the peak-hour problem is not the only challenge mass transit must cope with. The rise of suburbia, and metropolitan growth in general, has led to an increase in passenger trips that are made within the suburbs themselves. The volume of travel to and from the central business district (CBD), although significant, does not play as important a part as it once did. In fact, many cities reached their peak in downtown traffic several years ago.

In urban centers with populations of 150,000 or more, travel from the CBD makes up only one fourth of the total trips, and, in urban areas of two million or more, less than 10 percent.[16] In fact, more than half of all persons who enter the downtown area do not want to be there at all; they are traveling to another location, which they can reach only by passing through the CBD.[17]

As suburban employment totals rise, urban work trips shift patterns correspondingly. In the past, such trips were mainly inbound to the CBD in the morning and outbound at night. Today's pattern is more widely diffused; the origins and destinations of workers have scattered. A modern traffic-flow chart will show many major routes, often lightly traveled, between various points within any metropolitan complex. And as we have already noted, work trips to suburban employment centers will soon outnumber those to jobs in the central city.

Thus, the decentralizing of residential areas, as well as of employment districts, is producing diverse transportation patterns. While urban population densities continue to strain transportation facilities, the increases in population, diffusion, origins, destinations, and routes pose new problems. The significance of these developments for modern urban transportation is immeasurable. No longer can public transportation be planned with the sole assumption of extreme population density. Rather, these facilities must provide for the broader needs of wide, but still heavily populated, land areas. The immense demands upon transportation facilities can be met only by tremendous commitments of finances, planning, and leadership.

Motorized transportation has had an almost devastating impact on today's metropolitan areas. At one time compelled to concentrate along fixed travel lines, urban growth has been freed by the automobile to expand in every direction. Many urban-area residents have become almost totally dependent on their cars for mobility, and thereby have trapped themselves in a vicious circle of traffic congestion which negates the original advantages of the auto. This total dependence is reflected by the fact that over 80 percent of all commuters ride to and from work in a car.[18] The automobile accounts for over 85 percent of all shopping and recreation trips.[19] In fact, nonwork trips, which account for two out of every three trips are almost all made by private auto.[20] In urban areas of over fifty thousand, an astounding 90 percent of all travel is by car.[21] By 1980, the average number of daily trips made in each automobile is expected to jump from four in 1960 to nearly five. In the metropolitan area, this will swell daily automobile travel per urban resident from seven to ten miles per day.[22]

Both in numbers and in relation to population, the ownership of cars in the United States is phenomenal. More than 100 million automobiles are privately owned in the United States today, and ten thousand more leave the factories each day.[23] More than 80 percent of all families own at least one automobile; more than 30 percent own more than one. In 1968 alone, 9.4 million new cars were registered in the United States, a 12.7 percent increase over 1967 and a new sales record for the automobile industry. Lowell Bridwell, former Under Secretary of Commerce for Transportation, asserted that in a few years a U.S. population of 225 million will include 126 million licensed drivers operating 118 million vehicles.[24]

Barring a drastic change in the status of the automobile, these trends seem certain to continue. While our population expands 39 percent in the years between 1960 and 1980, car ownership is expected to increase 64 percent in the same period. These trends have special significance for our metropolitan areas, because an enormous share of the new autos will be bought by urban residents. Estimates indicate that, while the 1960 average was one auto for every 3.2 metropolitan residents, the ratio will change to one for every 2.5 by 1980.[25]

Several factors account for this remarkable trend. Perhaps the most important is that rising levels of economic activity, higher incomes, and more equal distribution of personal income have accompanied our population growth. Also, used cars are now available at prices within the range of low incomes. Higher income brackets (where auto ownership is nearly universal) are gaining more and more families. At the same time, in 1967, over half of the families with incomes as low as $2,000-$3,000 owned cars.[26] The automobile is now within reach of more people than ever before, and the response to the lure of car ownership is reflected in the rapid proliferation of the auto market.

Economy is one of the most important advantages to choosing the private car (although the typical motorist does not take into account all costs involved in automobile travel). Gas and oil to keep his car running, plus occasional repairs, account for an out-of-pocket total of as little as 3.7 cents per mile.[27] And, because his automobile can carry additional passengers at no extra cost, the per-person figure may be further reduced. For example, an automobile carrying two passengers may reduce out-of-pocket costs to 1.85 cents per passenger-mile. With four or more passengers, this sum would be less than one cent.[28] The auto has a certain psychological advantage in the area of economy. The motorist rarely thinks of money when he drives off in his car, for he does not have to lay out tangible and immediate fares.

Although price is an important influence in the choice of mode, probably a greater boon the car offers is convenient service. The motorist can walk a few feet to his garage, drive away, and park close to his destination. Not confined to fixed routes and schedules, he goes where he wants, when he wants.

Automobiles provide privacy and comfort, as well as the opportunity for personal preference in vehicle style. The car has achieved a unique position as a status symbol in our nation, a competitive advantage that has been put to good use by the automotive industry through a long-term advertising campaign geared to molding consumer preference for the private auto.

Paralleling the accelerated usage of the automobile is the vast rise in truck travel since World War II. In our urban areas alone, motor-truck travel more than doubled, from 21 billion miles in 1940 to 47 billion in 1960.[29] At the same time, motor-truck ownership promises to keep growing at a rate faster than that of our population. The growth in population predicted for the twenty-year period from 1960 to 1980 will be far outstripped by the 61 percent increase in truck ownership during the same period.[30] One reason for this extraordinary increase is a standard of living that requires trucks to provide more and more specialized services to urban dwellers and businesses. Residential-area truck trips include everything from home delivery of milk and fuel to service calls by the telephone repairman and the plumber. Other truck services range from store deliveries and industrial hauling to post-office pickups and deliveries.

Burgeoning automotive traffic has frustrated efforts to accommodate it. In the average city, most street and highway facilities are already obsolete, inadequate, and inefficient. Nevertheless, they carry more than half of the nation's total traffic.[31] In the light of the problem, our urban areas are the site of continuous construction of an extensive network of complex highways. Some 6,700 miles of Interstate-Highway freeways are being built within the boundaries of urban regions so that by 1980 almost one fourth of the total network will be located in metropolitan areas.[32] Planned freeways will carry about half of all future urban motor travel.[33]

To many, these developments seem an efficient and essential boon to urban transportation. But masked as progress, urban highway building imperils the safety, economy, beauty, and security of our metropolitan areas.

Freeway construction turns valuable land in already overcrowded regions into cold rivers of concrete. Established homes, schools, parks, churches, and stores are swallowed up in the road building. Highways tend to isolate non-auto owners and seal off ghetto areas, as in the strife-torn Watts section of Los Angeles. Inner-city blacks find their neighborhoods razed to make way for what they resent as the "white man's highway." Although the federal government's right of eminent domain allows it to tear down anything that stands in its way, almost no attempt is made by government officials to provide alternate dwellings, or to reestablish disrupted neighborhood cohesiveness. Inevitably, such bulldozing breeds discontentment and even violence. Former Michigan Governor George Romney told a Senate committee that freeway construction was a major cause of Detroit's 1967 riots.[34]

Besides devouring land and buildings, freeways actually aggravate the congestion they are designed to alleviate. The new roads attract automobiles into the city which clog streets and strain parking facilities. Mass transit vehicles, particularly buses, are unable to run efficiently in the wake of so many cars. Ridership declines, and raised fares and deterioration of facilities follow.

In her book, *Superhighway—Superhoax*, Helen Leavitt applies to the highway Parkinson's Law that expenditures rise to meet income. She contends that traffic will increase to the limit of road accommodations and in support of this cites the example of the New Jersey Turnpike, which was constructed to relieve United States Highway Number 1. But within two and a half years, the new Turnpike was carrying as much traffic as Highway Number 1, and Highway Number 1 had 5 percent more traffic than originally. Twice as many cars crowded between Trenton and New York simply because additional freeway space had been made available.[35]

Los Angeles is another prime example. The Hollywood Freeway was opened in 1954 and designers predicted that it would carry an ultimate daily volume of 100,000 vehicles. Yet it took only one year from opening date for the traffic rate to exceed 168,000 vehicles per day.[36] Los Angeles has devoted no less than 85 percent of its downtown area to automobiles in one way or another, but still is unable to control its escalating traffic mess.[37]

The highway planners' response to congestion is more highways, more tunnels, double-decked lanes of expressways, and more bridges to siphon still more automobiles into cities. Yet not even the total gross public and private investment of more than $5.2 billion in car-storage facilities by 1962 could satisfy the nation's parking demands.[38] If everyone in Manhattan relied on the automobile for transportation, it would require at least nine stories of every structure just to store automobiles. So even if highways could magically accommodate a tremendously increased volume of traffic, parking the vehicles would be physically impossible.[39]

Highway backers often insist that building more roads in the urban area would stimulate the city's dying economy. Experience indicates the opposite is true, for suburban stores continue to usurp more and more business from the city. Between 1958 and 1963, Boston lost 9 percent of its total retail sales, despite considerable freeway construction. San Francisco, on the other hand, halted all freeway construction in 1966, and by 1967 sales had increased 16 percent over 1963.[40]

The social costs of congestion cannot be easily measured. How much less productive is a worker on the job because of the fatigue and anxiety created by the physical and mental challenge of driving to work? On the Long Island Expressway, cars move bumper to bumper at an average speed of five miles per hour.[41] Commuting in such congestion is a waste of both work and pleasure time.

Originally, the Interstate System was not intended to be bull-dozed through inner-cities. It was conceived in 1944 to serve only intercity traffic for long-haul and defense purposes. The vehicles were to consist solely of trucks, buses, and a few private interurban cars. But, by the end of World War II, highway boosters had determined that the automobile should become the dominant form of intra-urban transportation. The 1956 Federal Highway Act specified that the Interstate System "may be located in both urban and rural areas." It also allowed federal funds to subsidize 90 percent of the highway financing. Thus the strangulation of our cities began when the first interstate highway entered city limits. Excessive parking lots, air pollution, congestion, and other traffic ills have created the crisis our cities witness today. Yet dollars are continually being poured by the billions into highway construction.

Total outlays of funds between 1955 and 1985 are estimated to reach an expected $297 billion, and as much as a third of this amount has been allotted for urban areas. The cost for individual freeways is enormous. Ten miles of Los Angeles' Hollywood

Freeway required a capital expenditure of $55 million, and eight miles of Chicago's Congress Street Expressway required about $50 million.[42] New York's proposed Lower Manhattan Expressway would cost an estimated $100 million per mile.[43]

The vast bulk of these highway-project costs has been borne by a combination of federal, state, and local efforts. The Highway Trust Fund, which receives its money from "road-user" taxes on gasoline, oil, and auto accessories, produced $5 billion in 1969 alone.[44] Trust Fund supporters assert that extensive road building from these funds is justified, no matter how much it may cost. They point out that the taxes come from those who use and thus support the highways, but at the same time forget or ignore the fact that millions of Americans use the roads and the auto not by choice, but because they have absolutely no other alternative.

Undoubtedly, the most pressing problem of excessive ownership and use of motor vehicles is the "slaughter on the highways." In the United States today, traffic accidents are the leading cause of death among all persons in the 5-31 age bracket.[45] Since the turn of the century, half a million people have been killed on city streets, and millions more have been injured.[46] Traffic deaths soared 30 percent, from 38,000 in 1960 to 55,000 in 1969, and a total of 1.8 million persons were injured on the roads that year.[47] The National Safety Council estimates that more Americans have been killed by automobiles than in all the wars this country has ever fought.[48]

Fortunately, not all of our nation's highways are equally accident-prone. Deaths per million passenger-miles are less than one third as great on expressways as on other roads.

What can we do about the automobile and highway influx? In the following chapters, we will examine what must be viewed as the only way to maintain the vitality and livability of our metropolitan areas: urban mass transit.

The Mass Transit Showdown

The automotive age has permeated our society, and has not only affected the pattern of urbanization in America but also seriously undermined the nation's urban mass transit systems. Mass transit has been neglected. It has become outmoded, inefficient, and often downright unpleasant. As more and more people begin driving regularly, transit facilities worsen because fare-box funds decrease. As physical deterioration spirals, ridership slumps even further, in a vicious cycle of declining patronage, financial losses, and decaying facilities and services.

Since World War II, the entire mass transportation industry has declined. The total number of surface and rapid transit urban passengers fell from 24 billion in 1945 to about 8 billion in 1970.[49] Since 1945, the bus and rapid transit industries not only lost two thirds of their passengers, but also decreased their vehicle miles by over 40 percent, from 3.2 billion to 1.9 billion in 1968.[50]

This declining trend is challenging cities all over the United States. In 1963, the number of transit riders in Chicago, for instance, amounted to little more than half the 1940 total. Boston suffered a 62 percent decline in ridership. Philadelphia suffered a 52 percent decline.[51]

Slumping fare-box revenues have effected a long-term financial crisis in mass transit. As a result, between 1950 and 1969, some three hundred transit companies abandoned operations and many cities were without transit service. The 1,100 remaining companies[52] must battle an ever-widening gap between operating expenses and gross revenues. Since 1945, the operating income for public mass transportation has plummetted from a $149 million profit to a $130 million deficit in 1968.[53] Just to stay in business, the transit companies have continually raised rates, and thus driven away more and more riders.

Several factors account for the ever-rising cost of operating mass transit in this country. Traffic congestion is certainly not the least of these. Transit vehicles caught in jams expend large amounts of fuel and labor time without any compensating increase in passenger revenues. It has been estimated that delays in downtown traffic absorb as much as 18 percent of total running time. One transit company in Seattle reported that an increase in average vehicle speed of only one mile per hour reduced operating costs by at least 10 percent.[54] Taxes are another significant burden for the transit industry. In 1969, the tax bill for the industry as a whole was over 6 percent of operating revenues of $100 million.[55]

However, management states that the greatest financial problem for the industry is labor cost. For every dollar spent on transit operations, sixty to seventy cents goes for labor.[56] The mass transit company must be able to meet the high equipment and manpower costs dictated by peak-hour and peak-day needs. During off-peak periods, much equipment is idle, although employees needed to handle the four peak hours must still be paid for a full day.

With the decline of population densities as indicated in the earlier analysis, many existing mass-transit routes have become unprofitable, but cannot be abandoned because of political and public pressure. In the newly developing suburban areas, origin-destination patterns are often so scattered that moneymaking transportation hardly seems feasible. If mass transit companies decide to experiment with new suburban routes, they do so warily, with the knowledge that the residents and local officials may insist that an experimental line become permanent, despite losses.

Perhaps the most significant consequence of these problems is that, while scraping for revenue to cover basic operating costs and taxes, most urban mass-transit systems are unable to spend funds for modernizing. One estimate places that need at nearly $10 billion between 1962 and 1971 alone.[57] For many years, obsolete and antiquated equipment has been used. Between 1950 and 1967, transit companies abandoned about 29,000 vehicles, and the number remaining in operation dropped from 87,000 to 58,000.[58]

Obsolete equipment drives away passengers, as do poor ventilation, overcrowding, and dirty, unattractive interiors. The ride itself is often bumpy and noisy, and when a patron must stand for the entire trip, or sit with a fat elbow in his ribs or a newspaper in his face, mass transit becomes intolerable.

On top of these discomforts, subways, rapid transits, and buses are the scenes of some crimes, which threaten the security and lives of patrons. Many people will not ride mass transit for fear of being robbed, injured, or killed in bus and subway stations, or in the vehicles themselves.

Fare hikes further discourage potential riders, who simply refuse to pay more for progressively deteriorating services and facilities. And because so many drivers have been robbed, a growing majority of transit companies now require exact fare. If a passenger refuses, or forgets to keep enough dimes and quarters in his pocket, he must overpay or not ride.

To add to the woes, mass transportation today is painfully slow. The bus, operating on the same right-of-way as the auto, is especially disadvantaged: aside from the normal stopping to load and unload, the bus must cope with time-consuming congestion. In Cleveland, surveys indicate that cars average twenty-eight miles per hour downtown, whereas the transit vehicles travel at about eleven miles per hour.[59]

A traveler must also bear the inconvenience and time loss of getting to and from mass transit routes, of transferring from one route to another, and of waiting for the vehicle. Even systems that operate on their own rights-of-way (such as rapid transits) offer delays of this sort. Although a passenger may spend less time in the vehicle than he would in his car, his total trip time is almost always longer that it would be if he had driven.

Passengers seem to prefer bus transportation over fixed-line rail transportation because the bus has an inherently more flexible routing system. In 1935, 78.6 percent of urban passengers traveled on railways (either surface, subway, or elevated) and trolleys. By 1967, buses accounted for 70 percent of all urban mass transit rides.[60] Fixed-line transportation is more difficult to reach. Rapid stations are accessible by car, but they offer few parking spaces. Those who want to ride on commuter rails today must arrange for someone to drop them off and pick them up. During rush hours, hordes of waiting wives circle the station in their cars, and thus cause traffic jams.

Until now, progress in this country has meant accepting what is new because it is new, and rejecting what is old because it is old. Most Americans regard the auto as progress, and mass transit as an outdated, second-class means of travel to be tolerated only by those who are too old, too young, or too poor to drive. But progress should be cumulative. Otherwise, the advantages of a new invention are lost as we automatically discard all that is still useful in earlier methods. The rise of the auto is an obvious sign of progress, but if, in its wake, it leaves a crippled mass-transit industry, its blessings may be dwarfed by the resulting problems.

Contrary to the contentions of the auto advocates, mass transit boasts potential benefits that cars cannot provide. The greatest advantage of mass transportation is in capacity. In one hour, a lane of highway can accommodate only 1,200 cars, moving at an average speed of seventy miles per hour. (This assumes minimum bumper clearance as recommended by the National Safety Council.) Even if every auto held five passengers (more than double the normal number), only six thousand persons an hour could safely move over a single lane.[61]

Mass transportation, on the other hand, can carry up to eight times as many people in the same time period—120 fifty-seat motorbuses, for example, can carry 6,720 riders one way in an hour. In the same time span, sixty of the old three-car units in a streetcar system could carry 14,400 passengers one way, and forty rapid transit cars can accommodate as many as 48,000 patrons.[62] To carry the same number of people as these transit cars do in an hour, urban planners and transportation engineers would have to design twenty-one one-way highway lanes that could accommodate 32,000 automobiles every sixty minutes![63] With mass transit, more people could travel, with less congestion and fewer highways as happy side-effects.

If urban residents are concerned about ever-rising taxes, mass transportation is a money saver compared with highway construction. Jean Gottman's *Megalopolis* includes a chart comparing construction costs of handling increased peak-hour loads in Philadelphia and New York City. Highway costs invariably exceeded costs of building mass-transit facilities.[64]

Additional savings may result from the fact that some cities already have extensive track for rapid transit and commuter railroads which need only be improved and extended.

Mass transportation also conserves land. Train and transit tracks take up less area than highways, with the added bonus of being well-suited to operating for long distances in tunnels or on elevated structures. Streets and buildings may be built right over the tunnels, and neighborhoods remain cohesive. One need only look at Manhattan to realize what a tremendous land-saver transit can be. Furthermore, the electrically powered vehicles are a vital advantage for any urban area, for their propulsion does not cause air pollution. We must, however, balance the elimination of car-exhaust pollution with the pollution which may result from the electric-generating plants.

One of the passengers' greatest gripes is the inconvenience caused by mass transit route inflexibility. But, as we shall soon see, this problem can be easily remedied so that riders could be picked up at or near their doors, and deposited exactly where they wish to be. If commuter roads and rapid transits are used to their fullest potential, they will prove more convenient than the automobile. They can go underground to drop off passengers directly in the centers of dense business and shopping districts. Such bus and rapid transit service would eliminate the search for a parking space and the long walk afterwards. Mass transport vehicles (including buses, if special bus lanes were installed) could defy all traffic snarls, challenge adverse weather conditions, and provide greater safety for patrons than could the private automobile.

Automobile	Cost (Thousands)	Suburban RR Cost		Cost Ratio
1. Phila.-Paoli Expressway	$ 720,000	1. Construction of high-level platform	$ 11,000	
2. Phila.-Media Expressway	300,000	2. Additional terminal station facilities	55,000	
3. Phila.-Chestnut Hill Expressway	324,000	3. Additional storage tracks	8,000	
4. Phila.-Wilmington Expressway	567,000	4. Additional electrification facilities	40,000	
5. Phila.-Trenton Expressway	780,000	5. Signal changes	7,000	
6. Center-city parking facilities	400,000	6. Additional parking at suburban stations	173,000	
		7. Additional equipment requirements	170,730	
TOTAL, PHILADELPHIA AREA	$3,091,000		$464,730	7:1
1. Trenton-Newark Expressway	$1,022,000	1. Construction of high-level platforms	$ 6,000	
2. Bayhead-Railway Expressway	1,064,000	2. Additional terminal station facilities	10,000	
3. Newark-New York Expressway	2,400,000	3. Additional storage tracks	9,000	
4. Center-city parking facilities	266,700	4. Additional electrification facilities	22,000	
		5. Signal changes	7,000	
		6. Additional parking at suburban stations	115,000	
		7. Additional equipment requirements	114,120	
TOTAL, NEW YORK AREA	$4,752,700		$283,120	16:1
GRAND TOTAL COST	$7,843,700		$747,850	10:1

The psychological benefits of public mass transportation are enormous. Driving to work, especially in congested cities, strains nerves and boosts blood pressure, wastes productive time, and endangers life and limb. If mass-transit facilities were modernized and expanded, the commuter could travel to and from his job in ease and comfort. Untroubled with driver's responsibilities, free from worry, anger, and frustration, he can work, read, or even sleep if he chooses, and arrive on the job relaxed and in good humor.

All of the blessings of mass transportation can be had for no more money than the auto. Car operation is more expensive than most people think. Direct operating expenses such as gasoline, oil, tires, and maintenance, as well as fixed charges such as depreciation, insurance, and license fees, all swell the total operating costs and bring the real cost of running a car to about eleven cents per passenger mile, plus parking and garaging. So, for a single individual to travel downtown and home again for a total distance of, say, twenty miles, operating costs and parking fees can total $3.20. Out-of-pocket costs alone could total $1.74, compared with the dollar or less required for a round trip via mass transit.[65] Of course, sometimes additional persons are added as "free" passengers to the auto, reducing the average cost per person, but a full 68 percent of drivers still go to and from work alone.[66]

Besides its potential advantages for the public as a whole, mass transportation offers the only mobility for a large portion of the population that simply does not have access to cars. In spite of the boom in car ownership, 20 percent of U.S. families, including 40 percent of all families with incomes under $4,000, have no autos.[67] An analysis of some major urban areas reveals even more dramatic figures: 46.8 percent of the households in the standard metropolitan area of New York have no auto; in New Orleans, it is 34.2 percent; and in Chicago, 27 percent.[68] United States Secretary of Transportation John Volpe stated in a recent address that half of the minority-group families in the nation do not own an automobile.[69] Thus, a sizable group requires some mode of transportation other than the private car.

Even if a family owns a car, not all members can use it at once, and some members may be incapable of driving because of age or disability. In Chicago, surveys showed that 73 percent of all bus and 40 percent of all rapid transit riders could not have made their trips by auto. In Pittsburgh, 85 percent of those who rode mass transit could not drive or did not have cars available.[70]

Improvement of public transportation must be vigorously supported, not only to alleviate the highway problem and offer the public more comfortable and efficient means of travel, but also to give those who do not own or drive autos the conveniences they deserve. Can the various available modes be integrated into a balanced system? What use can be made of innovative techniques and mechanisms?

Pulling Things Together

The concept of a varied system implies, first, that the various modes be coordinated as well as competitive, and second, that coordination be directed toward local, regional, or national goals. Therefore, competent planning of a truly balanced system requires not only consideration of area needs, but, equally important, consideration of the best possible combination of modes to fit those needs.

A basic step in planning mass-transportation improvements is analyzing the potential market and determining its specific needs. Urban planners have divided this market into three basic groups: those who cannot drive, commuters, and the marginal riders. We have already discussed the large percentage of people who must depend on mass transit totally, and who should have pleasant and wide-reaching facilities. Commuters constitute a second major group requiring mass transportation, especially those traveling to and from the CBD.

Almost one out of every five workers in the 190 largest metropolitan areas uses surface railroad, subway, elevated railway, bus, or streetcar to travel to work and back.[71] In many cities, commuters rely even more heavily on mass transit to and from the CBD. The New York example has been cited often: 86 percent of those entering that CBD do so by mass transit. In Chicago, Newark, Philadelphia, Richmond, Boston, Atlanta, Cleveland, and other cities, one half to two thirds of the trips to the CBD are by public transportation.[72] These commuters need extensive, frequent service, especially during peak-hour periods.

Besides the nondrivers and the commuters, a third potentially large source of patronage for mass transportation is the marginal rider, who now uses private transportation but who could be persuaded to switch. This group includes commuters who drive but who would actually prefer attractive mass transit, drivers who dislike the auto but have no other alternative, and those who, although they cannot drive, depend on others to chauffeur them around in cars.

Some demonstration projects conducted since 1960 suggest that the marginal rider group could be significant. In a joint effort in 1962, the Housing and Home Finance Agency, the Department of Street Railways, the Department of Streets and Traffic, and Wayne State University improved bus service in the Detroit area. The site of the project was the fourteen-mile Grand River Avenue bus route, which connects downtown Detroit with the northwestern part of the city and some suburbs. Bus service was increased up to 70 percent during rush hours, as well as on Saturdays and Sundays. A 12 percent increase in patronage was recorded, and by the eighth week of the project, revenues exceeded the base period intake by 8.6 percent.[73]

Before mass transportation can hope to fully win over the public, an integrated system of transit modes must be developed. Some cities, notably Cleveland and Boston, have extended rapid transit rails into the suburbs, with feeder bus lines to the transit stations. The free, 3,800-car parking facilities along Cleveland's West Side rapid line are filled to capacity daily. A survey showed that nearly a third of those using the free lots had formerly driven their autos the entire length of their trip.[74] Cleveland's free parking lots are often cheaper than feeder bus service; patrons need not face the time-consuming collection of parking fees. The only drawback, of course, is the limited capacity of the lots.

Another means of intermodal integration is the linking of rail rapid transit to an airport. Metropolitan airports are handicapped if they offer no speedy means of transportation to the core of the city. Often passengers spend more time traveling from the airport to the central city than they do in the air. However, Cleveland, as of 1970, was the only American city that had forged a rapid transit link between downtown and the airport.

Whatever the particular needs of the urban area, combining the various modes of public and private transportation into a balanced system is a sensible way of meeting those needs.

The most basic need in planning a balanced system of urban transportation, according to a growing number of experts, is a metropolitan authority. In many communities, responsibility for each form of transportation is now often divided among several different agencies, without provisions for one unit of government able to organize a cohesive network. As a result, there is no unified approach to a workable, integrated transportation system.

Until March 1968, New York City was an excellent example of transportation disunity. The Port of New York Authority was responsible for interstate bridges and tunnels, bus and truck terminals, and airports. The Triborough Bridge and Tunnel Authority had responsibility for intrastate water crossings, including seven bridges and two tunnels, as well as parking facilities and the East Side Airline Terminal. All other bridges were built by the city and maintained by the Department of Public Works. In mass transportation, the New York City Transit Authority, several private bus lines, and several private rail commuter lines all shared responsibility. The same dispersion of authority existed in the administration of highways. Within this maze of administration, unified action was impossible.

Few local agencies in any U.S. city are empowered to go beyond the boundaries of the legal divisions which created them. As a result, few can manage urban transportation on a sufficiently broad geographical basis to encompass the dimensions of an area's transport problems.

The traditional pattern of local government action has lagged behind urbanization trends. Furthermore, metropolitan problems—especially in transportation—do not confine themselves to predetermined legal boundaries. Accordingly, it seems most metropolitan areas need not only a single transportation authority, but also an agency authorized to prescribe direction for the entire area's transportation needs. Few such metropolitan planning organizations exist.

Progress toward comprehensive metropolitan transportation planning has been spurred, however, during the last eight years by stipulations in federal legislation which require comprehensive metropolitan transportation plans before federal funds for transportation purposes can be obtained. For example, in 1964, the old Massachusetts Transit Authority of Boston, which ran rapid transit, trackless trolleys, and buses in Boston, was transformed into the Metropolitan Bay Transportation Authority (MBTA), which was credited with coordinating and, in some cases, absorbing outright all public transportation in Boston and the surrounding seventy-eight suburban communities in the metropolitan area.

The MBTA regional master-plan took one and a half years to draw up and called for the construction of thirty more miles of rapid transit, progressive integration of rail commuter services, and the purchase of new rapid transit cars and buses. In March 1968, New York state legislators established one master organization—the Metropolitan Transportation Authority—to coordinate into the CBD of Manhattan the movement of people via land, water, and air. Likewise, the 123 suburban municipalities of the Chicago Urbanized Area each have agreed to cooperate with the Chicago Area Transportation Study (CATS), an organization which prepares regional transportation plans. The CATS takes inventories of existing area transit facilities and tries to forecast future needs consistent with economic activity and consequent land development. The Chicago Transit Authority has already acted on some of its recommended projects. Thus, some urban areas are responding to the need for long-term, area-wide transportation planning.

Scraping Up the Funds. One of the greatest obstacles to building a balanced system is a lack of funds. The federal government and the states provide an overabundance of money for urban highways, and all but neglect public mass transportation. In 1967 alone, $2.6 billion was consumed by municipal extensions of the state and interstate highway systems. Most of this money came from the federal government. But if municipalities want to construct or revitalize transit systems, the financial burden falls, for the most part, on the cities themselves. A mere $200 million yearly is available under the Urban Mass Transit Act of 1964.

If an urban transit company faces financial setbacks and can no longer maintain adequate service, the city it serves has four alternatives. It can reduce or completely exempt the company from franchise payments, taxes, and other state and municipal charges; or it can pay a direct subsidy to the transit company. A third alternative would allow the city to assume ownership of the mass transportation organization. The city's fourth choice is to apply for a federal grant under the 1964 Mass Transit Act.

In 1962, voters of San Francisco, Alameda, and Contra Costa counties approved a $792 million bond issue to finance their Bay Area Rapid Transit system. In 1969, Rochester, New York, and Kansas City, Missouri, received federal grants to purchase their transit systems. The Massachusetts legislature, in 1964, levied a tobacco tax which provided $225 million to underwrite improvements in the Massachusetts Bay Transportation Authority's system. In 1966 alone, Boston received $4.5 million from the federal government for rapid transit improvements. In 1967, the voters of Chicago, Philadelphia, and New York approved bond issues to finance new mass transportation. In 1968, voters in Maryland and Virginia suburbs approved a bond issue to finance construction of a rapid transit system for Washington, D.C., but in the same year, citizens of other metropolitan areas found bond issues too burdensome. Voters in Los Angeles, Seattle, and Atlanta turned down bond issues which would have provided for new and improved mass transportation facilities. Seattle voters again rejected a bond issue in 1970.

As capital needs skyrocket and costs of operation continue to climb, public support of the kind given to highways is demanded by mass transportation. In early 1970, the Nixon administration promised a twelve-year, $10 billion mass transit program. Congress, according to the wishes of the administration, passed legislation which recognized that success in the area of urban mass transportation "will require a federal commitment for the expenditure of at least $10,000,000,000 over a twelve-year period." Yet, Congress did not see fit to appropriate this sum of money. The Urban Mass Transportation Act of 1970 (Public Law 91-453) authorized the Secretary of Transportation to finance loans and grants totaling only $3.1 billion. The legislation does, however, provide that the Secretary of Transportation, after consulting with state and public agencies, can submit to Congress requests for additional appropriations for fiscal years 1976 through 1982. The legislation directs the Secretary of Transportation to utilize the funds available "to assist state and local public bodies and agencies thereof in financing the acquisition, reconstruction, and improvement of facilities and equipment for use, by operation or lease or otherwise, in mass transportation service in urban areas and in coordinating such service with highway and other transportation in such areas."

The legislation also demonstrated Congress' new-found concern with the condition of our environment. The Secretary of Transportation must assure that in the planning, designing, and construction of urban mass transit projects, a special effort will be made "to preserve the national beauty of the countryside, public park and recreation lands, wildlife and waterfowl refuges, and important historical and cultural assets."

The legislation also expresses a congressional awareness that the elderly and handicapped persons have special transportation needs which must be met by improved public transportation. The Secretary of Transportation is authorized to make special loans and grants for the specific purpose of developing programs to meet the needs of elderly or handicapped citizens.

Despite the congressional recognition of the need for a long-range mass transit financing program, critics are very disappointed with the 1970 legislation. They contend that the funds are far too meager. Prior to July 1, 1972, the Secretary of Transportation cannot commit the federal government to loans and grants totaling more than $310 million. Yet, this sum is hardly large enough to take care of the needs of even one large city. Furthermore, mass transit advocates wanted the federal government to adopt a trust fund approach to financing similar to the one adopted for financing highways and airports. Some wanted the federal government to siphon off money from the Highway Trust Fund to finance mass transit. In short, the 1970 Urban Mass Transit Act represents a continuation of a very low-keyed financing program for the facilities of our nation's cities. In no way does it represent a significant commitment to reduce the nation's reliance on the automobile for movement into and out of cities.

Looking Toward Tomorrow

To solve our cities' transportation plight, urban planners, architects, sociologists, and inventors have been pooling their creative and intellectual resources. Their suggestions range from staggering work hours and putting tolls on all auto traffic, to some startling technological innovations in mass transportation. All of these could help salvage our floundering urban areas.

Staggering work hours would be one aid to reducing rush-hour congestion in central cities and on suburban facilities. At present, urban transportation facilities are deluged with traffic for about two hours in the morning and two hours in the evening. Expressways and transit facilities have been designed for extremely high capacities and yet remain doomed to peak-hour congestion and to non-peak hour lulls. The Second World War cut the use and production of private automobiles. To help mass transit handle the great influx of patrons who formerly drove cars, staggering of work hours became a necessity. This did alleviate peak-hour problems in seventy cities during the war years, but it created new problems by disrupting normal business schedules.

The attractiveness of the staggered-hour proposal is enhanced by the growing trend toward a shorter work-week. Since 1900, the average work-week has declined at the rate of nearly three hours per decade—from sixty to forty hours or less.[75] Thus, in the next two decades, a thirty-two-hour work-week may become standard for most urban jobs. The five-day work-week with fewer hours could adapt neatly to a staggering of starting times between 7:00 A.M. and noon, and closings between 1:00 P.M. and 6:00 P.M.

Negative reactions, however, could arise from the disruption of traditional living and working patterns which staggered hours would cause. Family life and social responsibilities may be disturbed when friends or members of the same family leave for work and return home at different times. Persons in similar lines of business may need to be at work at the same time. Nonetheless, the opportunity for easing urban traffic congestion and regulating the load on mass transportation may make this proposal worth consideration.

The most obvious way to relieve congestion in the city is to discourage auto traffic. Experts have reasoned that one deterrent would be to charge for the use of public roads. One plan would equip every vehicle with an identification unit which could be scanned by a roadside monitoring device at designated boundaries. As the vehicle passes from zone to zone, its progress would be recorded and transferred to a central data processor. The motorist would then be billed for the use of the streets and highways. Several similar electronic devices have been suggested, all with the same objective—discouraging traffic through tolls.

But even supporters of highway tolls concede that the idea has inherent inequities. Additional charging for auto use discriminates against those who are not wealthy enough to support this added financial burden and leaves the relatively rich to enjoy the freedom of the private auto on fairly uncluttered roads. And if planners continue to ignore mass-transit systems while implementing the road tolls, those who could not afford the tolls would be relegated to overcrowded, unreliable, uncomfortable mass transportation. Similar suggestions, such as raising downtown parking rates to discourage auto use, would be equally unfair.

The solution apparently favored by most present-day planners would sharply curtail highway construction in inner-cities, and divert federal freeway funds to mass transit. Subsidized fares, for example, would undoubtedly increase patronage, not only during peak hours, but throughout the day, by people who ordinarily make no trip at all.

Other ideas show promise. For instance, since buses on normal highways not only aggravate congestion but must travel at the mercy of the hundreds of cars on the street, some experts have proposed the construction of road facilities for buses only. Their suggestions were finally realized in September 1970, when the U.S. Department of Transportation decided to instruct the states to use the rest of the $5 billion Highway Trust Fund for exclusive bus highways, bus lanes, and other forms of preferential bus treatment. Secretary of Transportation John Volpe told federal road engineers in all the states to "encourage the greatest use of buses in preference to individual automobiles" so that our cities can breathe again.[76] These actions can relieve congestion not only by segregating the buses, but also by convincing more riders to switch to buses from their cars.

Some experts have proposed free mass transportation to attract riders. But even free use of transit facilities and increased patronage might not prove effective in reducing significantly the number of automobiles. Some drivers will prefer to use their own cars despite all costs and inconveniences, unless mass transit is made as comfortable and as flexible as the auto.

Although fresh technology is always needed, it is far more essential that the wealth of available techniques be implemented. The attractiveness of ultramodern innovation should not entice experts away from examining and adapting what has already been proposed for the transportation market. Air conditioning, for example, has been available for many years. But despite the marketing appeal it provides, this relatively inexpensive improvement was generally ignored until recently in the transport field. Washington, D.C., and Pittsburgh have embarked upon substantial programs to air condition their bus fleets, and Chicago, New York, and Cleveland have bought air-conditioned cars for their rapid transit systems. With increased use, air-conditioning equipment could well become a very attractive selling point.[77]

A structural change in rapid transit—the use of rubber wheels on rail-guided cars—is another improvement which is already available. Montreal pioneered the use of these cars which provide a smoother ride and have definite advantages in performance over the traditional rapid transit cars. Acceleration requires less power and grade ability improves greatly. Still, transit companies continue to give their passengers a noisy, bumpy ride, even though improvements are within easy reach.

Engineers and designers have also sought new means of support and propulsion for mass-transit vehicles. One invention called "ground effect," uses a low-pressure cushion of air for vehicle support. This principle can be applied to private vehicles or to rail systems; in either case, both friction and the needed propulsion power are reduced.

Ingenious experts have come up with even more farsighted ideas. For example, RRollaway, advanced by General American Transportation Corporation, combines the speed and efficiency of rail transport with the mobility of the auto. Using a rail vehicle which resembles the fuselage of a giant airliner, RRollaway could accommodate a dozen autos in each of its cars. Each electrically powered RRollaway car would measure 24 feet by 128 feet and operate at speeds up to two hundred miles per hour. The motorist would drive his auto to a RRollaway plaza and pass through automated toll gates onto a RRollaway coach. Automatic doors on both sides of the coach would provide the means of entrance and exit for the auto. Once on board, the motorist could stroll from his auto to a restaurant or lounge car on the train as he is sped to his destination. Upon reaching his departure point, he could simply drive away. Experts assert that the charge to the motorist would be no more than he now pays out-of-pocket for driving his auto.

Unbelievable as the concept may sound, high-speed tubes are already in the experimental stage. Vehicles using pneumatic propulsion in a tube system could travel at speeds estimated as high as five hundred miles per hour. Such a system would probably be less expensive to construct than high-speed railroads such as the famed Tokaido trains in Japan. Tokaido was built at an average cost of $6 million per mile, whereas a tube-transport system should cost no more than $5 million per mile.[78]

New ideas for monorail also seem quite promising. Efficient suspension methods which distribute vehicle weight evenly and produce little vibration would reduce the obtrusiveness of unsightly supporting structures. Vehicles would carry relatively small passenger loads, with lighter weights and lower profiles. The appealing Montreal Expo 67 monorail system is an excellent example of swift, efficient, and attractive elevated transport. However, as of now, no one has come up with a solution to the problem of switching cars on a monorail. As a result, monorail operations have been restricted to small-scale, direct-route service.

Schedule inflexibility and the unpleasant prospect of dragging to and from takeoff points discourage unlimited numbers of potential public-transport riders. The Dial-a-Bus system, which eliminates these woes, would greatly benefit the transportation cause. Dial-a-Bus, a cross between the conventional bus and the taxi, would pick up passengers at their doors or at a nearby bus stop soon after they have telephoned for service. A station computer would know the location of its vehicles, how many riders were on them, and where they were heading. It would select just the right vehicle and dispatch it to the caller on the system's quickest route. Investigation indicates that, depending on demand, door-to-door transit can serve patrons almost as fast as a taxi, but at one quarter to one half the price. Dial-a-Bus systems financed by the U.S. Department of Transportation are now successfully serving Peoria, Illinois, and Mansfield, Ohio. In Peoria, bus ridership quickly rose by 53 percent, proving the Dial-a-Bus a success in at least one experiment.

Another convenient and inventive means of travel, the personal rapid transit (PRT), would be of special value to persons living in low-density areas, who now must rely solely on their cars to get them to and from the central city. The PRT would consist of small vehicles, each carrying the same number of persons as an auto. These vehicles would travel from station to station over a city-wide right-of-way network, either over standard lines or over automatically calculated, individual routes. The roadbed for the vehicles might consist of steel or rubber wheels or air pads, and propulsion could be either in the vehicle or in the roadbed itself. Empty PRT vehicles or "capsules" would be available at each station on the network. The travelers would enter one, select and register their destination, and then automatically be transported there nonstop. A network of personal rapid transit could serve up to ten thousand persons an hour in a single travel corridor. This system would allow riders minimum waiting time, as well as private and secure accommodations.

Conveyor belts may soon supplement transport improvements by carrying passenger pallet cars at speeds up to fifteen miles per hour. The pallet extends the moving sidewalk concept to include longer-distance travelers who want to sit down during their trips. The cars decelerate to 1 ½ miles per hour at the loading stations, receive their passengers, and glide away. San Jose, California, plans to install a six-mile conveyor system in its downtown area, with construction of the first phase tentatively set for mid-1972. Unfortunately, little has been done to implement these sophisticated proposals because they all require apparently prohibitive capital investments.

Since the passage of the High-Speed Ground Transportation Act in 1965, research has been conducted with the guidance and financial assistance of the Office of High-Speed Ground Transportation (a subdivision of the U.S. Department of Transportation). The Office collects all information on possible technological innovations in the area of ground transportation, decides which are feasible, and then proceeds to financially assist all potentially useful projects. The Office, for example, recently announced plans for the first tracked air-cushion vehicle operation, which will serve the Los Angeles International Airport. The project will cost over $50 million and should go into operation by late 1972.

But not all of the suggested improvements are innovations or adaptions of surface modes. Metropolitan helicopter service, for example, may also play an increasingly important role in future years. During 1963, U.S. helicopter lines traveled 1.5 million miles in metropolitan areas. Most of this traffic was confined to New York, Miami, San Francisco, and Los Angeles, where service was largely an extension of airline travel (either to and from airport to central city, or between airports).[79] As commuter demands increase, however, today's relatively costly helicopter services may become cheaper. This could become a valuable addition to a balanced metropolitan transportation system.

Tomorrow's transportation needs cannot be met by antiquated solutions. The innovations which have been suggested to improve our transport network are ready and waiting. As knowledge of urban travel markets grows and technological skills advance, still newer innovations will undoubtedly arise. But those available must also be used—and used today—to help provide the present patrons of mass transit with quick, convenient, safe, and comfortable rides at relatively low cost.

CHAPTER 3

CASE STUDIES

Cities handle their transportation problems with varying degrees of intelligence and efficiency. Some, like Stockholm and Tokyo, have implemented systems which provide swift and obliging service. Others, like Los Angeles, seem to have worked their way into an inescapable rut. A look at the situations in these and other cities may provide some insight into today's crucial transportation problems.

San Francisco

Partitioned by both the Santa Cruz Mountain Range and the San Francisco Bay, this city has few natural traffic corridors and, therefore, little room for massive auto flow. Concerned with the threat of highways to the natural beauty of their metropolitan area, the citizens of Alameda, Contra Costa, and San Francisco Counties decided to build the first new mass-transit system in the United States since 1907. In 1962, they passed a $792 million bond issue for the development of the Bay Area Rapid Transit System (BART), and in return accepted an average increase in annual property taxes of about $25. Construction funds came from two other sources as well: $133 million from surplus Bay Bridge tolls furnished by the state of California and $71 million from anticipated revenues of the transit system itself. But a greater-than-expected rate of inflation upped the cost of the project from $144 million to an anticipated total of $1.2 billion. This unexpected increase has delayed the system's scheduled opening date until at least 1972. Although $180 million has come from California's toll-collecting division, $792 million from the bond issue, and $80 million from the federal government under the provisions of the 1964 Urban Mass Transit Act, BART still needs an additional $50 million for rolling stock and a final $144 million to finish the job.

BART promises superior public facilities to serve at least half of the area's peak-hour and peak-direction commuters. Besides lowering transportation costs to two or three cents a mile, it expects to attract patrons with such features as speed, safety, comfort, dependability, aesthetic appeal, frequent service, and a smooth, quiet ride. These advantages will substantiate BART's advertising campaign and may, in fact, tip the psychological balance in favor of mass transit. The commuter will be guaranteed an upholstered seat, as comfortable as those he uses at home, in a transit car with air-conditioning and eye-appealing interior. During peak hours, BART cars will run every ninety seconds; their average speed will be fifty miles per hour, with top speeds exceeding eighty miles per hour. The whole system will be controlled by a complex computer.

The entire undertaking encompasses seventy-five miles of specially designed, wide-gauge track, sixteen miles of subway tunnel, and a four-mile tube under San Francisco Bay. The BART project has also generated a building boom along its right-of-way. Even now, before the system is operating, at least $300 million of new construction is either planned or already in the building stage.

Despite its contemporary transportation spirit, San Francisco has not foresaken the picturesque past. In mid-1970, the city's transit system, the Municipal Rail, decided to invest about $19.9 million in new streetcars and, perhaps, $7.5 million in trolley buses, to the amusement and delight of nostalgic citizens. These vehicles are quieter than buses and do not pollute the air. Whereas buses have a hard time climbing the steep San Francisco hillsides, the electrically powered transports can master the heights with ease. The greatest support came from the general public, which, concerned with air pollution and urban noise, campaigned for the streetcar and the trolley bus (or "trackless trolley") with slogans, signs, and bumper stickers.

While San Francisco builds public mass transportation, it also challenges auto problems more directly. In 1968, for example, the Golden Gate Bridge inaugurated a successful one-way toll collection program which later was extended to most other Bay crossings. Vehicles must maneuver into toll booths, stop, and pay the toll only once during a round trip over the Bridge. As a result, congestion and delays in the free direction have been reduced substantially, and in one year the number of toll-stop accidents dropped from one hundred to five.[1]

In late 1969, a state law was passed permitting the Golden Gate Bridge to experiment with any mode of transportation that could lessen congestion on the Bridge. The law created the Golden Gate Bridge District to formulate a long-range plan to be submitted to the legislature in 1971. If the lawmakers reject the plan, they can abolish the Bridge District and the law that created it. As part of the project, the District began experimenting with a passenger ferry system in 1969.

San Francisco is among the few major municipalities to stand up to the auto. The courage and foresight of its citizens have preserved the delightful charm and convivial atmosphere of one of America's best-loved cities.

Los Angeles

Unlike San Francisco, California's largest city has almost surrendered to the automobile. Planners decided to put all eggs in the freeway basket and, in doing so, have encountered little opposition to what has proved a questionable decision. The seductive availability of federal highway funds led politicians and administrators to rejoice in the sight of new concrete.

Two thirds of downtown Los Angeles is devoted to moving, storing, or servicing the auto. Three hundred twenty-six miles of freeway make up the urban highway system. Cars are multiplying even faster than people, so that the present 3.5 million cars in Los Angeles County could double in the next decade.[2] Financially oppressed voters turned down the city's first attempt at a rapid transit bond issue in 1968, and this dimmed hopes for any form of mass transportation in the immediate future.

The city's sprawling geography may partly account for its freeway obsession. The concentration of people in the CBD is only about half that of Chicago, a metropolis of comparable size. Thus some 7 million residents are forced to drive their cars to an extent well beyond established national averages.[3] The preoccupation with the automobile has induced a certain myopia with respect to future transit requirements. Of the more than 500 communities in the Los Angeles area, at least 321 have no rail facilities at all and are served exclusively by motor vehicles. Moreover, as residents rely more and more on their cars, transit patronage declines. Transit passengers in 1963 numbered only 60 percent of the 1940 total,[4] and in that same year, all street and interurban railway service for passengers was ended.

Age has finally caught up with Los Angeles' freeway system. Nearly one third of the network suffers from rush-hour congestion and cannot cope with the onslaught of commuters. More than 300,000 motorists suffer some delay each day. Proposed solutions call only for new lanes, automated roadways, and redesigned ramps. The only suggestion even vaguely related to mass transportation is one calling for two special bus lanes along eleven miles of freeway between the city and suburban El Monte.

Consequences of the Los Angeles highway frenzy are notorious. The city's concrete metastasis has aggravated air pollution, traffic jams, accidents, and perhaps even the riots in freeway-walled ghettos. Planners must begin to recognize that transportation policy also shapes total environment.

Chicago

Chicago has made noble efforts to develop a balanced transportation network, with public transportation playing a key role. This city has a system of five interconnecting expressways, as well as a network of radical highways streaming from the central city. But decreasing availability of land has prompted city authorities to abandon road construction. Since then, three main factors have helped the area deal with its mass-transportation problems: first, the cooperation among the suburban private commuter lines, the communities they serve, and the Chicago Transit Authority (CTA); second, the intensive planning and intelligent use of facilities and space by CTA; and finally, the willingness of political subdivisions and private corporations to pool all available resources to maximize financial capability.

Five privately owned commuter railroads serve Chicago's suburbs—Illinois Central, Chicago and North Western, Rock Island, Milwaukee and South Shore, and Great Northern. These lines constantly better themselves through purchases of modern equipment, increased service, improved parking facilities at terminals, fewer and fewer stops, and simplified fare schedules. For example, the Chicago and North Western has spent a total of about $58 million for improvements since 1956. In 1968, the line purchased twenty new, double-deck cars for its 84,000 daily commuters at a cost of $3.5 million. Furthermore, the commuter service has operated at a profit every year but two since 1959. In 1969, the line showed a $2 million profit.[5]

The Illinois Central recently ordered 130 new high-speed air-conditioned cars for its 37,000 to 40,000 daily commuters. DOT, under the provisions of the Mass Transit Act of 1964, will provide a grant of two thirds of the total $37 million cost. In order to get the money, citizens served by the Illinois Central formed a mass-transit district to comply with the federal regulation that only local communities, not private corporations, are eligible for transit grants. This Chicago South Suburban Mass Transit District leases the new equipment to the Illinois Central. Cooperation between the district and the CTA (a municipal corporation) also helps give continuous and extensive service to commuters. The agreement of both organizations to link the terminals of train lines makes transfer from one system to another easy and convenient.

Supplementing this railroad service is the Chicago Transit Authority's fleet of about 3,200 buses and 1,300 rapid transit cars. CTA serves millions of weekday riders over 135 bus routes and eight rapid transit routes. Integrated bus-rapid transit service makes use of extensive parking facilities at terminals, modern equipment, and capital improvements. The rapid transit cars are new and well-lit, with large windows and air conditioning. Terminals are also being revamped for better service.

Among the many innovative programs initiated by the CTA, the *Skokie Swift* project and the rapid transit lines which operate along expressway median strips contain special merit. By pooling their resources, the village of Skokie, the CTA, and the Department of Housing and Urban Development reestablished commuter railroad service between Skokie and neighboring Evanston over the abandoned tracks of an interurban railway. At Evanston, the system connects with the CTA's elevated rapid transit service into central Chicago. According to George Krambles, CTA research and planning superintendent, between 7,500 and 8,000 riders are served each weekday—five times the number predicted by CTA planners.[6]

Riders apparently are not attracted to the *Skokie Swift* by lower fares. An Illinois Central line which serves an area of comparable size and distance from the downtown area at a lower rate carries only five hundred riders per day. The *Swift's* riders are responding to better services that include improved terminals, parking lots, and ramps to deliver riders to their trains.

The types of riders attracted may well be more important than the simple fact of increased patronage. About 40 percent of the *Skokie Swift's* patrons are converts to the CTA. At least one quarter recently switched to mass transit, despite the fact that four fifths of them own autos and more than half come from homes with two or more cars. The experiment has been so successful that nine out of ten people in the area served by the *Skokie Swift* are favorably impressed by it.[7]

The CTA also embarked on two new median strip rapid lines which were completed in 1969. The first was a 9.8-mile rapid transit extension in the median strip of the Dan Ryan Expressway which runs south from the CBD. The system extends from an existing south-side elevated structure between 16th and 18th Streets to 95th Street. Two stations along the route are available for transfers to other bus lines. The second project is a 4.7-mile extension of rapid transit line in the median strip of the Kennedy Expressway which runs northwest from the CBD and extends from an old elevated terminal in Logan Square to a terminal link-up with the Chicago and North Western commuter facilities at Jefferson Station. The project also included the purchase of 150 air-conditioned cars. Total cost was $84 million, of which two thirds was paid by the federal government under provisions of the Urban Mass Transit Act. The city paid its share from transit bond funds approved under a 1966 capital improvement bond referendum.

A major reason for the city's relative success in moving people is its stress on a fairly balanced system. For example, the bulk of the $4.5 million in CTA's 1969 capital budget went toward new buses and bus facilities. Furthermore, the CTA harmonized two modes of travel by inaugurating a bus service between O'Hare Airport and the Jefferson Park rapid station in February 1970.[8] Chicago also wants to implement direct rail service to and from the airport, and authorities have considered extending CTA's Kennedy Expressway rapid transit for that purpose. The downtown-to-airport trip would take thirty-five minutes, which is the same amount of time required for a trip by car or by limousine. The committee that proposed the line feels that it "may not be competitive during non-rush hours."

The CTA and the Chicago and North Western have opened a pair of rail-to-rail links which make it easier for commuters to transfer stations. One project, the Northwest Passage, links the Central and North Western downtown station with the Clinton-Lake Streets Elevated Railway station. The six-hundred-foot passageway gives commuters full weather protection while transferring from one service to the other, and features carpeted walkways and piped-in music. Another joint project was the installation of two escalators linking the C&NW station platforms to a new pedestrian tunnel under the tracks. The tunnel leads to CTA's Jefferson Park rail terminal where the Kennedy Expressway transit line ends. These two massive projects cost about $1 million. Sharing the cost are the U.S. Department of Transportation, the city of Chicago, and the C&NW Railroad. The CTA looks upon the coordinated effort as a giant step to break down long-standing transportation barriers and to make job opportunities in the outer suburbs more attractive and accessible to inner-city residents. Meanwhile, the link-up at both points will benefit suburbanites who prefer riding public transportation to work if connections are good.

Other experiments involved various automatic monitoring systems which will soon be available for mass transit. The CTA is providing automatic routing for its Dan Ryan median-strip trains, both northbound and southbound. The Monitor-CTA project for buses consists of a computerized vehicle-location-and-identification system that will monitor bus schedules; a silent-alarm radio system that will instantly transmit the location, bus, and run numbers of an operator in need of help; and a two-way radio system that will provide full-time communications between the operator and a central dispatcher. In emergencies, a special alarm system will enable the bus driver to push a foot switch which will communicate his location to the dispatcher's unit. The alarm lets off no telltale beeps or flashes in the bus that might upset passengers or tip off would-be thieves.

Chicago's concern with a balanced system helped prompt Chicago and North Western President Larry S. Provo to propose an area-wide transportation authority for the six-county metropolitan area of Northern Illinois. The agency would be independent of the state, county, or Chicago governments, and would have broad authority to plan, implement, and operate all systems of mass movement. The system, which would be similar to New

York's MTA, could buy, lease, and operate suburban bus lines and railroads, and exercise control over the CTA system and highway improvements influencing mass transit.

This move may further progress towards a well-coordinated system. Although 90 percent of Chicagoans entering the CBD use public facilities, the city, troubled and complex, still has transportation problems, but refuses to surrender to them.

Cleveland

Starting with the viable elements of a balanced transportation system, Cleveland is striving to develop and expand its facilities. The problem seems to be one of implementing ideas that authorities and planners already feel are workable.

Cleveland's mass transit system has run into substantial difficulties in recent years. Ridership dropped by 120,000 from 1967 to 1968, the eighth consecutive year of decline. The city-owned Transit System faced a deficit of $57.6 million in 1969 as expenses soared.[9] These financial difficulties have led to pressure for the purchase of the system by Cuyahoga County, which encompasses Cleveland and its suburbs.

One explanation for the Cleveland Transit System's (CTS) problem is the loss of many of its passengers to a new 120-mile network of interstate freeways. Besides, fare increases and cutbacks in service have annoyed and alienated customers. Even so, CTS has made advances. On November 21, 1968, Cleveland became the first city in the country to link its airport with the downtown area by rail rapid transit. The west-side rapid line was extended 4.5 miles to reach Cleveland Hopkins Airport, eleven miles from downtown. The extension cost $18 million, much of it paid by the federal government under the grant-in-aid provisions of the Urban Mass Transit Act. The extension serves a dual purpose: it links the airport to the downtown business district and it offers rapid transit to employees of large industrial plants near the airport. The train, running at a ten-minute headway, now serves about fourteen thousand riders per day. The trip from downtown costs forty cents, and takes only twenty-two minutes, a substantial savings in time and money over cab or limousine.

Despite its inherent advantages, the rapid has not drawn the patronage CTS had hoped for. Several drawbacks account for this. Luggage accommodations are limited to a couple of under-sized platforms next to the doors, and unless the owner is constantly vigilant, a thief might easily make off with his property. The lack of luggage service forces people who want to play it safe to keep their suitcases at their seats during the entire trip. Furthermore, the train's drab, dingy interior discourages travelers, and the absence of conductors frightens away many for whom a lack of supervision poses a threat.

In 1969, the Cleveland-Seven County Transportation Land Use Study Group (SCOTS), an intergovernmental planning body, devised a program to meet the transportation needs of the region through 1990. The study group forecast that by 1990 the region's estimated 3.8 million people will be driving 1.6 million cars[10] and recommended the construction of seventy more miles of rapid-transit facilities, including sixteen miles of subway; extensions of existing rapid lines; and the creation of new lines northwest, southwest, and northeast from the downtown area. But when the Department of Transportation rejected the plan, SCOTS fell apart. A new group, the Areawide Co-ordinating Agency, has taken its place and is using the SCOTS plan as a basis for further study and planning. Perhaps they can motivate Cleveland to improve its troubled transportation network.

New York

The largest urban complex in the United States, New York boasts a highly developed system of public transportation. The city's working force depends on this system to such an extent that on a typical working day in 1960, of the one and a half million people who entered Manhattan south of Sixty-first Street between 7:00 and 10:00 A.M., only 14 percent used autos, taxis, or trucks. A full 86 percent used some form of public mass transportation, mostly subway.[11] By 1968, an estimated 4 million people who entered the CBD daily were continuing to rely heavily on public transportation.[12]

Nevertheless, New York has crippling traffic problems. Some 700,000 motorists still creep, honk, and squeeze their way into Manhattan each day, bumper to bumper. Recently, the Automobile Club of New York, an organization of some forty thousand motorists, drew up a list of the city's worst bottlenecks, which range from the Bronx's "kamikaze circle" (where three expressways meet in the antiquated Bruckner Traffic Circle) to that famed masterpiece of poor planning, the Long Island Expressway.[13] The number of vehicles clogging Manhattan's streets keeps increasing at a rate of 3.5 percent per year and overwhelming the highways despite computerized traffic lights, new signal systems, and even a new "pusher service" to expedite removal of broken-down cars.

To begin remedying the congestion, the New York State Legislature created the innovative Metropolitan Transportation Authority (MTA) in order to coordinate the movement of people by land, water, and air into Manhattan. The Authority has jurisdiction and control over all mass-transit facilities in New York City and its seven neighboring upstate and Long Island counties. Facilities previously controlled by the New York City Transit Authority, the Triborough Bridge and Tunnel Authority, and the Long Island Railroad (LIRR) have been turned over to MTA. Further activities will be coordinated with the Port of New York Authority, a self-supporting, nonpolitical agency of the states of New York and New Jersey, which controls the three area airports. New York voters first displayed their support of transportation improvement in 1967 when they approved a $2.5-billion bond issue earmarked for projects over a five-year period. When the MTA was born a year later, it proposed to use these funds for a massive, multi-faceted $2.9-billion project. It acquired additional proceeds from the Triborough Bridge and Tunnel Authority and from an increase on the state mortgage-recording tax.

In 1969, plans were approved for new subway and commuter lines, and a $70 million contract was awarded to three firms for construction of a double-deck rail tunnel. The tunnel will run from Sixty-third Street and York Avenue, under the East River, to Long Island City in Queens. The MTA also won permission to create a rail route on existing LIRR track from Penn Station to Kennedy Airport. The service would be nonstop, and all that is needed to meet its 1973 completion goal is $50 million. MTA also plans a second subway route which would run from Forty-eighth Street and Third Avenue to Kennedy Airport, but the line, which would use the proposed East River Tunnel, could not be ready before 1977. Also at 48th Street and Third Avenue, a proposed transportation center would coordinate existing and new subways with a new LIRR terminal and, eventually, with a passenger-distribution system of conveyors or guided cars. It would also serve as a midtown terminal for Kennedy where travelers could check in, deposit baggage, and be carried by rail in twenty minutes to the airport.

In still another phase, the Kennedy Airport Access Project is putting into service a whole fleet of dual-mode vehicles that are half-bus and half-train. The plan calls for by passing the worst of Manhattan's traffic by on-railing the buses to the tracks of the Long Island Railroad, where they will travel for about eight miles. Then, in a relatively free-from-traffic area, they will be off-railed and proceed the rest of the distance as conventional buses.

In a speech in fall 1969, Governor Rockefeller promised that in a few months, the Long Island Railroad would be the best commuting road in the nation, yet the road has been continuing to run downhill ever since. The MTA has ordered 620 new air-conditioned cars for the LIRR, but those already received have been plagued with operating failures. And although the cars are more clean and comfortable, the trains themselves are still jammed and breakdowns are maddeningly frequent. To add to the burden, the railroad recently hit its ninety thousand passengers with a substantial fare increase. Enraged customers revolted. Several riders refused to hand in their commuter tickets and had to be escorted off the train by police. One man attempted to seize control of an idle locomotive in Penn Station, and another is suing the LIRR for "commuter neurosis." In an unprecedented move, train-operating personnel threatened to strike unless given police protection from menacing commuters.

In addition to improvements of the LIRR, the MTA has promised that the commuter services of other private railroads (such as the Penn Central, the Staten Island Rapid Transit, and the New York portions of the Erie-Lackawanna) will be renovated. This might require a paper transfer of ownership from the private corporations to the state, since New York law forbids the use of public funds to improve private facilities. Once ownership is transferred, the railroads could operate their lines under a service contract from MTA. All in all, a total of two hundred miles of transit lines is planned for the metropolitan area.

A criticism of MTA's master plan is that it neglects the area west of Times Square, where large skyscrapers are going up rapidly. Transportation in this district is already poor and surely could not withstand a huge influx of new commuters. The MTA, however, is being encouraged to attach higher priority to this area in its overall plans.

Many cities throughout the country look to MTA with eager

interest and hope. If this first organization of its kind in the country is successful with the awesome monster, New York, it will probably work anywhere.

Baltimore

The threat of the superhighway has been met head-on by Baltimore. The city suffered from traffic paralysis as early as the 1940s when officials called in New York public works promoter Robert Moses for consultation. Moses recommended an expressway across the center of the city, through a section known as Franklin Mulberry. Although never really acted upon, Moses' recommendation accelerated the deterioration of that neighborhood, which eventually became a slum. Thus, Baltimore was given a preview of what expressways can do.

For the next twenty years, officials allocated $15 million for studies of alternate routes and plans for mass transit. Meanwhile, three interstate highways barreled up to the city's edges, and engineers pressed to channel traffic from all three into a single, massive expressway which would devour $28 million worth of land, send a fourteen-lane bridge across the city's lovely old harbor, and wipe out four-thousand homes and six-thousand jobs.

Baltimoreans began to organize against the superhighway.[14] In 1967, they originated a design-concept team composed of engineers, architects, sociologists, and urban planners, to create a road that would not destroy but serve. Once established, however, the team ran into difficulties. The interstate highway points of entry into the city seemed impossible to change because nearly all the condemnation ordinances along the originally proposed route had been passed and the land had already begun to deteriorate. The engineers clung to the Moses plan, refusing to cooperate with the "petunia-planting, bird-watching do-gooders" who threatened their pet project. And looming ahead was the deadline when federal funds needed for the road would expire.

When the concept team eventually reached a stalemate, Baltimore's mayor, Thomas D'Aleasandro, called a final meeting where he listened to lengthy arguments for and against the superhighway. At last, he threw his support to the architects and "urbanologists," promoting what they considered a functional, efficient, safe, and aesthetically acceptable freeway system. Part of the road will go underground to permit surface space to be used for community facilities. One section of the road will run submerged for a mile and a half through Franklin Mulberry. Above it will stand a school, a shopping center, and a rapid-transit station. The transit line will run between the lanes of the expressway. This road will not disturb local street patterns or fragment neighborhoods.

The long period of controversy and conflict appears to have ended with the mayor's decision. Newspapers and the community at large have accepted the road plan, and the concept team's contract has been renewed with another $4.7 million from the (U.S., city or state) Department of Transportation. Detailed planning of the 22.4 miles of roadway is in progress, and private and civic developers show possibilities of advancing as much as $600 million toward various aspects of the project. Baltimore's concept-team approach, despite its difficulties, has proven that at least one major U.S. city is concerned with environment and not just expediency.

Toronto

Resisting the demands of highway enthusiasts, Toronto has relied heavily on an extensive subway to meet its transportation problems. Starting with a 6.6-mile, north-south subway line on its main street, Yonge Street, Toronto has added a number of extensions within the last three years. In 1966, an eight-mile, east-west route (the Bloom-Danforth Route) opened up. Two years later, three miles were added to each end of Bloom-Danforth, as well as a four-mile extension to the Yonge Street line, with both additions increasing the length of Toronto Transit Company's subway system to twenty-four miles.

Patronage of the system rose 6 percent in 1966 over the previous year, and this directly reflected the addition of the Bloom-Danforth line.[15] All subway cars have modern, automated identification systems which correspond with receiving units along the tracks. These units arrange the proper alignment of routes and light train destination signs on station platforms. The system operates from 6:00 A.M. to 2:00 P.M., with a daily rush-hour headway of 2¼ minutes. Normal headway is 3¼ minutes; Saturday, 3½; and Sunday, 4½. From 2:00 to 6:00 A.M., the Toronto Transit Company provides bus service on lines parallel to the subway. Longer-range planning calls for the construction of a second Yonge Street extension, an east-west subway line south of the Bloom-Danforth Route, and a north-south rapid transit route in the median strip of the Spadina Expressway.

On May 23, 1967, the government of Ontario Province began a subsidized high-speed train between Hamilton, Ontario, on the west and Pickering' on the east, via the Toronto Union Station. Within Toronto's municipality, the train makes convenient stops near the subway lines. The sixty-mile system cost the government $15 million in capital expenditures, plus a $2-million annual subsidy. The system is operated by the Ontario Department of Highways, which regards the train service as a cheaper and more efficient alternative to further highway construction. The equipment was designed with fast, reliable service and passenger comfort in mind. The 17,500 daily riders have established the fact that an efficient train can lure people from their automobiles. Surveys have estimated that 46 percent of the system's riders formerly commuted by auto. In addition, 22 percent asserted that the location of train stations influenced their choice of residence.[16]

Toronto is also experimenting with six transit cars to increase passenger comfort and reduce power costs. The cars have air springs, acoustic insulation to cut transmission of noise and vibrations to the car body, and special three-layer panels for doors and interior linings. Ventilation through ceiling ducts rather than by open fans prevents harsh noise from the tunnel roofs.

To simplify transit operations, the Toronto Transit Commission (TTC) recently opened a $1-million control center with fifty-four emergency and supervisory vehicles, two-way communications with all subway trains, and a network of telephone lines connecting it with the police and fire departments. The two control systems allow the TTC to monitor and operate the main line track and signal system, and to run all electric transit substations.

Canadian transportation authorities have made great contributions to the development of one of the fastest-growing downtown areas in North America.

Stockholm

The citizens of Stockholm enjoy one of the most highly developed rapid transit systems in the world. The city's geography forced residents to turn to the subway much earlier than other cities of comparable size. Since Stockholm rests on fourteen islands on Lake Malaren and the Baltic Sea, road space is at a premium, and modern transportation would have been impossible without a highly sophisticated rapid transit system.

The first subway, which opened in 1957, runs into the center of Stockholm from the western and southern suburbs and swings around through the main business district. A out a half million passengers a day ride the twenty-five-mile line, which includes forty-seven stations and 430 cars. In 1964, a second underground system, which runs from the southwestern to the northeastern sections of the city, opened up. Trains (each consisting of eight cars—with total capacity of 1,100) operate at a 2½-minute headway during rush hours. The subway is so successful that 87 percent of the commuters entering the CBD in 1961 used public transportation.[17] In 1965, legislation was passed which provided aid for subway construction from gasoline and automobile taxes. The city has also established a metropolitan body responsible for planning and coordinating all area transportation. Furthermore, since 1950, suburban residences have sprung up within short distances of rapid transit stations.

Nonetheless, car ownership has been increasing at a rate of 12 percent a year. City planners are constructing freeways to carry traffic through and around the central city. But Stockholm's planners continue to depend on rapid transit as the more practical way of maintaining mobility in a modern city and controlling traffic downtown.

London

Approximately 90 percent of the 1.2 million commuters entering the Central Business District of London use some form of public transportation. On an average weekday morning in 1965, approximately 490,000 commuters traveled on the suburban facilities of the British Rail, 590,000 on the subway and buses, and 120,000 in private autos or motor scooters.[18] But the existing facilities have not been modernized or expanded enough to meet present demands, and the future poses ever greater problems for London. Automobile registrations in the area showed a 50 percent increase from 1960 to 1965, from

1.3 million to almost 2 million. The number of cars entering the CBD has increased accordingly (from forty thousand in 1955 to seventy thousand in 1965), whereas the average number of persons per car has declined.

The London highways have been unable to deal with such a rapid influx of cars. For example, the central-city buses lost 3.7 million miles in 1965 due to congestion, compared with 2 million miles lost in 1963.[19] To add to the headache, the suburban rail service from the south is reaching saturation level. Underground facilities within the CBD that were built in the nineteenth century desperately need renovation and expansion. The London Transportation Study indicated that, compared with 1963, twice as many London-area families will own automobiles by 1981.[20] Furthermore, London's businesses are decentralizing and shifting to the suburbs. The government's National Plan, published in 1965, reported that total employment within London's CBD has actually stopped growing.[21]

One of the major roadblocks to effective improvement and integration of public transportation is the fact that suburban rail passengers do not have fast, reliable service from train stations to downtown areas. Since there is no government subsidy of transportation, both the London Transport Board and British Rails must pay for all their improvements from the fare box. Their revenues are not sufficient to finance substantial modernization and extensions of facilities, much less the increased maintenance and labor costs.

Recently, however, two new projects have aided London's transportation to some extent. The British Rail finished converting the London Midland line out of Euston to electric power, and a sizable increase in ridership resulted. The second plan, a subway extension between Victoria and Walthamstow, was completed in 1969. Officials had dallied for thirteen years before they finally allowed the London Transport Board to proceed with this expenditure.

The task for London's planners clearly rests with public mass transit. Experts must devise new methods of financing both better facilities in the CBD and extensions of facilities into the suburbs. Hopefully, they will act soon.

Tokyo

Japan's capital city faces a highly complex transportation

problem, for nearly 16 million persons live within a thirty-mile radius of the city. Tokyo, however, has met the challenge squarely by planning and constructing both an extensive freeway system and excellent public transportation.

In 1959, the Metropolitan Freeway Corporation was established, financed half by the central government and half by the Tokyo metropolitan government. The Corporation planned eight radial lines emanating from the center of the city and one ringed line totaling seventy-seven miles. Another recent project, the 8.5-mile freeway line between Yokohama and Tokyo, runs from Tokyo International Airport to the center of Yokohama.

Yet the number of private car owners is rising so fast that the volume of road traffic in rush hours will inevitably exceed road capacities. As of July 1966, 1.2 million automobiles were registered in Tokyo—an average of one automobile for every two and a half families. Residents of Tokyo are buying thousands of cars per month. This boom in car ownership has led to an appalling increase in accidents. The number of people injured in traffic accidents rose from 68,692 in 1966 to 88,283 in 1967.[22]

Both the shortage of land available for freeway construction and the increase in automobile accidents have encouraged the city leaders to push an extensive system of public transportation. Present subways serve some 2.1 million citizens daily at intervals of two to three minutes. The subway network covers fifty miles in the metropolitan area on six different lines. The two private corporations which operate the subway systems (Teito Rapid Transit Authority and Metropolitan Bureau of Transportation) plan to extend their modern subway service ninety-five more miles.

In addition to this vast subway network, Tokyo has an 8.2-mile monorail link between the center of the city and Tokyo International Airport. The monorail, which began service in September 1964, is operated by the Tokyo Monorail Company. It covers the route in fifteen minutes—a tremendous saving over the automobile trip, which often takes more than an hour because of congested highways.

One of the most intriguing projects has been the construction of a $38 million transportation center (the Shinjuu Station) in uptown Tokyo. The station handles an average of 3 million passengers each day. In addition, the eight-story, 5,530-square-foot structure has 350 stores, dining halls, wedding halls, and a school. In fact, the station, combined with its neighborhood, is developing as a sub-city center to decentralize activities.

Tokyo's emphasis on public transportation has been matched throughout Japan with the vast construction of high-speed intercity railroad systems. Opened in 1964, the new $1-billion Tokaido Line serves passengers in the 320-mile Tokyo-Osaka corridor. High Speeds, moderate fares, frequent schedules, and passenger comfort have made the train one of the best known in the world, as well as a profitable enterprise. With speeds averaging over 100 miles per hour, the entire trip takes only three hours and ten minutes.

The train's success has led to the construction of a 100-mile extension west along the Inland Sea from Osaka to Okayama. Later, Tokaido will expand further west to Hiroshima, and eventually to Hakata, a total of four hundred miles. In the eastern half of the island, the train will extend north from Tokyo 330 miles to Morioka, so that when the entire expansion program is finished, total mileage will reach 1,050.

One American visitor to Tokyo was amazed at the refreshingly decent service he received on Japan's high-speed train from Tokyo to Nagoya. He reported: "We cruised at 130 miles per hour, but the ride was smooth as silk. The seats are spacious even for a Westerner, and they swivel, so you can turn around and talk with your friends. You can buy snacks and drinks at your seat."[23] What the American apparently considered remarkable is part of the daily Japanese experience.

CHAPTER 4

INTERCITY TRANSPORTATION

Statistical data on intercity travel is far less refined than that on metropolitan transport. But available data does indicate clearly that the automobile is predominant in intercity as well as metropolitan transportation.

No matter what the purpose of the trip, Americans use the car more than any other mode. It accounts for about 68 percent of all business trips, 88 percent of all pleasure trips, and 85 percent of all trips for personal and family affairs.[1]

The following table discloses the percentage of intercity trips of various distances which are made by auto:[2]

Percentage of All Trips by Auto	Distance
95	under 50 miles
96	50 to 99 miles
93.5	100 to 199 miles
81	200 to 499 miles
82	500 to 999 miles
55.5	1,000 miles or more

In relatively short trips, the private automobile is used almost exclusively. And, all told, it is used more than any other single mode.

The shifting fortunes of different transportation modes took place in an environment characterized by a lack of significant growth in the common-carrier travel. Except for a boom in airplane travel, most mass transportation has declined. The degree of stagnation is illustrated in the following statistical table:[3]

Intercity Travel
Revenue Passenger Miles
(millions)

Year	Airlines	Railroads	Motor Bus	Total	Airline Share %
1944	2,200	97,700	26,900	126,800	1.7
1950	10,000	32,500	26,400	68,900	14.5
1960	34,000	21,600	19,900	75,500	45.0
1961	34,600	21,500	19,700	74,800	46.3
1962	37,500	20,200	21,300	78,000	47.5
1963	42,800	18,600	21,900	83,100	51.5
1964	49,500	18,300	22,700	90,500	54.7
1965	58,000	17,400	23,300	98,700	59.9
1966	67,700	17,200	25,000	109,900	61.6
1967	87,200	15,300	24,900	127,400	68.4
1968	101,200	13,300	26,200	140,700	71.1
1969p.	111,000	12,000	26,000	149,000	74.5

Because of its speed and comfort, domestic air travel has been soaring, especially since World War II. From a meager 2 percent of all common-carrier passenger mileage at the war's start, air travel had surpassed railroads as the leading common carrier of passengers by 1957.[4]

Airlines have reached new peaks both in passengers carried and in miles traveled. Whereas in 1950 air travel accommodated 17.5 million revenue passengers, by 1964 the total was 73 million and growing.[5] In recent years, plane travel has accelerated so that between 1963 and 1969, air passenger miles increased 39 percent.[6] Airline traffic may have reached a temporary peak, however, as passenger miles in 1970 showed no increase over the 1969 level. Since World War II, the airlines have developed a definite clientele. Continued technological advances and imaginative promotion figure importantly in increasing airline patronage. Pricing devices such as youth fares and family plans also continue to boost air travel.

But airlines are not without their share of difficulties. Despite unprecedented increases throughout the 1950s and 1960s, passenger airline growth is not without limits. In fact, airlines have run into serious financial problems. The total loss of $101 million during the first half of 1970 by three major air carriers— United, American, and Trans World Airlines—certainly cannot be dismissed as trivial. In their efforts to stay in the race, airlines have outbid one another in the purchase of new equipment and amount of scheduling. Also, the major airlines are forever rushing to buy each new aircraft developed by leading aerospace manufacturers. The costs of each new undertaking soared in the late 1960s, along with interest rates for borrowed money.[7]

Caught up in the advertising war, airlines have often petitioned the Civil Aeronautics Board (CAB) for permission to schedule flights between major cities every hour on the hour. Such flights cannot possibly be filled anywhere near capacity. On short-haul flights (under three hundred miles), airlines need 80 to 90 percent capacity to cover operating expenses, but they schedule too many flights between cities to achieve this goal; many flights are only 20 to 30 percent filled. Businessmen, crucial to the airline industry, have of late reflected the general pessimism of the national economy by avoiding business trips by air to cut down expenses.

In August 1970, these occurrences led the airlines to petition the CAB for the right to discontinue a number of passenger flights. To many, this situation sounds all too familiar. Unless authorities attack the air crisis right away, the transportation field may find another railroad situation on its hands.

Despite the growing dominance of quicker and more sophisticated modes, the intercity bus has managed to hold its own. With the development of limited-access interstate highways, terminal-to-terminal bus service has grown. Bus and depot facilities continue to be improved and the scheduling of nonstop routes, coupled with other service conveniences, reflects a major effort by this mode to woo passengers. In 1966, bus patronage in the United States rose to 690 million, an increase of almost 13 million passengers from 1965. At the same time, revenues jumped over $30 million in one year to a total of $729 million.[8] More recent figures are somewhat less impressive, but still verify that the bus's clientele will remain stable for quite some time. This popularity, enhanced by the flexibility of routing on an expanding network of government-built superhighways, and relatively low fares, has placed the intercity bus in a strong competitive position, second among all common passenger carriers.[9]

Nevertheless, by limiting more and more trips to interstate highways, the bus companies are effectively eliminating service to many smaller cities which are by passed by the interstate system. Thus, increases in bus travel between major cities are offset by declines in bus travel between smaller cities. Many small cities whose locations are inconvenient with respect to the interstate highway system are left without intercity public transportation.

The decline of the passenger train has severely upset the balance of our transportation network. In 1944, passenger miles were at an all-time peak of nearly 100 billion.[10] Since then, rail-passenger travel has drastically fallen until, in 1967, the number of passengers dropped to a new twentieth-century low of 297 million, while passenger miles continued their decline to a total of a little over 15 billion.[11] A crucial problem in intercity passenger service is the continuing deterioration of effective rail service. The estimated twenty thousand passenger trains serving the nation in 1929 have tumbled to a present grand total of 366.[12] Between many large cities, rail service for passengers has virtually disappeared. The last passenger train between Cleveland and Pittsburgh made its final run in 1965. The few remaining prestige runs, such as Santa Fe's *Super Chief* and the Burlington Northern's *Empire Builder,* are feeble testimony to the days when railroads dominated even long-range passenger service. The *Lark,* which travels between Los Angeles and San Francisco, once carried three hundred passengers per run in comfort and leisure. Now the Southern Pacific Railroad has requested permission from the California Public Utilities Commission to discontinue its service, since only ninety-five round-trip passengers ride the *Lark* each day. Meanwhile, frequent and swift air service between these two cities daily attracts 7,700 passengers.[13]

Several factors explain the deterioration in rail service. For one, the trains are too slow. The Wabash *Cannon Ball* covers the 489 miles between Detroit and St. Louis in the relatively inefficient time of ten and a half hours. A second factor is lack of adequate service. The only train between Memphis and Birmingham (a distance of 253 miles) is a night run with nothing but coach cars.

These examples are by far the rule, not the exception.

High on the list of problems is the difficulty of mobilizing capital to modernize equipment. Although railroads have added some new passenger cars, the total number in operation decreased by more than three thousand between 1967 and 1968. As a result of this neglect, 60 percent of the nation's rail passenger cars are over thirty years old.[14]

Because the railroads have allowed their passenger services to stagnate for so many years, they now find it almost impossible to generate the large funds needed to modernize rolling stock, upgrade track, and restore terminals. These investments are postponed to a more and more remote future, until the possibility of modernization almost vanishes.

The problem of rate-making, examined in general in preceding pages, plagues the railroad industry in a unique way. Restrictions imposed by the Interstate Commerce Commission (ICC) have almost frozen the rate structure. This regulatory albatross inhibits any marketing scheme that might lure commuters from other modes.

In addition to the particular problem of rate determination, the whole environment of railroad regulation is decidedly unfavorable to experimentation. Even if companies do decide to risk capital on experimental lines, the regulatory framework may make it impossible to stop operating them. Carriers are forced to tie up their limited research funds in the operation of experimental lines which may have already proven unprofitable. Therefore, the ability of the railroad to assess the results of its experiments and decide rationally which service warrants keeping is severely limited.

A clear illustration of this conflict between regulation in the "public interest" and potential experimentation is the speed limitations imposed upon railroads. After World War II, the Interstate Commerce Commission declared that trains could not exceed eighty miles per hour, unless their locomotives were equipped with cab signals (instruments which the engineer can read even when trackside signals are obscured by poor weather) and automatic safety devices to stop the train in the event of engineer disability. Because the Burlington does not have cab signals along the entire length of its track between Chicago and St. Paul, its *Afternoon Zephyr,* one of the fastest trains in the United States, averages only 67.4 miles per hour. Rates of speed on this railroad have actually declined, since that same run was completed twenty minutes faster a generation ago. Most intercity trains were slower in the 1960s than they were in the 1920s when the "streamliners" commonly ran at top speeds of one hundred miles per hour.[15] The railroads in general feel that even on main lines traffic is too light to justify investment in this equipment. But if they want to test the success of new high-speed lines, they must first invest in cab signals and safety devices, a move they are not about to make for a mere experiment.

Perhaps the greatest danger to passenger train service is the railroad's apparent desire to eliminate passenger runs. Before 1958, state commissions exercised stringent controls over the supply of passenger trains within their respective states. These local authorities were reluctant to let the railroads drop passenger runs, but Section 13a of the Interstate Commerce Act, passed in 1958, placed railroads under control of the Interstate Commerce Commission, stating that the ICC must allow discontinuances of passenger lines not proven to be "required by the public convenience and necessity." The railroads did not hesitate to take advantage of the new standards. In 1955, about 121,000 miles of road were operated for passengers; in 1967, the number had shrunk to an estimated 68,000.[16]

The railroads were apparently convinced that there was no money to be made in carrying people. Competition for that business was fierce, and, in large measure, government subsidized. Airlines got free port facilities and an enormous boost in federal, defense-related research. Buses and private autos traveled on rights-of-way paid for with tax money. While other carriers steadily upgraded their equipment and services, the railroads fell steadily behind even what they had been able to offer before World War I. Besides, overhauling their facilities to make them competitive with other modes would require huge investments with little prospect of immediate profit. They centered their attention, therefore, on the instantly profitable freight business.

Now, thanks to ICC regulations, the abandonment of passenger lines was much easier. To liquidate a run, the railroad needed only to prove it was not "required by public convenience and necessity." The instrument for such "proof" also was provided in the controversial "ICC accounting formula," which permitted railroads to figure passenger service expenditures as approximately half the total right-of-way cost, a split of about fifty-fifty with freight. Passenger sales, however, seldom matched the cost levels thus computed, and the ICC got "proof" after "proof" that lines had to be abandoned.

As lines are abandoned, gaps appear in what once were tightly woven passenger networks. Abandonment of the Cleveland-to-Columbus segment of the Cleveland-to-Cincinnati run, for example, made possible the dropping of the Cleveland-to-Cincinnati and, eventually, the Cleveland-to-Columbus trips as well. Each time a run was dropped from the schedule it spelled doom for one or two others.

The ICC also has been criticized for its willingness to accept the figures in abandonment petitions as final and correct, not even subject to independent audits that might expose prejudicial calculating or human error. Asked whether certain railroad-reported figures were accurate, Commissioner Kenneth H. Tuggle simply replied, "We assume so."[17]

The combination of the ICC's unorthodox system of cost calculation and unquestioned acceptance of figures submitted by the railroads to support their own case is considered by many transportation authorities as the ultimate blow to rail passenger service. Until those factors came into play, the railroads faced two alternatives—either revive passenger service and make it attractive and competitive, or dismember it piecemeal until it ceased to be a system and deteriorated into a patchwork of orphaned lines in obviously poor financial straits.

Critics insisted that more equitable cost-accounting yardsticks be used to measure passenger line profitability—compare their income with the costs they alone incur, assuming the total expenses would be necessary even if passenger trains were removed and the properties cleared for exclusive freight use.

In 1967, the ICC responded to that pressure by releasing a study showing that the costs relating to passenger trains alone (repairs to passenger cars, fuel for passenger train locomotives, wages for ticket agents and porters, maintenance for passenger stations) exceeded operating revenues by $72 million. The railroads, using the old cost-accounting formula, reported their deficit for the same year: $485 million. In evaluating petitions for abandonment, however, the Interstate Commerce Commission stuck with the old method.[18]

The railroads insist that people have deserted them for other modes, but they have done very little to win back the passenger patronage. Instead, they have neglected advertising and downgraded facilities in many ways actually discouraged potential riders. Reliable information from railroad sources reveals that many roads have special teams of employees whose task it is to devise ways to discourage passengers from taking the train. And between 1950 and 1957, when aviation advertising in magazines grew 125 percent, railroad advertising dropped 24 percent.[19]

Some feel that since the passenger train is dying, we should let it go in peace. Others point out that, in some areas of the country, the railroad industry provides the only intercity public transportation. They also argue that the train has advantages over other forms of transportation. Its tracks bring passengers right into the middle of big cities. It remains unaffected by almost all weather conditions, and does not pollute the air. It is not delayed by traffic jams, offers an extremely low cost per passenger, and may be designed for excellent passenger comfort.

Although the railroads and the ICC assert that passenger service is no longer demanded between cities, surveys indicate that the demand still exists, if only decent service were offered. A recent questionnaire, given to Milwaukee businessmen, showed that 94 percent of those sampled felt that frequent, clean, reliable, fast, and modern trains between Chicago and Milwaukee would lure more riders; 55 percent said they would use the train themselves.[20]

Finally, early in 1970, a crisis atmosphere developed around the fate of rail passenger service. More and more government bureaucrats, Congressmen, concerned citizen groups, and labor organizations came to realize that unless drastic measures were taken, the collapse of the U.S. passenger network was imminent. The ICC had proven helpless to protect the public's access to fast, efficient intercity rail passenger service. In the absence of aid from the federal government, the railroads themselves felt no obligation to provide such service.

The Department of Transportation's Federal Railroad Administration came forward with a proposal to establish a semi-public corporation to take over the railroad passenger business, to develop new, fast trains for the highly populated corridors between the major cities. As a result of the FRA's efforts and the efforts of concerned citizen groups, Congress passed the Rail Passenger Service (Railpax) Act of 1970 (Public Law 91-518) which was signed into law on October 30, 1970.

Railpax represents a congressional recognition that "modern, efficient, intercity railroad passenger service is a necessary part of a balanced transportation system . . . and that rail passenger service can help to end the congestion on our highways and the overcrowding of airways and airports." In order to achieve these goals, Congress authorized the establishment of the National Railroad Passenger Corporation, a "for-profit," semi-public corporation, whose purpose is "to provide intercity rail passenger service, employing innovative operating and marketing concepts so as to fully develop the potential of modern rail service." The corporation will have fifteen directors on its board. Eight will be appointed by the President with the advice and consent of the Senate, three will be elected by common stockholders, four by preferred stockholders. The other two will be the Secretary of Transportation and a consumer representative.

The National Railroad Passenger Corporation will operate a network prescribed by the Secretary of Transportation. He is authorized to specify points between which intercity passenger trains will operate, to identify all routes over which service may be provided, and to designate basic service characteristics within the basic system. In selecting a national rail passenger network, Congress required the Secretary to consider:

1. Adequacy of other transportation facilities servicing the same points.

2. Unique characteristics and advantages of rail service.

3. Potential profitability of service.

4. Opportunities for faster, more convenient service, service to more centers of population, and service at lower cost.

The legislation directed the Secretary to initially designate an intercity rail passenger network on a preliminary basis. Congress provided that the initial proposal be subjected to review by the ICC, state railroad commissions, and representatives of railroads and labor organizations. According to the terms of the legislation, the Secretary of Transportation would review the findings of these organizations and submit a final binding report on the rail passenger network. The final report would have to specify why the suggestions of interested parties were or were not followed.

The entire system will be operated without change by the Corporation from May 1, 1971, until July 1, 1973. If after July 1, 1973, certain segments of the basic system prove not to be required, then trains may be discontinued in accordance with Section 13a of the Interstate Commerce Act.

At any time, Railpax may add new lines to the designated intercity network, if such additions are "consistent with prudent management." After two years of operation, any train designated in this manner becomes part of the basic system. Any state, regional or local agency may request more service, and the Corporation will add trains if the agency involved assumes 66 ⅔ percent of the solely related costs and associated capital costs, including interest on passenger equipment—minus revenues attributable to such service.

By entering into a Railpax contract on or before May 1, 1971, a railroad may be relieved of its entire responsibility as a common carrier of passengers under Part I of the Interstate Commerce Act or under any state or other law relating to the provision of intercity passenger service. Railroads which do not enter into such an agreement before May 1, 1971, may do so on or after March 1, 1973, but before January 1, 1975. Railroads joining the Corporation must agree to pay to it each year for three years an amount equal to one third of 50 percent of the fully distributed passenger service deficit for the railroad as reported to the ICC for the year ending December 31, 1969. Railroads have two methods of payment available to them. The railroad's contribution to the Corporation may be in the form of cash or (at the option of the Corporation) in the form of equipment (transferred to the Corporation). The legislation makes provision for the railroads to receive a tax deduction equal in amount to the cash they pay to the Corporation or to the value of the equipment they transfer.

Realizing that the nations's passenger service could not be refurbished without new capital, Congress provided for financial assistance to Railpax—$40 million in the form of grants to be utilized for improving reservation systems and advertising; for serving, maintaining, and repairing railroad equipment; for conducting research and development; and for developing and testing new rolling stock. The legislation also enables the Secretary of Transportation to guarantee up to $300 million for long-term loans into which the Corporation enters.

Early in December 1970, in accordance with the provisions of the legislation, Secretary of Transportation John Volpe announced an initial proposal for the basic system of rail passenger trains. This proved disappointing for many transportation experts. Some pointed out that only 156 of the present 366 intercity passenger trains—40 percent—would be included. Twenty-seven major metropolitan areas now enjoying substantial rail passenger service would have no guarantee of service under Volpe's plan. Certain omissions also were cited. On the West Coast, no direct rail service was offered to connect San Diego, Los Angeles, San Francisco, and Portland, even though population in the West has risen 24 percent in the last decade. There are now 35 million Western Americans—7 million more than in 1960. The Volpe plan included no direct service throughout the Southwest that would link New Orleans, San Antonio, El Paso, Phoenix, and San Diego. An increasing number of elderly citizens, who have the leisure to utilize train facilities, live in this area.

Although Volpe filled in some of these specific missing links in the final Railpax network announced in January 1971, the new plan represented no change in Volpe's underlying premises. According the Volpe, the first guiding assumption in the selection of routes is: "Intercity rail passenger service will survive only if demand for it increases sufficiently to reverse the decline in ridership and the resultant mounting losses experienced to date in providing such service." He also stated that, because of limited resources, the Corporation ought to concentrate funds "on a limited number of routes which show some promise of profitability."

Most advocates of rail passenger service apparently disagree with these fundamental assumptions. They point out that when Congress decided to build the Interstate Highway System or a modern merchant marine fleet, it did not set up rigid standards of profitability. The *New York Times* in an editorial stated an alternative assumption for consideration by the Secretary of Transportation:

> Intercity rail passenger service is essential in a civilized, urbanized society. Its operating deficit, if any, will be supportable if riders are provided with clean, comfortable, conveniently scheduled, dependable service. As with highways and airports, the capital investment in rolling stock and roadbed will be written off by the Government.[21]

Conceding that profitability is always a desirable goal, advocates of increased intercity rail passenger service contend that the money allocated is so inadequate that such a goal is thoroughly unrealistic. The sum of $40 million in grants could at best enable the Corporation to develop fast, efficient service between two or three major cities, and $40 million for the entire country may do little more than continue the present, admittedly inadequate service.

Also challenged in the Volpe program is his emphasis on long-haul (over two hundred miles) train routes. No effort is made to optimize quantity and quality of service between cities within the dense corridors. Many experts argue that rail service will not generate sufficient ridership if, as in Volpe's proposal, it is concentrated on distances of over two hundred miles.

Many intercity rail passenger advocates have come to the rather stunning conclusion that the entire Rail Passenger Service program, although noble in concept, is doomed to failure. They insist that the lack of adequate funds to improve existing service rules out any hope for reasonable testing of the viability and acceptability of rail passenger service. According to the legislative intent, the National Railroad Passenger Corporation must work in close cooperation with railroad personnel responsible for passenger service, most of whom, over the past twelve years, have been assigned to build cases to present to the ICC which would minimize the value of intercity passenger service. Railroads have shifted talented managerial employees from passenger operations to freight. In short, the legislation relies too heavily on railroad personnel who have demonstrated the most competence in getting passenger service removed.

Megalopolis

Along major transportation routes between many large cities, urban growth has coalesced to form one large urban area. This interesting population phenomenon, the so-called "urban corridor," is not entirely new. Along the Atlantic Coast, for example, and in the Great Lakes community centered in Chicago, it has long been difficult for the citizens to tell precisely where one municipal spread ended and another began. In recent years, however, similar developments have taken place in all parts of the nation, some of the largest being between Los Angeles and San Diego, Dallas and Fort Worth, Pittsburgh and Cleveland, and the 250 miles around Lake Michigan in the South Bend-Chicago-Milwaukee area. The core cities are linked by a series of suburban developments; the suburbs provide the attractiveness of urban life along with the advantages of low population density.

The oldest of these regional urban complexes, a center of commerce, industry, and culture, is the Northeast seaboard of the United States. This region constitutes an almost continuous stretch of urban and suburban development, from southern New

Hampshire to northern Virginia and from the Atlantic shore to the eastern foothills of the Appalachians. The area has been nicknamed Megalopolis after the ancient Greek city-state which strove to become the largest of Greek cities.

Megalopolis encompasses all of Massachusetts, Rhode Island, Connecticut, New Jersey, Delaware, and the District of Columbia, as well as portions of Maryland, New York, Pennsylvania, New Hampshire, and Virginia. Five of the nation's largest metropolitan areas—New York City, Boston, Philadelphia, Baltimore, and Washington—lie within its boundaries. Although comprising only 2 percent of the nation's land area, it contains about one fourth of the nation's population.[22]

High density is one of its most outstanding characteristics. The 53,575 square miles hold nearly seven hundred persons per square mile. In the whole world, only West Germany, Britain, northern Italy, the Nile Valley, Japan, India, and China have population densities that match or surpass that of Megalopolis, U.S.A.

This population density has generated abnormally large transportation demands. Studies of the Northeast Corridor prepared by the U.S. Department of Commerce predict that demands for all modes of transportation may well triple within twenty years.[23] Although more people need more transportation facilities, the evolution of intercity transport patterns themselves rarely differ from those in other parts of urban America. More Megalopolitans are using automobiles and airplanes, while fewer and fewer resort to trains and buses. Consequently, intercity mass transit facilities are floundering to the point of extinction.

Automobile traffic is expected to triple between Baltimore and Washington in the next two decades. However, in the same period of time, the number of available highways is only expected to double, and this widens the gap between requirements and capacity all the more.[24]

The airways of the Northeast Corridor are already crowded. In Washington, air traffic has outstripped the capacity of National Airport, and the airlines are compelled to ration flights. New York began rationing flights also, as a reaction to a 1968 prediction that the average airliner would be delayed for two hours by 1970. True to prophecy, delays have become so commonplace that one out of every three flights from Kennedy Airport is held up. When the weather deteriorates and the field can be used only intermittently, delays at Kennedy may be as great as four hours, with as many as eighty aircraft jammed nose to tail awaiting clearance for departure.[25]

Private losses due to air traffic congestion are enormous. A Senate Commerce Committee report asserts that these delays cost traveling businessmen alone several million dollars of productive time each year. The cost to airlines is put at more than $40 million annually,[26] but this figure cannot include losses from ill will engendered in millions of inconvenienced passengers.

The Office of High-Speed Ground Transportation (OHSGT), a federal agency, directly aids stricken Megalopolis by implementing the provisions of the High-Speed Ground Transportation Act of 1965. This act authorized research in high-speed transportation, demonstration projects to determine effectiveness in intercity travel, and a unified national program to improve the scope and availability of transportation statistics. As part of its research program, the OHSGT carries out its Northeast Corridor project, analyzes the intercity passenger and freight requirements of Megalopolis through 1980 and beyond and develops plans to meet those requirements. The Northeast Corridor project is not limited to the study of ground transportation, for experiments with VTOL (vertical takeoff and landing) vehicles also play a significant part in OHSGT's program. The Office feeds results of its research to the Northeast Corridor project, where experts work to apply it to the specific needs of intercity travel along the northeastern seaboard. Through fiscal 1968, $52 million had been authorized for the OHSGT programs, and in 1969, an additional $13 million was allotted by the federal government. The office regards its money not as interest and government subsidy, but rather as seed capital to spur private interest and investment.[27]

In order to make high-speed rail transportation between major cities feasible, the OHSGT has concentrated the largest portion of its budget on two experimental railroads for the Northeast Corridor. The projects were completed in 1969, linking Boston and New York on one line, and New York and Washington, D.C., on the other. Their total cost was $81 million, of which the federal government provided about $22 million, and private industry the rest. Both trains operate up to speeds of 110 miles per hour, but average about seventy-five miles per hour for the entire run.

The Boston-New York project was started in 1966 when the Department of Transportation contracted with the United Aircraft Corporation to build two three-car Turbo-Trains. The DOT turned over operations of the completed line to the New York, New Haven and Hartford Railroads, and the train began to draw patrons immediately. Consisting of one passenger car in between two power-dome cars, the Turbo carries 148 passengers and takes about three and a half hours to complete the 229-mile trip—a full hour faster than the previous train speed record. In a speech on January 13, 1970, Federal Railroad Administrator Reginald N. Whitman expressed satisfaction with the new system:

> On the Turbo-Train there were almost 57,000 people who used the service between April, when it started, and November 1969. The average load factor for the one daily round trip has increased to around 66 percent since July, 1969. While we have some maintenance problems, we are very pleased with passenger response to these trains.[28]

In the New York-Washington corridor, Penn-Central and the DOT combined resources to provide the Metroliner, another experiment in high-speed rail transportation. Total cost of the program, which began service on January 15, 1969, was about $57 million of which the Penn Central's share was $45 million and DOT's about $12 million. Budd Company received the contract to provide fifty electrically powered Metroliner cars (twenty passenger coaches, twenty snack-bar coaches, and ten parlor coaches). The company used both General Electric and Westinghouse as major subcontractors for supplying the electrical propulsion and braking equipment for the train. Metroliner's success is a good example of the potential high-speed corridor trains all over the country. By the end of 1969, 700,000 people had taken the train, and this accounted for a 46-percent increase in the number of rail passengers between the two cities over the previous year.[29]

In the same speech, Whitman pointed out that the Metroliner proves not only the need for a rail alternative in congested areas, but a definite preference by many people for trains. A survey indicates that, in its first six months, the Metroliner gained half of its 228,000 passengers from other modes.[30] The train's powerful competition, Eastern Airlines, showed almost no increase in its passenger total over the previous year, whereas its normal yearly increase had been 3 to 15 percent.[31] Riders are attracted to the Metroliner's speed (the journey takes about three hours), as well as its comfort, which is emphasized by such enticing features as complete air conditioning, individual reading lamps, and incoming and outgoing telephone service. The train has almost no delays and even adverse weather does not stop it from running.

One of the most significant and revealing factors of Metroliner's success is the youth and affluence of its passengers. Penn Central Company's *Metroliner Facts*, issued on the first anniversary of the train's inauguration, says that "Metroliner passengers are active, affluent." A U.S. Department of Transportation survey disclosed that one third are between twenty-one and thirty-five, another third between thirty-five and fifty. Two thirds have family incomes over $15,000.[32] These facts challenge the argument that only the poor and aged will ride trains.

As the demand for a varied network of intercity transport becomes more compelling, the federal government is asked to assume a greater responsibility for transportation policy and finances. Long a trend-setter for the nation as a whole, the Northeast Corridor forecasts the coalescing of urbanites into large sprawling supercities. Freight, meanwhile, is following consumers in equally disorganized patterns. Movement of both passengers and goods is fast presenting problems for entire regions instead of individual cities.

Along with urban growth, the emphasis must be on regional transportation planning, with all its political disunity, rather than on urban planning. And to coordinate activities across regions, federal planning is called for. The 1966 establishment of the Department of Transportation in the President's cabinet is but a small advance when federal transportation policy remains neither consistent nor cohesive. Government involvement must be reevaluated and readapted to today's needs. So, in our following report, we will define, analyze, and hopefully clarify government's increasingly vital role in transportation.

Reprinted with the permission from "U.S. Petroleum and Gas Transportation Capacities" (1967) a Report of the National Petroleum Council.

Reprinted with the permission from "U.S. Petroleum and Gas Transportation Capacities" (1967) a Report of the National Petroleum Council.

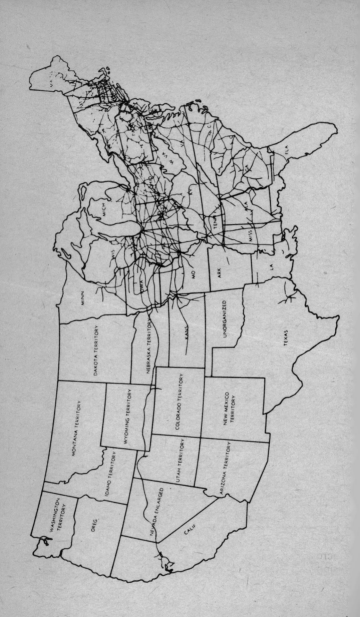

During the decade 1830-1840, the total length of completed railroad lines increased from 23 to 2,808 miles, and during the next ten years, more than 6,200 miles of railroad were opened, bringing the total network up to 9,021 miles. In the first twenty years of railway development the population of the United States nearly doubled.

Association of American Railroads.

Map (left): Although the Civil War temporarily halted railway development, many projects were resumed or initiated soon after and the nation's network increased from 30,626 miles in 1860 to 52,922 miles in 1870. An outstanding development of the decade was the construction of the first railroad to the Pacific Ocean, making it possible to travel all the way across the country by rail. Railway development in the Mississippi and Missouri valleys were notable during this period.

Association of American Railroads.

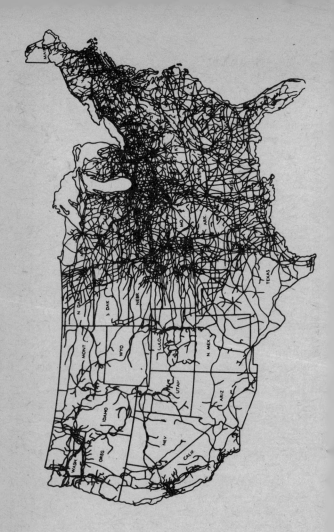

Class I railroads operate 209,000 miles of rail lines in th
U. S. The total track mileage owned by line-haul and switchin
and terminal companies is estimated at 340,000.

Association of American Railroads.

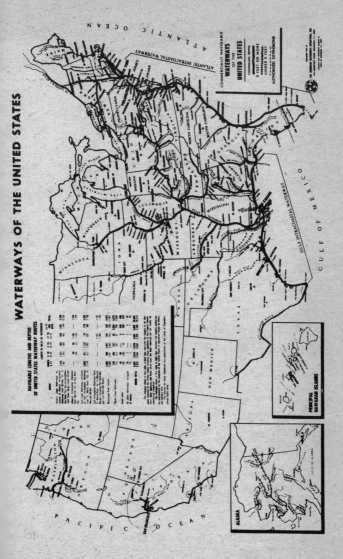

WATERWAYS OF THE UNITED STATES

Courtesy of THE AMERICAN WATERWAYS OPERATORS, INC.

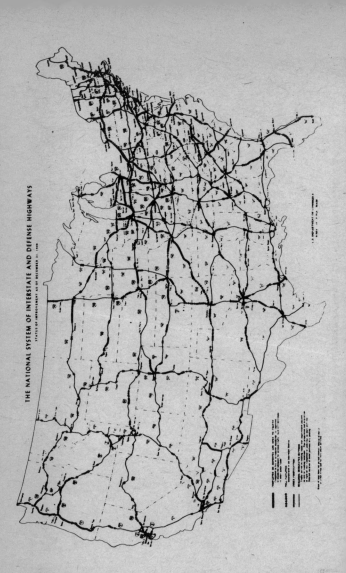

Map: Courtesy of the U.S. Department of Transportation, Federal Highway Administration.

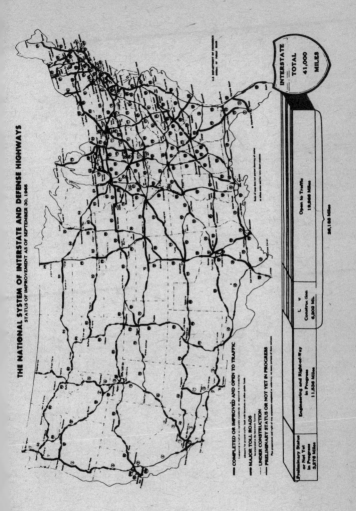

Map: Courtesy of the U.S. Department of Transportation, Federal Highway Administration.

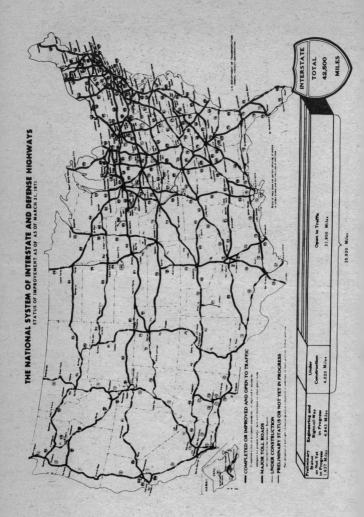

Map: Courtesy of the U.S. Department of Transportation, Federal Highway Administration.

GOVERNMENT
ROLE IN
TRANSPORTATION

INTRODUCTION

Despite its shortcomings, the federal government deserves sympathy for its touchy and complicated responsibilities in an elaborate economic and political system. Vast, complex America forces her officials onto a tightrope, with the result that they must struggle to keep a delicate balance. They must both assert authority and remain passive; they must work for the general welfare while maintaining an awareness of the needs of wealthy but essential businesses. Usually, the government keeps this balance with relative skill, but all too often it may sway far to one side or another, sometimes with unhappy consequences.

For example, government may hold minimal controls over one industry, dealing with it in a spirit of unrestricted laissez faire. This may result in a tight scramble for markets, penny-pinching on wages that drives competent workers into other fields, ambivalence on quality products or service, with weaker firms drifting toward bankruptcy and the strong toward monopoly—all problems that command government's attention.

On the other hand, government may overstep its boundaries and assert power which is neither necessary nor beneficial. It freezes rates and holds back innovation, and the public pays inflated prices for inferior services.

Always shaking the tightrope and threatening the balance are the lobbyists. Always eager to placate, the government often responds to the richest and loudest pleaders. Ideally, the government will have the wisdom to decide which requests from lobbyists are motivated by selfish financial interests and which by a concern for the needs of the country, and then will have the honesty and the courage to respond accordingly.

Both government involvement and government neglect have accompanied the development of transportation in the United States. History provides some excellent examples of each, while establishing the erratic pattern of government actions.

When the United States Constitution was ratified, the steam engine was still an infant and the internal combustion engine not yet even a dream. The Constitution's transportation analyst recognized water and, to a lesser degree, land transportation as the only major modes of travel.

Even this limited travel network won little attention from the young federal government. In 1786, several state governments granted John Fitch the exclusive right to operate steamboats on their waters, but they did so more to humor him than to admit the practicality of his enterprise. Fitch had already petitioned Congress: "The subscriber begs leave to lay at the feet of Congress an attempt to facilitate the internal navigation of the United States"; but he was virtually ignored. Benjamin Franklin and George Washington politely turned him away. Thus government, preoccupied with weightier matters in managing a new nation, let the steamboat flounder until Fulton's New York-Albany run twenty years later.

During the colonial and early national periods government provided for the construction of post roads; however, government did not provide regulations for stagecoach lines which operated over public roads. Unchecked competition among stagecoach lines, which were then the standard means of land travel, grew into bitter rivalries among companies that ran parallel routes. If a new competitor threatened an established line, a fare-cutting war usually followed, forcing one or the other out of business. One such war, on the Boston-Providence Line, reached the point where the two rivals did away with fares entirely and were serving a meal and a bottle of wine to every delighted passenger. The government did, however, take steps to cut down on casualties resulting from poor stagecoach operation. During the early 1800s, laws were passed for the protection of passengers; one required lamps at night and another imposed fines on drivers who were found intoxicated on duty.

The need for better roads was compelling, but the federal government and most of the new states were too poor to appropriate necessary funds. Private companies took charge of road-building, and turnpikes and tollgates appeared throughout the East. The roads proved unprofitable for their promoters, so in 1806 Congress authorized a survey to select a route for a roadway leading west from Cumberland, Maryland. Five years later, work began, and by 1838 Congress had spent nearly $3 million on the road which reached as far west as Vandalia, Illinois.[1] So began federal involvement in highways.

Canals were not new in the United States when New York State leaders began dreaming of one connecting the Hudson River to the Great Lakes. When the federal government refused to help, New York undertook the project alone. The Erie Canal was so successful that the travel time from New York City to Buffalo was reduced from twenty days to six, and the cost to ship a ton of goods that distance decreased from $125 to $5. Transportation experts lost no time reacting to the obvious message. By 1850, canals covered 4,460 miles.[2]

The 1830s were a decade of canal construction, but they also witnessed the birth of the railroad industry. The first railroad line, the Baltimore and Ohio (B&O), was started to compete with the Erie Canal. Since the federal government did no more for this new mode than supply army engineers, construction financing depended entirely on the citizens of Baltimore and Frederick, Maryland. The cars were horse-drawn, for steam engines did not come into use until Peter Cooper's *Tom Thumb* convinced the B&O in 1831. The South Carolina Railroad had been using steam locomotives since its beginning in 1830. By 1860, railroads had replaced canals as the predominant travel mode east of the Mississippi.

For nearly twenty years, railroad builders had sought federal aid in vain and were forced to rely on private, state, and local funds. In 1850, however, the scene changed through the efforts of Stephen A. Douglas, U.S. Senator from Illinois, who convinced the federal government to grant between 150 and 160 million acres of land during a twenty-two-year period.[3] The Illinois Central was the first railroad built with the assistance of federal land grants. In the early 1860s, when visionaries suggested a transcontinental railroad, the government responded with enthusiasm. The Union Pacific and Central Pacific lines were chartered by Congress and guaranteed financial aid ranging from $16,000 to $48,000 per completed mile.[4] But Congress had failed to specify a meeting place for the two lines, which had begun to race. Day by day, they came closer until finally, on parallel roadbeds and only yards apart, they began passing each other. In their eagerness to dig into the federal coffers, both roads intended to keep on laying track until stopped by the oceans. To remedy the oversight, Congress designated Promontory Point, Utah, as the meeting place and there, on May 10, 1869, the two companies performed the ceremony of linking the first transcontinental railroad.

The railroads continued to expand, almost exclusively under private management. The government followed a policy of promotion but not ownership, although it supplied substantial subsidies. To gather the huge capital needed to build railroads, the railroads often practiced excesses in promotion and financing which were foreshadowed in the transcontinental project. Overcapitalization, together with frenzied competition, led to business practices ranging from inefficient to reprehensible. Shipping costs varied not according to distance and bulk, but according to which routes involved less competition. Rochester, New York, merchants found that shipping goods east through New York City and then west—right back through Rochester—to Cincinnati, cost them much less than shipping directly to Cincinnati. In 1885, an Ohio railroad charged the Standard Oil Company ten cents per barrel to ship oil from Macksburg, Ohio, to Marietta, Ohio. The same railroad charged smaller independents thirty-five cents per barrel, and even turned over the extra twenty-five cents to Standard Oil.[5]

This discrimination caused such a furor that in 1887 the federal government embarked on its first major venture in railroad regulation. Congress passed the Act to Regulate Commerce and created the Interstate Commerce Commission, which still administers the Act and its amendments today.

Meanwhile, federal action during the Civil War unintentionally brought about the demise of the steamboat. An embargo denying shippers the use of the rivers forced merchants to turn to railroads. Even after the war, when river traffic was permitted to resume, most customers stayed with the rails.

Perhaps impressed with the shocking consequences of its prodigal permissiveness toward the railroads, the government began showing a lively interest in new transportation modes as they came onto the scene. From their inception, both the automotive and airline industries were spurred on by injections of public funds.

In 1863, the internal combustion engine was invented, and in 1881 the Duryea brothers made and operated the first gasoline-propelled vehicles in the United States. The automobile was on its way, but it needed better roads to ride on. So in 1900, the United States Office of Road Inquiry started pressuring various states to take action. State and local governments began investing more heavily in road construction, and by 1908, sixteen states had highway commissions.[6] At the time, the need for roads was obvious, but the government continued promoting highways even after planners offered evidence that the nation's transportation system was being buried in concrete. The Depression spurred massive road building, a favorite government way to create jobs. During World War II, highway construction lagged, only to intensify in the postwar years. Thus the government paved the way for the supremacy of motor-vehicle travel and the inevitable decline of other modes.

By establishing airmail service after World War I, the government became godfather at the christening of American commercial aviation. Still, the young industry needed the nourishment of a vital civilian market, so the federal government founded the Aeronautical Chamber of Commerce (ACC) to promote research and sell flying to the American public. The ACC sponsored and financed headline-making feats which gripped imaginations and emotions everywhere. But it remained for another war to push air transportation forward. A tremendous expansion in air-passenger traffic followed World War II and, since government-funded research helped develop the jet, air freight also gained popularity.

Government today holds life-and-death power over the various transportation modes. History may trace a general pattern of involvement, but it does not fully reveal the impact and significance of federal, state, and local action. The failure to recognize the precise nature of government involvement in transportation development may stem from a confusion in terms. In fact, the very words used to designate the government role have become hazy because of frequent misuse. Terms such as "involvement," "action," "decision," and "impact" are often mistakenly interchanged. For example, government "involvement" need not necessarily come about through specific decisions or actions.

"Impact" may range from the economic effects of government financing to the psychological effects on the public market.

Careless interchanging of terms abounds in legislation, court decisions, policy statements, political party platforms, and so on. Often cited as a masterpiece of muddled thinking is the Transportation Act of 1940, the nation's first attempt at a written transportation policy. The document declared that from that day on, it would be the duty of Congress:

> . . . to provide for fair and impartial regulation of all modes of transportation subject to provisions of the Act, so administered as to recognize and preserve the inherent advantages of each; to promote safe, adequate, economical, and efficient service and foster sound economic conditions in transportation and among the several carriers; to encourage the establishment and maintenance of reasonable charges for transportation services, without unjust discriminations, undue preferences or advantages, or unfair or destructive competitive practices; to cooperate with the several States and the duly authorized officials thereof; and to encourage fair wages and equitable working conditions—all to the end of developing, coordinating, and preserving a national transportation system by water, highway, and rail, as well as other means, adequate to meet the needs of the commerce of the United States, of the Postal Service, and of the national defense . . . [7]

The meaning of "efficient utilization" has been so ceaselessly debated that lawmakers use it as they please. The Act's most serious pitfall is the total ambiguity of the relationship between "balance," "coordination," and "competition," conflicting terms which are tossed about mindlessly and almost without distinctions. The authors of the Act were too bound by political strings to recognize priorities.

Transportation experts envision "coordination" as a placing of each mode in its proper perspective so that wasteful overlapping of facilities may be eliminated, leaving the modes to complement each other's services, and the network as a whole to run like a fine watch. Meanwhile, "competition" implies a lack of coordination. The result is a situation in which each service attempts to displace the other and overlapping is inevitable. The Transportation Act of 1940 calls for some balance among conflicting practices, but it neither defines this balance nor explains how it is to be achieved.

Another major source of confusion lies in the word "mode" itself, bandied about by every institution from the ICC to GOP. The Interstate Commerce Commission employs the five groupings of railroads, motor vehicles, water transports, pipelines, and airplanes in its regulatory framework.[8] For some reason, the Republican platform definition of mode does not include the automobile.[9] In his *Economics of Transportation*, Dr. Philip Locklin, a widely recognized expert, includes five modes: railroads, water transportation, pipelines, transportation by air, and motor vehicles on public highways.[10] Locklin's list is a carbon copy of the ICC's, with one significant three-word addition: "on public highways" introduces the enormously complex concept of right-of-way.

The GOP, the ICC, and Professor Locklin demonstrate the inconsistency and confusion connected with a word so vital that its misuse has caused gross imbalance and injustices in government's treatment of the transportation network. Many policies were designed to promote one mode over another, or even certain aspects of one mode, merely because officials could define the word as they pleased. To avoid such terminological chaos, we will use a specific but all-encompassing definition which includes four components: vehicle, right-of-way, service facilities, and corporate structure.

The railroad is the perfect model of this definition. Its vehicle consists of engine and rolling stock, and its right-of-way involves land and track. Service facilities—stations and terminals—make the operation of the rails possible and, equally important, the corporate structure decides policy crucial to all who use the industry's services.

Pipelines, a second major mode, are perhaps the most homogeneous of all. Their construction is sufficiently standardized for them to be considered one vehicle and, like the railroads, rights-of-way and service facilities remain similar throughout the industry. Pipelines are, however, a divided legal identity. From the standpoint of the ICC, they are either private, common, or contract carriers.

The other modes do not fit the definition as neatly, for several of their components vary. We consider water transportation to be the third major mode, even though only its rights-of-way are constant. The vehicles differ, as do the service facilities and the corporate structures. The Republican platform of 1968 anticipated this confusion and so designated only the barge as a major mode. But tempting as it may seem, the other types of craft operating on our waterways must not be ignored if the meaning of mode is to be at all consistent. As it does for pipelines, the ICC defines three legal types of water carriers; private, common, or contract.

The fourth major mode, motor vehicle, is as diverse as water transportation. These vehicles range from auto to truck and bus and, to further complicate matters. the truck has a divided legal identity, as do both pipelines and water carriers. The ICC classifies trucks as either private, common, or contract carriers. Although all three types of motor vehicles operate on public highways, buses and trucks are sometimes restricted from residential roads because of local weight and size regulations. So although the vehicles share a common right-of-way, there are still some important exceptions. Service facilities vary also within the mode, from passenger terminals for buses to special freight-loading docks for trucks. And the truck and the bus are operated by corporate systems, whereas, for the most part, private individuals own and run the auto.

The fifth mode poses still greater problems of definition. The airplane is constructed according to rigid standards, and its access to the airways is also controlled to some extent. It shares a right-of-way, the federal airways system, which has an elaborate system of traffic control, and it likewise uses common terminal facilities.

But complications set in with the locations of airports. Because most are situated some distance from the cities they serve, construction of access roads and transit lines has been a prerequisite for efficient operation. Thus, the complex notion of intermodality crops up, with attendant legal and technical arguments.

As much as the diversity of these modes is a vital concept, we must also understand the complex interrelationships between modes and their components if we are to form a true picture of government impact on transportation. The railroad's components are perfectly cohesive. One company, with its individual corporate structure, owns right-of-way and service facilities which exist solely for the railroad. Although the track and terminals are shared with other lines, the owning company still finances them, maintains them, and pays taxes on them. This legal relationship of corporate structure to right-of-way and facilities, which also describes private pipelines, does not characterize the association between airplanes and the airways, between motor vehicles and the highways, between watercraft and the waterways, and between common-carrier pipelines and their rights-of-way. Roads, waters, and skies serve any vehicles able to travel on them. No one industry or company may own right-of-way on them, and none must finance or maintain them.

Equally essential to understanding government's transportation involvement is the concept of intermodality, the linking of modes for optimum efficiency in the movement of passengers or goods. The best known example is the piggyback operation, by which railroad flatcars carry truck vans, and the airport-highway tie-in mentioned earlier.

But perhaps the greatest barrier to intelligent discussion and analysis is the cloudy language used in defining the government role. The Transportation Act of 1940 is an example of how terminology juggling can paralyze thought and judgment. Clearly needed is a single unifying term to express the meanings of every term from "government action" and "participation" to "response" and "intervention." An interesting suggestion is "investment" for, although not entirely original, it appears to offer the best possibilities for comprehensive analysis.

"Investment" is, in simplest terms, the addition or subtraction or reassignment of resources by any level of government which affects transportation. Carrying no implication of goals or influences, it underscores the fact that what appears to be an investment in one mode may simultaneously have negative results for another or, ultimately, no net effect on either.

To further clarify the definition, let us fit four factors into the overall term "resources": land, labor, capital, and entrepreneurial ability. *Land* refers to all natural resources and so, somewhat paradoxically, represents waterways and airways as well. *Labor* is even more flexible. It not only designates construction and maintenance workers, but also any labor input for projects such as government-financed or government-directed surveys. *Capital* encompasses facilities such as machinery and vehicles, as well as stocks, bonds, loans, and grants, all of which government has invested in transportation at one time or another. The fourth factor, *entrepreneurial ability*, represents human resources in the managing or decision-making realm, including government's own personnel, who sometimes sit on the boards of directors of certain public corporations.

These subdivisions are not cut-and-dried, however. Some aspects of government investment fail to fall neatly into any of the four compartments of land, labor, capital, and entrepreneurial ability. Taxation, for example, could easily be viewed as a subtraction of capital. At the same time, it may have a negative effect on entrepreneurial ability, acting as a potential incentive-killer. And in the case of property tax, it takes resources from the land. So for convenience, let us place taxation in the capital category and set our primary focus on the treasury of the company involved.

Many resources fit no category at all. *Corporate structure* is altered by the government in many instances. Interventions, such as antitrust laws which attack monopolistic structures and lay ground rules for new corporations, may be regarded as forms of investment. *Research and development programs* comprise still another brand of resource, for they often influence transportation development. Even research which government undertakes without transportation in mind but which has side effects on the industry may be defined as investment.

Without directly donating or removing resources, government may still affect transportation. Because it controls the economy as a whole, it determines how much money may be available at any time for the transport industries. It holds psychological sway over the *investment and general business climate*. At times, government has even acted as a financial intermediary by arranging the exchange of funds (in the form of securities) between private investors. By insuring the rate of return, government can encourage investors to put their money into transportation. Although this type of government investment involves no direct transfer of resources from the public treasury to the transport industries, it nevertheless brings powerful influence to bear on transportation development.

Although it furnishes a framework for analyzing virtually all areas of government action, the concept of investment must be supplemented by two additional concepts—promotion and regulation. The essential distinction between these terms and investment is that, whereas investment implies only the action itself, promotion and regulation denote objectives and goals.

Regulation is a type of investment, but it more specifically refers to the actual decisions of regulatory bodies which organize and balance the transportation industries. Promotion is investment linked to goals which may range from community well-being to economic development for the country as a whole. Government may cater to short-term or long-term objectives in its promotional schemes. In some cases, regulation and promotion interact. The Civil Aeronautics Board (CAB) commissioned to promote adequate, efficient, and economical air service also is required to regulate air transportation. By using its regulatory powers to control competition, however, it underwrites growth and development of existing airlines to the detriment of would-be competitors.

The guiding concepts and definitions discussed in this chapter will be dealt with later in more detail. Hopefully, the terms and definitions chosen here will help illuminate a subject long shrouded in semantic fog.

CHAPTER 1

INVESTMENT

Local, state, and federal governments have many ways of investing in transportation. They may provide resources to the private establishment itself, or they may give money to individual private firms for the purchase of these resources. Government may also engage directly in transportation, sometimes in competition with private enterprise. It may also create, augment, reduce, or eliminate the demand for transportation by guiding the location of economic activities through zoning regulation and through different taxing policies. The definition of "resources" offered in the preceding chapter—land (or natural resources), labor, capital, entrepreneurial ability, corporate structure, research and development, and a stable business climate—is useful in analyzing such factors as legislation, regulatory decisions, and court verdicts. With the breaking down of "mode" into four components—vehicle, right-of-way, corporate structure, and service facilities—the various forms of investment come into sharper focus.

Natural Resources

The most outstanding example of natural resource investment by the federal government is the awarding of public land (either through land grants or through the right of eminent domain) to the rights-of-way of privately owned wagon roads, canals, and railroads. The railroads were the greatest beneficiaries, gaining not only right-of-way, but squares of land adjacent to the area over which the tracks ran.

Conservative estimates place federal land grants to railroads at 131.4 million acres,[1] at an average value of nearly a dollar per acre.[2] This figure does not include some 49 million acres that the United States gave the states to distribute among the railroads. The railroads were free to do as they pleased with the land. They sold or mortgaged it and often used the profits for railroad construction or to buy other land rich in the timber and minerals needed for railroad maintenance.

Land grants were investments with staggered payoffs for the railroads. Besides the immediate benefit of the right-of-way, the added sections of land allowed speculation which often yielded tremendous profit. Owners held the extra land until most of the cheaper federal land was gone, then sold it at a premium. The completion of the railroad also enhanced the value of the surrounding property.

While land grants gave the rails profit and incentive, they also caused problems. Discrimination was practically inevitable. The federal government won extra privileges in return for its land gifts. Mail, soldiers, and government property were transported at special rates, saving the federal government what some historians estimate at $600 million (throughout World War II), with at least one estimate at $900 million.[3]

The government refused to renounce complete legal control over the waterways as it had over land. In 1824 the Supreme Court ruled in *Gibbons* v. *Ogden* that the waters of a state, when they constitute a highway for interstate of foreign commerce, are within the jurisdiction of Congress. Thus the states could not grant exclusive rights for water navigation, nor could they parcel out their waterways as they had done with their land. The rivers and lakes were for everyone's use, and businessmen could invest in water transport without facing the outrageous monopolistic fees so common in the rail industry.

Labor

Surveys, planning, construction, and maintenance comprise the bases for government's investment in transportation labor resources.

The federal government spurred transportation development by sponsoring or requiring extensive surveys and planning of states and localities applying for federal funds. The General Survey Bill of 1824 authorized the President to order the necessary surveys, plans, and estimates for certain roads and canal routes. Although railroads were not specifically mentioned in this legislation, Congress appropriated funds for them too.

The federal government is responsible for most of the survey and planning work in waterway construction. In 1819 the Corps of Army Engineers was delegated to evaluate proposed river and harbor improvements. Legislation in 1902 directed the Chief of Army Engineers to come up with a plan for the improvement and development of waterways, which is submitted annually to Congress. The 1902 Act also created the Board of Army Engineers to examine, from technical and economic standpoints, the waterway projects submitted by the Army Engineers.

The national government actively plans airports as well. The Federal Airport Act of 1946 required the Civil Aeronautics Authority (now the Federal Aviation Agency—FAA) to form and annually update a national plan for airports. The FAA must approve all designs, plans, and construction to insure that airports meet federal standards.

Highways demand much survey work and extensive, detailed plans. The 1930s marked the beginning of what was to become a tremendous federal-aid program. Statewide surveys have supplied data for the past thirty years, and more recently, federal policy began stressing wide-area coordination of transportation and land-use. Such overall planning is now a prerequisite for any federal assistance to state and local governments.[4]

All levels of government undertake various construction projects, and the work is usually contracted to a private firm. But in relatively rare cases (for example, during the Depression), the federal government has placed construction laborers on its own payroll.

When private industry could not be persuaded to invest in the transportation services government deemed necessary, federal authorities took over. National defense, too, required construction for which the government hired labor directly. This kind of federal participation is usually welcomed, but sometimes it arouses political resentment at the state and local levels. The very first federal highway project, for instance, so threatened state powers that it became necessary for Washington to give up control of the national road it had built. Since then, the states and localities have been the primary movers in constructing and maintaining highways and the federal role has been confined primarily to providing grants. However, the federal government did designate a basic pattern for the Interstate Highway System, but left to state and local administrators the job of planning the exact highway alignment.

Mostly because private enterprise kept out of the picture, the states themselves built many canals and railroads. New York labored over its Erie Canal, while Ohio, Indiana, and Illinois undertook their own major projects.[5] But financial difficulties and the Supreme Court, which gave the federal government jurisdiction over navigable rivers, made the states reduce their waterway improvement programs. Between 1947 and 1971 the federal government will have contributed $9 billion and the states and localities $5 million for waterways.[6] Federal money went for inland and intracoastal waterways, Great Lakes and coastal harbors, operation and maintenance of canals and harbors, locks and dams, alteration of bridges over navigable rivers, and advanced engineering design. The states have contributed funds which were utilized by private entrepreneurs or local port authorities to construct terminal facilities.

Pennsylvania built two railroads as part of its public works program, as did Illinois, Michigan, Georgia, and Virginia. But financial panics essentially finished off state programs of construction and maintenance.[7] Since the turn of the century, railroads for the most part have been owned and kept up privately, except during the two world wars. Also during the past few years, some local governments have assumed ownership of commuter road facilities.

The Federal Aviation Agency controls the airways, maintaining and operating the system, as well as establishing new facilities. In *Economics of Transportation*, Dr. Philip Locklin described the airway as an:

> ... elaborate network of navigation aids such as radio signal stations, beacon lights, continuous weather service, intermediate landing fields, instrumental approach systems, air-route traffic-control centers, and radar-approach facilities.[8]

Approximately $11 billion will have been spent for these operations by 1971, with an additional $3 billion for federal construction and maintenance of airports.[9]

Finance Capital

Bonds. Government investment through the sale of bonds follows a devious path because the relationship between government on the one hand and private buyers and sellers on the other is inconsistent. Local, state, or federal governments would either buy transportation bonds from certain industries, or offer loans or outright gifts to a carrier. If the government did not directly participate in buying or selling bonds, the private corporation still needed the approval of state legislatures before it could place bonds on the open market.

The first important use of bonds was to help finance construction of the Erie Canal. From that time, state governments, noted in the late 1820s for their relatively small debts and good reputations in international markets, decided to assist canal construction by selling bonds. These state bond programs rose swiftly from $13 million between 1820-1824 to $108 million between 1835-1837.[10] But the Panic of 1837 undercut the success of the bond program, leaving many states near bankruptcy.

Government investment with bonds also appeared in railroad financing, but railroad bonds are remembered more for their unhappy demise than for any positive financial contribution. Minnesota at first refused to honor its railroad bonds of 1860 and later agreed to compromise. In Missouri, a large part of the local railroad bond debt was scaled down after a drawn-out controversy.[11]

Federal bonds were important but not really critical to the building of the Union Pacific Railroad. While proceeds from bond sales amounted to $27.1 million, the money was by no means enough to pay the cost of the road.[12] So many state governments oversubscribed and so many railroads defaulted on payments, that several states—Ohio, Michigan, Tennessee, and Iowa, among others—amended their constitutions to ban state aid for public works.[13]

Government bonds played only a small part in pipeline planning and construction, but have been extensively used for constructing airports. States often raise funds through bond sales to meet the required 50 percent of cost they must pay in order to get the remainder in federal funds.

Revenue from the sale of government bonds, although not nearly as prevalent as in other years, is still important, particularly in urban mass transit. The first phase of the New York Metro-

politan Transportation Authority modernization plan required
$1.6 million in funds from a $2.5-billion bond issue approved by
New York voters in 1967.[14] The Chicago Transit Authority
bought rights-of-way from the Chicago, Milwaukee, St. Paul, and
Pacific Railroad through the sale of revenue bonds to private
investors.[15] The CTA had put $1.3 million worth of equipment
trust certificates on the market by the close of 1967. The voters of
three Bay Area counties endorsed a $792-million issue of general
obligation bonds to help finance San Francisco's BART.[16]

Stocks. Government bought stock in private companies to provide important financial resources for the early construction of
turnpikes and railroads. Pennsylvania, Virginia, and Ohio
bought stock in turnpike companies, although exactly how much
is not known. George R. Taylor, author of an important work on
antebellum transportation, candidly admits that "the total
amount of the investment by states in turnpikes is unknown, but
it was surely a fairly substantial sum."[17] The same obscurity sur-
rounds the municipalities' contributions.

Data on government stock purchases in canal-building companies are also spotty and poorly organized, but all levels of
government bought these stocks. By 1840, Pennsylvania had invested over $600,000 in the canal and navigation company
stock.[18] To encourage the building of the Union Canal, it granted
valuable lottery privileges and guaranteed a 6 percent return to
Union Canal subscribers.

Eventually the states placed ceilings on amounts of bonds that
could be sold, and the railroads began to make more important
use of stocks. Statistics on purchases during this period are more
abundant and better organized. In 1938 the federal Coordinator
of Transportation estimated the total state aid to railroads in the
form of stock purchases at about $40.1 million.[19] The state
governments rarely relied on one method of investment, but
generally packaged several types of aid best suited to the
particular needs of the receiving company. Upon its completion
in 1841, the Western Railroad in Massachusetts had been given
$4.6 million from the legislature, $600,000 in investment in the
company's stock, and the remainder in a secured loan.[20] The state
often offered to buy stock as an incentive to building,
foreshadowing the matching grant technique of highway
legislation. Virginia, in particular, gave special impetus to railroad construction when it agreed to take three fifths of the stock
of a railroad company, as soon as the other two fifths had been

sold. (This was a common ploy, not only with stocks but with other forms of public aid: the states and cities involved would only grant bonuses, land, etc., after the rails had completed construction to a particular point.)[21]

In some cases, the government owned a company outright and held all of its stock—even while daily direction of the company remained in private hands. In other instances the government created a corporation, supporting it by purchasing its stock. In 1924 Congress created the Inland Waterways Corporation, which ran a barge service, and the federal government held all its stock until 1953, when it sold the company to private owners.[22]

Loans. In 1957, the first legislation was passed in which the federal government promised to back up loans that banks made to private airlines for the purchase of new equipment. If, for some reason, the company could not pay back the loan, the government would pay it, and the banks, thus assured that their money would be returned, were more willing to lend. Congress initiated the law to make equipment financing easier for local service carriers and certified helicopter operators. Similarly, the Transportation Act of 1958 authorized the ICC to back up loans made by public or private agencies to railroad companies for capital expenditures or maintenance work. Loans made to intercity trains, as well as urban lines, were covered. The one major drawback was that railroad managements were reluctant to negotiate loans with financial intermediaries, claiming that their financial position was weak. Thus, that provision of the Act was allowed to expire in 1963.[23]

Meanwhile, the railroads had made it clear that only direct government loans would solve their financial difficulties. Since there was yet no Department of Transportation, railroad loan problems were assigned to the Housing and Home Finance Administrator in the Housing Act of 1961. The Act provided for the use of loans to "finance the acquisition, construction, reconstruction, and improvement of facilities and equipment for use, by operation or lease or otherwise, in mass transportation service in urban areas, and for use in coordinating highway bus, surface-rail, underground parking and other transportation facilities in such areas."[24] But since the Housing and Home Administration worked only on urban matters, many problem areas were neglected.

Another type of insurance provided by the federal government was the mortgage guarantee. Under the provisions of the Merchant Marine Acts of 1936 and 1970, carriers could obtain government-insured mortgages to help finance the construction of equipment.

Grants. A grant is a transfer of funds from one level of government to another, or from government to a private corporation. Since the turn of the century, grants have become more and more important in financing highway building, airports, and waterway improvements. In fact, the federal government has found it the most effective stimulus to private industry in transportation development.

Federal and state governments have become the main sources of funds for transportation improvements, including most of the planning and leadership. Actually, private corporations have depended mostly on Washington for their grants, and less on the states and municipalities.

At first, political pressure forced the federal government to hide its payments to private establishments in the form of mail "payments" which far exceeded the cost of the grant itself. But in 1935, in his message on the American merchant marine, President Roosevelt candidly told Congress:

> In many instances in our history the Congress has provided for various kinds of disguised subsidies to American shipping. . . . The Government today is paying annually about $30 million for the carrying of mails which would cost, under normal ocean rates, only $3 million. This $27 million difference is a subsidy and nothing but a subsidy . . . I believe that it (Congress) can well afford to call a subsidy by its right name . . . [25]

One outstanding feature of public investment in highway development has been the dramatic shift of financing from county and municipal governments to the rapidly maturing state and federal governments. In 1915, local governments provided 90 percent of all highway funds; the states, 10 percent; and the federal government, nothing. In 1921, federal aid took care of about 6 percent of all highway expenses, the states' share rose to 30 percent, and local authorities provided the rest. By 1965, the division was 29 percent, federal; 52 percent, state; and 19 percent, county and municipal. From $5 million in 1917, federal aid to highways sailed to $4.8 billion by 1969.[26]

Also through the years, highway-user charges have come to replace general funds (property and other tax receipts). Road-user taxes, which yielded only 3 percent of highway funds in 1915, accounted for nearly 75 percent of all road funds in 1965.[27] Congress' application of the user charge for highway financing shows its desire to have those who benefit from a transportation service pay for it.

In 1891, New Jersey created a state-aid highway system, paid one third of all improvements, and thus became the first state to succumb to the powerful rural-automobile-cyclist lobby.[28] By 1915, forty-five states had enacted state-aid laws, and forty had established highway departments. The Federal Aid Road Act of 1916 spurred on federal participation in highways by authorizing the government to split with the states fifty-fifty the costs of intercity highways.[29]

To be sure of reaping the full benefits of its investments, Congress, in 1921, restricted the use of federal funds to connected networks of highways, and thus focused federal funds on a limited major highway system. The networks were picked by the states and limited to 7 percent of their then existing road mileage.

The federal government made its first attempt to assist urban highway construction in 1928. An act of Congress made available Federal funds " . . . within municipalities of 2,500 or more, along those sections of highways on which the houses (were) . . . more than 200 feet apart on the average." [30] Obviously, this hardly describes a modern urban area, and the program represented no more than a token effort to aid urban highways. Only highways surrounding the thinly developed areas of large cities could profit.

During the Depression, however, emergency highway programs sprang up; states did not have to match federal funds, and federal money went into highway building as an effective way to ease unemployment. Regular federal highway aid resumed in 1936. Grants-in-aid assisted intercity highways in urban areas, but Congress made no specific allocation for city highways until 1944, with a program of federal fund distribution. The program divided the annual federal highway appropriation into 45 percent for a primary system, 30 percent for a secondary system, and 25 percent for urban projects.

The Highway Act of 1956 provided for the construction of a National System of Interstate and Defense Highways. This legislation authorized the federal govenment to pay up to 90 percent of the costs for acquisition of right-of-way and construction of any portion of the Interstate Highway System.

The federal government does not, however, provide funds for maintenance of highways thus constructed. Some states are experiencing difficulties in raising money to repair the extensive highway networks which they now have.

The most significant feature of the 1956 Act was its pay-as-you-go trust fund, which spent the receipts from gasoline and other road-related taxes for highways. The Highway Trust Fund provided the only means for federal-aid payments to the states.

The federal government alone has subsidized the airlines, recognizing the economic and military potential of a mighty air industry. The airmail subsidy payment of 1925 was a pioneer, albeit disguised, form of federal aid. At the time, public opposition to government assistance to private industry forced the federal government to rely on indirect and unidentifiable grants. The government would overpay for mail services, and the money kept the young airlines from floundering.

Between 1926 and 1933, state and local governments paid for airports because the Air Commerce Act of 1926 barred federal construction and operation. But during the Depression, the government again poured money into airport building to provide jobs and, when the nation was back on its feet, continued to aid airport construction under the supervision of the Civil Aeronautics Administration.

The Federal Airport Act of 1946 laid the foundation for intense federal assistance to states and municipalities for airport construction and improvement. About $1 billion has been doled out under this legislation, but the $4.5-billion contribution of states and municipalities has still far surpassed the federal share. [31] Locklin says:

> Federal participation assures that the airport facilities are meeting the needs of an expanding air transport system, and are preventing the waste of capital that would result from independent and uncoordinated airport planning by a host of local authorities with only local interests in mind. [32]

The subsidy, disguised as mail payments, enabled some of the first commercial airlines to compete successfully with the older modes. Since the passage of the Civil Aeronautics Act of 1938, which set up the Civil Aeronautics Board to determine subsidy payments, the federal government has presented over $1 billion in subsidies to domestic airlines. [33] The major trunk lines (United, Eastern, American, TWA) were once the main beneficiaries, but their aid has been gradually cut, and the bulk of federal money now goes to local air service carriers. The CAB, which administers the program, has continually reduced the overall subsidy and furthered its goal of eliminating subsidies entirely. The $84 million designated for airlines in 1964 dropped to $44 million by 1969.[34] The CAB could make this reduction by assigning more profitable routes to local carriers and inaugurating a "use it or lose it" policy.[35]

Federal subsidies to the merchant marine fleet began in 1845 in the form of mail contracts. The Ocean Mail Act of 1891 awarded mail payments to various classes of steamships and originated a trade-route system which remains unchanged to this day. Under the provisions of this Act, which stayed in effect until 1923, $29.6 million was handed out. The Merchant Marine Act of 1920 continued the provisions of the 1891 law, but required the U.S. Shipping Board and the Postmaster General to determine fair and reasonable subsidy rates. Thus the 1920 Act eliminated much of the excess payment which had bolstered the merchant marine, and only $4.8 million was given in mail subsidies between 1923 and 1929. Under a later act, the Merchant Marine Act of 1928, post office appropriations paid approximately $200 million for $25 million worth of services, the overpayment being mail subsidies.[36]

In 1936, a significant change occurred when federal aid to private companies was no longer disguised as mail payments. The traditional channeling of government aid through the post office ended, and in its place the U.S. Maritime Commission was created.[37] Joseph Sarisky outlined the specific guiding concepts of the legislation:

1. The Maritime Commission may grant a construction subsidy to vessels built, reconstructed, or reconditioned in the U.S. which are suitable for national defense purposes. This provision makes sure that American shipowners will no longer be attracted to foreign shipyards where construction costs are considerably less. A shipowner may receive up to 55 percent of the total cost of his vessel to compensate him for the higher American prices.

2. The Maritime Commission may also grant differential subsidies to vessels utilized on essential trade routes.

3. The Commission may make payments for national de-

fense features incorporated into a vessel, features which are often helpful to a vessel in peacetime as well.

4. The Federal government grants additional compensating subsidies to U.S. companies to offset the effects of government aid by other nations to their ocean fleets.[38]

The 1936 legislation spurred domestic shipbuilding and ship operation in the years before World War II and during the war itself. However, the position of the U.S. merchant fleet sagged badly during the 1950s and 1960s. The provision of $6.3-billion in federal subsidies between 1947 and 1969 did not reverse the unmistakable downward spiral.[39] The 1936 legislation provided assistance only to some U.S. shipowners who operated on essential fixed ship routes. All operators of bulk carriers were excluded from the subsidy benefit precisely because they did not operate with fixed schedules on fixed routes.

In the late 1960s, Congress began seriously discussing new proposals which would revitalize our merchant fleet. The result of nearly two years of discussion and debate was the Merchant Marine Act of 1970, signed into law by President Nixon in October 1970. The new legislation contained a commitment to construct three hundred new ships in American shipyards during the next decade. The new legislation eliminates the existing restriction on giving subsidies to shipowners who do not operate over fixed routes. As a consequence, operators of bulk carriers for the first time are eligible for the construction-differential and the operating-differential subsidy payments. The legislation also attempts to make the U.S. shipyards more efficient by limiting the percentage of total costs for which a shipyard or shipowner can be reimbursed. Presently, the federal government can pay up to 55 percent of the total cost. Under the new legislation, by 1976 the federal government will authorize the payment of only 35 percent of the total costs. The Secretary of Commerce may, however, pay a higher sum if he determines that the nation's commitment to the shipbuilding program will be damaged without the money. The new legislation also attempts to make the ship operator more efficient by limiting the funds available for operating-differential subsidies.

Between 1950 and 1970, all levels of government dabbled in mass transportation financing. Direct state and local grants, supplemented by loans, bonds, and grants, formed the backbone of mass transit funding. In 1958, Massachusetts paid the New

Haven Railroad $900,000 to insure continued commuter service.[40] Philadelphia also granted money to its transit company to buy equipment and to experiment with various fare cuts and service innovations on commuter lines.[41]

The Mass Transit Act of 1964 was the first legislation to provide for federal aid to mass transportation. It authorized the Housing and Home Finance Administration "to provide additional assistance for the development of comprehensive and coordinated mass transportation systems, both public and private, in metropolitan and other urban areas . . . "[42] Under this act, the federal government provides the needed capital to cover the high building and operating costs of mass transit systems. Federal funds thus may be used "for a wide variety of purposes, including purchases of right-of-way, parking facilities, buses, rail cars, signal equipment, stations, and terminals."[43] In 1968, the newly formed U.S. Department of Transportation took over the program. Lack of sufficient funds has somewhat slowed progress but the program has registered some gains: in 1969 alone, the government gave over $25 million to the Chicago South Suburban Mass Transit District for commuter cars, $28 million to San Francisco's Bay Area Rapid Transit District for BART cars and continued construction, and $27 million to the Massachusetts Bay Transportation Authority for new cars and a rapid transit extension. Since the beginning of the program in 1964 through fiscal year 1969, almost $572 million has been committed to 119 projects in thirty states.[44]

BART is a fine example of different forms of financing blended in one project. A voter-approved $792 million bond issue to be paid by a property tax over thirty-seven years will provide a substantial part of the total cost. The California legislature promised $180 million for the Trans-Bay Tube, the federal government has chipped in $52 million in matching funds towards the total project, and the Department of Transportation approved the additional grant of $28 million already mentioned.[45]

Taxation and Tax Exemptions. State and local property taxes are viewed by the railroads and pipelines as unfair burdens.[46] They point out that other modes operate tax-free on government-provided right-of-way, and even the user tax on motor carriers (for gasoline, registration, tires, etc.) does not hurt the automotive industry as a property tax would. Whereas the user tax goes into a trust fund which provides for highway construction and

112

maintenance, the property tax paid by the rails and pipelines goes into the general state and local treasuries. In 1947, the railroads paid $182 million in property taxes—a rate of 9.3 percent. This compares with the normal maximum rate of 3 or 4 percent for the general tax rate on other private property. Although their property taxes have declined in recent years, the railroads still paid over $161 million in 1965. The ad valorem property taxes paid by pipelines in 1959 was in the neighborhood of $1.5 million. Although the tax rate on pipeline right-of-way facilities is not overbearing (estimated at 2.5 to 3 percent of their property), the tax receipts go into state or local coffers, not into a fund for the construction and maintenance of pipelines. In addition to these tax inequities, the government has been charged with discriminating against railroads and pipelines in the assessment of their property values. In a 1965 study of twenty-one states, the Association of American Railroads indicated that rails had overpaid almost $72 million in taxes, which threatens their already shaky competitive position.[47]

When railroad commuter lines began to encounter financial pitfalls during the early 1950s, some states relieved them of their property tax burdens. New York was the first to come to the aid of its ailing Long Island Railroad by granting its full tax exemption in 1951. Later, New York froze all railroad taxes at their 1959 level and allowed certain exemptions to lines that lost money. The state also reimbursed local governments with 50 percent of any loss in city revenue due to railroad tax exemptions.[48]

New Jersey, in 1967, abolished all taxes on railroad rolling stock, and exempted property from taxes on right-of-way up to a width of a hundred feet. The state taxed other railroad-owned property at an established rate, and compensated municipalities and other taxing jurisdictions for loss of revenue by paying them a sum equal to the 1966 railroad taxes.[49]

Regulation

When regulatory agencies control transportation, they add and subtract resources from the carrier involved. Also, decisions and even the procedures may affect not only the carrier being directly regulated, but other carriers in the transportation network as well.

The regulatory procedure involves extensive legal costs. The carrier must hire lawyers, pay court fees, and spend expensive time preparing his case, while losing revenue as he waits for the commission to reach a decision.

The precise effect of a regulatory decision depends on long-term results. While the costs of additional mandatory devices on vehicles or rights-of-way, combined with heavy insurance requirements may mean a short-term subtraction from the carriers' resources, they may prove to be additions in the long run because of fewer accidents and less liability. The results of rate determination may likewise be unpredictable. Higher rates may effect an immediate rise in per-unit income, but lower rates may attract more patrons. Over a greater time period, the new rates may have unexpected results. The higher rates may prove profitable despite loss of traffic, or they may bring about losses in patronage which cause a drop in profits.

Some regulatory decisions, on the other hand, can have immediate and definable results. If, in the public interest, a commission forces a carrier to continue service to an area where it is unprofitable, this decision may comprise a subtraction of resources. Permitting a merger or consolidation of two or more firms within a mode may prove an addition to resources of both firms if the merger results in greater earnings. Finally, a decision to restrict entry into the market by denying an operating permit to a new carrier may add resources to another carrier by protecting his monopoly.

Entrepreneurial Ability

Government can directly invest its employees in the transportation industry, as the state and federal governments did when they appointed representatives of the "public" on boards of directors of so-called "mixed" corporations. The impact that direct government investment of entrepreneurs had on transportation companies is questionable. Theoretically, the "public" representatives acted as guardians of both the government investment in that corporation and the consumer interest in fair business practices. But the government officials often thought and acted so similarly to private management that policies rarely changed with their joining the boards of directors. There were reports that the federal directors who sat on the board of the Union Pacific hardly bothered to attend meetings. Businessmen defended this laxness by arguing that the best interests of both government and business coincided. Thus the daily direction of almost all corporations remained, for all practical purposes, in private hands.

Government's direct investment of entrepreneurs in private corporations proved little more than psychological, reminding the firms that their decisions had important social consequences. It is difficult, if not impossible, to determine whether this investment expanded management's social awareness.

Although specific research on the relationships between various forms of investment is inadequate, one relationship—that of land grants to railroad entrepreneurship—has been thoroughly explored. Undoubtedly land grants affected railroad investment decisions, but the importance of their influence is open to debate. Thomas Cochran has researched this area most intensively. In an article in the *Journal of Economic History*, he asserts that, although limited reading may lead one to believe that grants were essential in the building of the transcontinental railroad, a wide sampling of correspondence at the time shows the opposite. Cochran examined the letters of John Murray Forbes, nineteenth-century Boston railroad investor, and decided:

> The generalizations that might be drawn from the Forbes correspondence alone are that a land grant may have been essential to the successful financing of the Hannibal and St. Joseph in the decade of the fifties; that the Burlington and Missouri in Iowa could have been financed without a grant; that eastern financeers in the fifties would invest in trunk-line connections up to and somewhat beyond the Mississippi without a land subsidy; and finally that there were a number of business considerations other than the property value of the road that influenced major investors.[50]

The "other business considerations" Cochran refers to, along with property value, fall into a general category of "rate of return." While the value of land was important in determining the rate of return, it was not paramount. The lure of the land grant varied over time, depending on the type of road being built and the length of time the speculator wished to invest.

Further evidence points to the fact that land grants may not have been the great spur to railroad building that people think. Only two western roads were completed during the antebellum period. None of the land voted to Wisconsin and Iowa came into significant use until 1860. Approximately 35 million acres were forfeited back to the government because they were not used. Perhaps, then, the same railroad expansion might have been completed without the extensive federal land grants.

Corporate Structure

Since a firm's structure is largely responsible for its efficiency and output, and since government decisions influence organization patterns of transportation industries, government a on in relation to corporate structure is crucial. To be sure, the ιᵔderal government severely limited the ability of railroads to control rates, and both federal and state governments tried to curb certain kinds of corporate organization through antitrust legislation. At face value, these forms of government action appear to have seriously curtailed the economic freedom of private business. But corporations were not without ingenuity in their response. As government moved to control this or that abuse, business went searching for more sophisticated ways of circumventing the laws.

Overtly, the interlocking directorate or holding company is illegal. But less obtrusive techniques of business organization such as informal market shares and cooperative pricing policies exist nevertheless. Government legal policy, intended to regulate and control business organization and practices, may actually have been an unintentional investment in the corporate ingenuity of management! The original intention of regulation laws was to divest private business of some organization pattern options. Government accomplished that. But the remaining options may well have proven the more efficient and profitable techniques anyway. Government regulation, therefore, may have actually flushed out the best (albeit sometimes most devious) corporate techniques.

Financial Intermediaries

Government can exercise its role as financial intermediary in many ways. It may act purely as an agent to aid the transfer of resources from one firm to another, without directly adding any of its own financial resources to the transfer. (Handling the transaction, however, involves government cost that may be viewed as an investment.)

Government banks helped finance many nineteenth-century

railroads and served primarily as marketing agencies for the privately owned securities. The Bank of the United States, for example, figured highly in financing the Philadelphia, Wilmington, and Baltimore lines, and acted as fiscal agent for the Reading Railroad and other coal roads.[51] Some railroads that depended on government financial intermediaries might have survived without this assistance, but with difficulty.

Sometimes various levels of government joined to establish banks for the sole purpose of helping develop a particular mode. Railroad banks chartered in Georgia during 1835-1836 departed from Georgia's earlier policy of letting commercial banks control all financing.[52] But when the Bank of the United States closed, the states granted banking privileges to the railroad companies themselves. These quasi-public banks had no authority to make loans and expand the money supply, for all earnings were fed to the stockholders as dividends.

Government could employ its financial intermediaries in still another way. Because of its credit rating and financial capabilities, it could guarantee the successful completion of a project managed privately. The protection often took the form of a guaranteed rate of return on stocks or bonds, as in the construction of the transcontinental railroad. A guaranteed rate of return had tremendous impact on investors, an example of the interrelationship between government investment and stable climate.

But government's extension of banking privileges to railroads and its special role as fiscal agent for marketing railroad securities are exceptions rather than rules. The real contribution of government to the transportation network lies in the protection it provided for the smooth functioning of capital transfers. The Federal Deposit Insurance Corporation (FDIC) certainly helps allay fears of people who question the safety of the banks. Although taken for granted because pinning a price tag on this form of service is hard, the FDIC's activities are crucial to the financing of America's transportation network.

Research and Development

An important addition to private transportation's resources, government-financed research and development, speeds technological progress without substantial investment of private resources. Private companies carry out most government-sponsored research and development under contract to independent federal commissions such as the FAA, the Maritime Administration, the Federal Highway Administration, and the Department of Transportation.

The Department of Defense, for example, has contributed notably to civil aeronautics. The origin of every major commercial aircraft design can be traced to research by the armed forces. Commercial airline officials readily admit that without this help their companies would not and could not have developed their advanced modern aircraft. Today government is focusing its aeronautical research on hydrofoils and hydroskimmers, all-weather, longer range helicopters, and a vertical short takeoff and landing plane (V/STOL). The military is conducting all these projects, but their commercial uses are at least as valuable. In addition, the Defense Department is financing research on a mammoth military cargo plane which promises to be easily converted for commercial air freight. The FAA, active as well, is developing a substitute for the DC-3 on feeder airline routes.

Total federal research and development investment concentrates so heavily on aviation that funding for other modes is neglected.[53]

The Coast Guard's 1969 budget contained $31.1 million for research and development programs which include activities in oceanography, applied research in materials, marine vehicles, marine aids to navigation, and evaluation of electronic aids to navigation systems. Development programs include aids to navigation and techniques for control and removal of oil spills. During fiscal year 1969, the Department of Commerce appropriated $12 million to study means of reducing ocean shipping costs.[54]

Federal research and development obligations for highway construction and safety were priced at $30 million for fiscal 1970, and $39.5 million for 1971. The funds support comprehensive traffic safety research and development, new construction techniques, and a study of social and economic aspects of highways.[55]

Federal, state, and local governments—with the help of private industry—have undertaken research and development programs for mass transportation. The Housing Act of 1961 made federal funds available for "stimulating fresh thinking which will bring about improved service and greater efficiency in the mass transportation field."[56] These funds often went to state and local governments, as did $49 million BART received in 1963 to help pay for track and equipment tests and research in rapid transit technology. Similar projects are being continued under the Mass Transit Act of 1964. In addition, the Department of Transportation is contributing a wealth of knowledge through its Northeast Corridor experiments, undertaken jointly with the Penn Central Railroad, which, incidentally, has paid the bulk of expenditures so far. (Of course, Penn Central's recent bankruptcy has jeopardized possibilities of expanding the project.) The state of Pennsylvania is also sponsoring research in this area through a project between Philadelphia and Harrisburg.

Climate

Although this category of government investment is psychological rather than statistical, it determines the effectiveness of all other investment tools. Because business climate is intangible and cannot be quantitatively measured, treating it as investment may seem incongruous at first. How can government add or subtract climate from the transportation industries? But all government policy affects the market, whether it be specific decisions or just a general tone of optimism or pessimism set by the President and his administration.

Government insurance to private banks, government guarantees of rates of return, and government extension of land-grant incentives all operate to offset the naturally high risk factor of many transportation projects. (While land grants may not have been essential, their effect on business climate must have sped the construction of the Transcontinental Railroad.)

Although government investment may produce only a fraction of the necessary capital for a given project, it often catalyzes private investments. A strategically timed government investment, however great, may assuage businessmen's concern. A tax-incentive policy or tariff rebates on vital raw material imports can also influence private investment decisions. Of course, no one government tool is sufficient to draw private investors; much depends on how the individual businessman weighs the factors which will determine his rate of return. Even the most carefully planned government investment methods may not succeed in creating optimism. After all, a stable business climate still depends on human psychology.

CHAPTER 2

PROMOTION

Promotion is investment with a goal, and one of government's first goals is the material development of the components of a transportation network, the needs of one mode, or even one part of that mode.

Government may provide direct inputs of natural resources, labor, capital, or entrepreneurs in order to promote any aspect of transportation. It can aid the development of a mode by favoring that mode's corporate structures or credit ratings, or it can push intermodality through its role as financial intermediary by easing the transfer of resources from one mode to another. Any attempt to influence the thinking of private decision-makers is a form of promotion; however, it is usually money which influences most. Government can promote any type of system it wants simply by funding projects. In this way, it can combine material development with planning by adopting policies which subsidize material development but at the same time, insist on overall planning. Thus promotion policy may take three forms: promotion of material development and promotion of planning may be embodied in separate policies, or they may combine into a third policy.

The level of government involved also determines the effects of promotion. Each level has its own strengths and weaknesses; the most obvious disparity is in the resource capabilities of each level. Whereas the federal government, at least lately, has vast capital and tremendous potential growth of tax revenues, the poorer local and state governments tend to be less generous with their funds. On the other hand, the local and state governments may have the advantage in the vein of organization and planning, which requires detailed knowledge of local conditions.

To provide a better understanding of promotion, we can analyze government's goals and policies in relation to the modal components—right-of-way, vehicle, service facilities, and corporate structure—remembering that policies designed for one mode may also affect another mode. We will also try to determine whether the combined results of federal, state, and local policies have been internally consistent. Did state promotion of a particular mode or one of its components mesh well with federal policy in the same sphere? Finally, we must scrutinize mixed involvement of public and private concerns.

Government, to be sure, never invested in all modes in the same way, partly because available investment tools differed from mode to mode and goals likewise varied, since each mode grew in its own way, at its own pace. Government investment differed according to the mode's economic maturity. The relationship among investment tool, promotion goal, and maturity of mode cannot be ignored, since the future of effective transportation policy depends on it.

Even a long and hard search fails to produce a significant number of nineteenth- and twentieth-century statements of comprehensive government transportation policy. A few documents indicate that some policy-makers thought of the transportation network in terms of national needs and responses. In 1808, Albert Gallatin, Secretary of the Treasury, submitted his "Report on Roads and Canals" to the Senate. Gallatin's plan is noteworthy, for it represents the first major attempt to integrate the investment potential of the federal government, the resources of state and local government, and private capital and managerial skills. The plan, intertwining economic, political, and military objectives, rested on two assumptions: lack of private capital and the administrative power of the federal government. The United States, confined almost wholly to the Eastern Seaboard, anticipated expansion to the south and west. The country had to extend communications over the Appalachians and, in fact, strengthen transportation facilities along the entire coast. Gallatin responded to these broad needs with specific proposals for both roads and canals.

The four canals proposed for the Eastern Seaboard were all built. The Erie Canal, as well as four of the five trunk-line railroads, ultimately grew out of the report's suggestions. Today's inland waterways, as well as highway and railway connections, follow the general direction of Gallatin's plan. The plan was so influential that the federal government used its charts and surveys for investing labor input to develop what was then a comprehensive transportation program.

The plan made no claim on federal funds for construction, but merely suggested feasible policies. Federal subsidizing was probably not practical at the time; rigorous investment criteria were lacking and the planning aspects were incomplete.

The plan, despite its obvious value, still managed to draw powerful criticism. For example, in *Government Promotion of American Canals and Railroads, 1800-1890*, Carter Goodrich wrote:

> . . . the basis for selecting objects of truly national importance is indicated by example rather than precept; the alternate forms under which Federal action might be organized are discussed only briefly; and the choice between them is put forward, perhaps for tactical reasons, more as a matter of detail than of substance.[1]

And the question of conflicting state and local interests, though clearly seen, is resolved, says Goodrich, with a "hopeful phrase."[2]

The question of constitutionality, perhaps best dramatized in Andrew Jackson's veto of the Maysville Road Bill in 1830, alienated the federal government more and more from transport planning in the nineteenth century. Although Washington still provided finance capital to projects of national importance, it could not suggest a meaningful, integrated national plan. This general lack of federal planning was reversed during both the Civil War and World War I, but for the most part, the transportation industries functioned without federal help.

A few wartime patterns, however, did carry on into peacetime, and this greatly aided the development of the transportation network. One of these carry-overs, manifested in the Transportation Act of 1920, was the coordination of the railroads during World War I. The act contained elaborate provisions relating to railroad consolidations. It directed the ICC to prepare and adopt a plan for the consolidation of railway properties in the United States into a limited number of systems. The Commission's plan was announced in 1929 and an extreme revision for the East was issued in 1932. But these early plans effected few practical results. The rules were based on the regulatory apparatus of the federal government, and were open to much debate.

When the national government finally began to plan an overall transportation network, it focused only on the rails, the dominant mode at the time. The pattern of promoting only the dominant mode, or one of its components, characterized federal policy for quite some time. The Transportation Act of 1920 reflected the railroad hegemony, although this mode had admittedly declined from its heyday during the late nineteenth and early twentieth centuries.

The rise of the automobile, especially in the 1920s, stimulated government interest in highway construction. This interest became manifest in promotion policy for both planning and material development. Federal-aid legislation in the mid-1930s allowed the use of federal funds for secondary roads and for extensions of state highways through municipalities, thus extending federal highway interest into urban areas. The federal government also started to suggest how and where the roads should be built, although the planning was strictly unimodal.

Two key reports to Congress—"Toll Roads and Free Roads" (1939) and "Interregional Highways" (1944)—led to the authorization (but not financing) of the National System of Interstate and Defense Highways.[3] Not until President John F. Kennedy issued his transportation message in 1962, however, did the United States begin a real campaign to coordinate the system. It would be wrong to equate the 1962 message with a plan like Gallatin's, for Kennedy limited himself to criticizing the outlooks of many transportation agencies and did not detail specific projects. The President had decided that a much broader intermodal analysis of transportation needs was necessary. Congress promptly passed the Federal-Aid Highway Act of 1962, which, although still centering mainly on one mode, departed from previous highway financing legislation by requiring an assessment of the total impact of highway construction on urban environments.

While many hailed it as a step in the right direction, the 1962 Act still fell far short of a thorough appraisal of the effects of highway construction on other components of the motor vehicle industry, and of the impact of all modes on urban life. Urban-transit expert George Smerk did not issue an understatement when he noted that, as late as 1963, "what was obviously missing was a way for the Federal government to provide financial assistance to projects of a non-highway nature."[4] National promotion was passive and fragmentary; whatever mode or component appeared to dominate received the greatest share of federal attention. Perhaps this was (and is) the crux of the problem.

Water Transportation

Government investment in water transportation took three basic forms—labor, capital, and research and development. Firms within this mode could also take advantage of government's role as financial intermediary, which was spawned by the Merchant Marine Act of 1936. Services include a referred tax on deposits to capital, special reserve funds, credit aid, and war-risk insurance. If canals are considered an extension of natural waterways, then government invested natural resources in the water transportation mode. And finally, the government's effect on business climate influenced water transportation as it did all other modes.

Since the early 1800s, all levels of government have concerned themselves, to varying degrees, with planning and financing the material development of inland waterways. All levels of government, in one way or another, have surveyed, planned, constructed, operated, or maintained channels and harbors, locks and dams, and terminal and port facilities. The federal government, through the Gallatin plan, showed an early interest in developing an overall transportation plan, but did not tie the plan to any specific methods of funding projects. Until the Civil War, the finance vacuum left by the federal government was filled for the most part by state governments. But the states, which financed canal construction through a variety of mechanisms—bonds, stocks, loans, grants—tied their aid not to an overall program but to specific promotion plans. Compared with federal objectives, those of the Ohio, Illinois, and Pennsylvania canal programs were provincial. The possibility of conflicting state and federal goals, hinted at in the Gallatin Report, became a reality when the Erie Canal convinced state officials that trade patterns could be rerouted by constructing alternative canals. Each state, county, and even city had its own economic objectives and wanted its own separate canal. Needless to say, federal desires for one coordinated program were stymied throughout the 1830s by vicious competition among the states.

The federal government increased its revenues as well as its powers in the late nineteenth and early twentieth centuries. The planning, surveying, construction, and operation of inland channels and harbors, and of locks and dams, were financed largely by federal general revenues. (State and local governments focused their activities mostly on the construction of terminal and port facilities.) The Corps of Army Engineers was in charge of approving projects and proceeding with the construction and operation of these projects. Ideally, the Corps was to analyze from a strictly economic standpoint only those projects which benefited the entire country, and keep selfish localities and states from rushing into unnecessary and wasteful enterprises, but this ideal role was never recognized. Harold Mayer, professor of geography at Kent State University, focused on some of the Corps' shortcomings in a paper he prepared for the 1970 Conference of the United Transportation Union. According to Mayer, the Army Engineers have used extremely controversial methods to measure the costs and benefits of specific projects. When the potential benefits of a project are doubted, the Engineers settle the question by giving the green light. The Corps of Army Engineers is entangled in the influences of Congress and states. Congressmen such as the late Mendel Rivers and others took pride in citing the figures of Army Corps assistance they personally had secured for their districts. As Mayer states, "The pork barrel is not a myth. Even though the members of the Corps may be sincere, competent, and dedicated—which they are—external pressures may often be irresistible."[5] Thus the Corps of Army Engineers approves projects case by case, without considering overall needs or problems of the nation's inland waterway system, let alone the transportation network as a whole.

The consequences of the case-by-case uncoordinated policy of port development loom threateningly for years ahead. This is mainly due to containerization, the movement of freight in uniform sealed and reusable containers, which has revolutionized the shipment of goods and materials. Containers are initially attached to trucking cabins or placed on a flatbed railroad car to be carried to a port. Once on a dock, the containers are lifted by modern equipment, positioned in specially designed ship hulks, and transported to their destinations. The process results in a great saving of time and money by reducing the number of man-hours required to load and unload the ship's hold. Large cranes make possible the loading or unloading of twenty to twenty-five tons of goods in two and a half minutes; traditional methods of handling the same tonnage would require eighteen to twenty hours of work.[6]

When the full effects of containerization are realized, the number of international shipping ports is expected to drop significantly. Experts feel that only four ports will be needed on the West Coast and only one or two in the East, a prediction which, if accurate, will leave the United States with excess capacity of port and terminal facilities. This alone should perhaps warrant more restrictive policies by the Corps of Army Engineers, and should encourage Congress to develop a national plan for port development. If state, local, and private entrepreneurs continue to build port facilities at will, they will waste tremendous investments on obsolete and unnecessary equipment.

One last crucial question concerning the material development of the nation's waterways is who should pay. Doubtless, Congress has assumed, throughout the country's history, that improvements in the inland waterway system should benefit all Americans and should be paid for out of general tax revenue. Yet highway improvements, which benefit all Americans even more than waterways, are paid for by a user tax. Many people, including Presidents Kennedy and Johnson, have supported a user tax for waterways—those who benefit most from improvements in channels, harbors, and locks should pay for the improvements. Rather than enjoying their right-of-way cost free, the companies involved would be assessed a tax for using facilities built by the Corps of Army Engineers. Inland water transportation owes its existence to improvements financed by the federal government, a fact which gives weight to arguments for a user charge.

Primarily through subsidies and the enactment of certain legal requirements, Congress has promoted an oceanic merchant marine consisting of American ships operated by American businessmen and manned by American crews. The Jones Act requires that ships registered in the United States be built in the United States, and restricts domestic trade to vessels which are registered in the United States. The Act forces domestic shipowners to purchase American vessels at American building costs to stay in business. The legislative prohibition includes shipments not only between U.S. coastal ports but also those to Hawaii, Alaska, Guam, Puerto Rico, and Okinawa. With respect to certain cargoes which are generated by the government, the relevant government agency must assure that at least 50 percent of the gross tonnage be handled in privately owned ships which are registered in the United States and flying the American flag.

To compensate shipowners for paying higher American costs, government began, in 1845, to give capital in the form of mail subsidies. Prior to 1947, federal promotional subsidies for the development of a merchant marine fleet totaled a massive $16.8 billion.[7]

The impact of subsidies will stay obscure until their types and specific goals are carefully distinguished. Before the Marine Act of 1936 went into effect, government employed several types of subsidies, including the mail and construction subsidies. The construction subsidy related primarily to vehicles and service facilities; the mail subsidy became essential to a shipping firm's supply of capital. Before 1936, Congress refused to grant aid outright but helped indirectly through piecemeal mail carriage legislation. In 1936, Congress passed new legislation which ended the channeling of funds for shipping through the post office. Congress provided direct assistance to ocean shipping by authorizing construction-differential subsidies to offset the lower cost of ship construction in foreign ports. The legislation authorized the Secretary of Commerce to reimburse American ship operators for up to 55 percent of the total cost of ship construction in an American shipyard. The Act also made available operating-differential subsidies that compensated American ship operators directly for the added costs of hiring American crews and purchasing insurance, maintenance, and repair work from American sources. The legislation empowered the Secretary of Commerce to estimate what these items would reasonably cost if obtained from foreign sources and help the ship operator make up the differential. The 1936 legislation also provided for a third type of subsidy. A ship operator, receiving an operating-differential subsidy, was required to deposit certain portions of his earnings and depreciation credits (deposits which were exempt from federal taxes) into either a capital reserve or special reserve fund. The capital reserve fund was designed to enable the shipowners to have sufficient revenue to purchase new vessels and to pay off mortgages.

However, not all American ship operators were able to receive subsidies under the 1936 legislation. The intent of the legislation was to enable the United States to have a merchant marine capable of providing shipping service "on all routes" essential for maintaining the flow of foreign commerce. Hence, only shipowners whose vessels operated on fixed routes were eligible for either the construction-differential or the operating-differential subsidy.

The merchant marine subsidy program has faced criticism from supporters as well as from opponents. Many feel that the United States should have the world's best-equipped and largest merchant fleet because the foremost nation in the world, they argue, should not have to rely on foreign sources to carry the great volume of goods entering and leaving U.S. ports. Such a policy, they contend, does not make good economic sense. The U.S. balance-of-payments position is worsened because U.S. importers and exporters pay dollars to purchase services from foreign flagships. Such a flow of dollars would be reversed if American flagships were capable of carrying the volume of goods coming into and going out of this country. The United States, many believe, must also have a large merchant fleet if this nation hopes to influence world freight rates and the decisions of various world shipping conferences. In addition to these economic primacy arguments, some believe that a large, efficient merchant fleet is vital for national defense; the country must always be prepared for an emergency Defense Department call to transport goods and troops. Without a modern merchant marine fleet some fear that the United States would be subjecting itself to the whims and dictates of foreign nations. According to a report of the Senate's Committee on Commerce:

> To permit our security and economy to become totally dependent upon foreign vessels, operated by foreign crews, subject to the wishes of foreign governments would be to run an unacceptable risk. The presence of a viable U.S. merchant fleet is necessary to provide some assurances that this nation's security and foreign policy objectives will not be subject to the dictates of other nations, and that the ability of our export shippers to compete in world markets and the delivered price of our import commodities will not be unilaterally determined by foreign competitors.[8]

Yet the present merchant marine program has failed to make the United States the leading maritime nation. The percentage of the country's total trade (imports and exports) carried in U.S. flagships has declined sharply between 1950 and 1970. In 1950, ships bearing U.S. flags transported over 31 percent of the nation's dry goods, but by 1966, this had dropped to 8.1 percent. By 1970, the U.S. merchant fleet was capable of carrying only 5 percent of the nation's waterborne commerce. Over three fourths of the U.S. foreign trade fleet is more than twenty years of age. Approximately three fourths of the freighters operating under the American flag are over twenty years old, while only one fourth of the freighters with foreign flags are that old. While other nations have been producing twenty to thirty ocean vessels per year, the United States has been producing twelve or thirteen.[9]

At the request of the Nixon administration, Congress, in October 1970, passed the Merchant Marine Act of 1970 in an attempt to revitalize the sagging merchant fleet. Congress declared that the national merchant policy "requires that there should be authorized for fiscal years 1971 through 1980 such sums as may be necessary to construct 300 ships of such sizes, types and designs as the Secretary of Commerce may consider best suited to carry out the purposes and policy of this Act."

Congress firmly believed that without the new legislation the U.S. merchant fleet would be almost nonexistent by 1980. For example, the Senate Commerce Committee predicted that the present foreign trade fleet of the United States (650 ships) would be reduced to 272 ships by 1974. Without a strong merchant marine fleet, Congress felt that national security would be endangered. In addition, the new merchant marine program made good economic sense to Congress. The Nixon administration predicted that the U.S. balance of payments would be improved by $2.9 billion in the period prior to completion of the program and by approximately $600 million annually thereafter. Furthermore, the program would generate a boom in the nation's shipyards. The Senate Commerce Committee estimated that a minimum of 440,000 man-years of employment would be required.[10] Workers trained in the shipyards could also transfer their skills to other sectors of the economy.

The Merchant Marine Act of 1970 attempted to correct many of the shortcomings of the Merchant Marine Act of 1936. The 1936 legislation allowed assistance only to certain ocean carriers on certain strategically located trade routes; thus, many ocean carriers with U.S. flags were forced to compete with government-aided carriers. Furthermore, the 1936 legislation prohibited subsidies to bulk carrier operators because they did not operate on a specific, fixed route, but filled specific shippers' orders at random locations. The 1936 legislation also gave assistance only to ship operators and therefore excluded assistance to owners of shipyards.

The 1970 legislation, however, attempts to give all U.S. ocean shippers, even the owners of bulk cargo vessels, a chance to receive federal subsidies. Operators who have maintained bulk cargo vessels without government subsidization are given some priority in the effort to replace their over-age fleets. The legislation recognizes that even under the new program not all U.S. ship operators will be able to receive construction-differential or operation-differential subsidies. Therefore, Congress enabled all U.S. shipowners engaged in subsidized or unsubsidized foreign trade, in Great Lakes trade, in noncontiguous domestic trade (Alaska, Hawaii, and Puerto Rico), and the fisheries of the United States to establish a tax-deferred construction reserve fund. Ship operators may withdraw money from the reserve fund without paying any taxes if they utilize the money to acquire vessels for the trade specified above. The legislation puts specific limits on the amount of money which a shipowner can pay into the construction reserve fund. Hopefully, as a result of this fund, more ship operators will be in a stronger financial position to continue the ship-modernization program. The 1970 legislation also permits any shipyard in the United States, not just ship purchasers, to apply for construction-differential subsidies. Congress hoped that this reversal of former policy would encourage shipyards to participate in the design work on the vessels and, through their participation, help achieve economies of construction.

Another flaw of the 1936 Merchant Marine Act was that it included no provision to encourage builders and operators to conduct their businesses efficiently. No matter what the total cost, if the Maritime Administration had authorized the construction, it paid 55 percent of the total. In a recent article in the *Fordham Law Review*, Joseph Sarisky noted that "there is no built-in provision in the Merchant Marine Act to provide an incentive for 'efficiency and frugality.'"[11] The Merchant Marine Act of 1970 reduces the percentage of total construction costs which shipyards can recover from the federal government. The maximum subsidy permitted will be reduced to 45 percent in 1971, to 43 percent in 1972, to 41 percent in 1973, to 39 percent in 1975, and to 35 percent in 1976 and thereafter. The Secretary of Commerce is authorized to pay a higher construction-differential payment if failure to pay more is likely to jeopardize the commitment to the ship-construction program.

Unlike the 1936 legislation, the 1970 Merchant Marine Act limits the amount of money a ship operator may recover from the government for labor costs. The U.S. ship operator may recover the difference between the "collective bargaining costs" of a U.S. crew and the cost of securing a foreign crew. The ship operators will not, however, receive a reimbursement for costs relating to the officers or members of the crew that the Secretary of Commerce has "found to be unnecessary for the efficient and economical operation of such vessel." In determining whether or not certain members of a crew are necessary for efficient operation, the Secretary of Commerce must (1) afford representatives of the collective bargaining units responsible for the manning of a vessel an opportunity to express their opinions, and (2) give due consideration, but not be bound by, wage and manning scales and working conditions required by bona-fide collective-bargaining agreements. The "collective bargaining costs" of a U.S. shipowner will be determined by means of an index developed by the Bureau of Labor Statistics. The legislation specifies the following about the index:

> Such index shall consist of the average annual change in wages and benefits placed into effect for employees covered by collective bargaining agreements with equal weight given to changes affecting employees in the transportation industry (excluding the offshore maritime industry) and to changes affecting employees in private nonagricultural industries other than transportation.[12]

Although the merchant marine has its supporters, many vigorously oppose the Merchant Marine Acts of both 1936 and 1970. They believe that in light of significant cost disadvantages, the United States should stop all construction and operation of the ocean ships financed out of U.S. government coffers. All U.S. shipping, it is argued, could be done in foreign-built vessels with foreign manpower. According to many, such a policy would bolster the total economy and end a subsidization policy which puts a tiresome burden on American taxpayers. One example often cited is the subsidy to luxury-liner passenger ships. Between 1965 and 1970, luxury liners got more than $240 million in government funds. A special subsidy, originated for defense before World War II, now benefits only cruise ships. In 1970, for example, ten ships sailing in the South Pacific and in the Carribbean were the sole receivers of this aid. The economic crunch came even to these government-subsidized liners in late 1970 and in early 1971. The *S.S. Santa Paula*, in its journey from New York to Curaçao, Haiti, Jamaica, and St. Thomas, had been receiving four hundred dollars in federal aid for each passenger carried.[13] However, in January 1971, the *S.S. Santa Paula* was one of the six Grace-Prudential liners which were laid up. Only four oceangoing passenger ships (all in the Pacific) are in operation under the American flag at this writing.

Opponents, disputing the argument that national defense justifies larger merchant marine subsidies, point out that with the introduction of the C5-A cargo plane or "jumbo jet," most troop movement today is by air. If ships do become necessary in a limited conflict, the United States could move troops and supplies on foreign vessels. Furthermore, if an American merchant marine is needed for defense, then the Defense Department, opponents argue, should pay for it.[14] If such parochial considerations continue to motivate Congress, transportation policy will continue to permit waste and inefficiency as illustrated by the merchant marine.

Government investment in research and development became more vital as water carriers confronted stiff competition from other modes. Government enabled improvements in craft efficiency that led to a tremendous increase of barge traffic on the inland waterways. In 1931, for example, barge freight on the Mississippi was twice the volume moved in any year before 1900, and between 1953-1957 the average annual internal tonnage was almost $64 million.[15] Water carriers have similarly gained advantages from government research which helped develop more powerful towboats; larger, better-designed barges; more efficient towing arrangements; improved lock designs; and modernized terminals with mechanized loading and unloading equipment.[16]

The exact dimensions of government's role depend on both the monetary value of its research and development programs, and an examination of project payoffs. In 1968, the government budgeted $9 million for research and development of the maritime fleet.[17] The sum covered work on the hydrofoil *Denison* and considerable research in the mechanization of the cargo ships and advanced ship design.

In the nineteenth and twentieth centuries, government investment in transportation influenced the rate of technological change. And, as the government entered transport research in general and water transport research in particular, it demanded higher performance levels. The Maritime Administration today insists that ships built under its subsidy program be capable of faster than average speeds, and this hastens technological progress in ship and power plant design.

Research and development investment demonstrates the effectiveness of combined planning-financing promotion, for when government binds its investment to achievement of a particular goal or policy, it obtains striking results. Departing from its traditional role as passive reactor, the federal government promoted water transportation by investing in research and development projects that would yield a measurable payoff.

Railroads

The railroads have received many types of government investment, each to some extent related to the economic maturity of the rails. Before 1890, the fact that investment was diverse reflected the many promotion objectives of the federal, state, and local bodies. Generally, promotion in the railroad-building era was concerned only with maintenance and expansion of the physical plant. The promotion policies of the government did not involve either the structure of railroad companies or their rolling stock. As new construction reached a plateau during the 1890s, government gave fewer natural resources and less finance capital. After 1890, investment in the form of regulation dominated government involvement. Apart from special assistance during the two world wars and the Korean War, the federal government's only financial help to railroads until the Mass Transit Act of 1964 was the ICC program mentioned earlier. In the late 1960s and early 1970s, the financial plight of many railroads led to the possibility of resumed federal aid or nationalization.

Government promotion is hard to analyze. First, we must identify the exact point at which government intervened in the development of the railroad, and then sort out the diverse philosophies and strategies pursued by government and private investors. Any analysis must also consider overlapping of public and private investments, since government officials and private investors often were one and the same, each playing both roles.

Underlying all these considerations is the fact that railroad development followed several distinct periods. Although their edges are admittedly blurred, these periods provide discernible landmarks: authorities debated the questions of railroad versus canal in the 1820s, and the first important era of actual construction began in the 1830s and carried over into the 1840s. In discussing government investment in railroads during the 1830s and 1840s, contemporary historians reject the idea that government surrendered completely to laissez-faire practices, but at the same time they deny that government was immediately and extensively involved. Instead, they regard the economic tone of the 1830s and 1840s as a synthesis of both extremes. Investment varied largely with the stage of development of the particular railroad in question. Often when the rails were getting started and most needed government aid, federal and state authorities were afraid to risk funds, and only after the railroad proved successful did government decide to invest in them.

One case study, although incomplete and not entirely typical of the age, does give some indication of the government investment sequence during the 1830s and 1840s. The Boston and Albany Railroad, a union of two smaller roads—the Western and the Boston & Worcester—was opened in 1841 as the first major trunk line in the nation. Its history enhances the point that, although government money was vital, the timing of the investments varied. The railroad, when finished in 1842, represented a total capital investment of $9 million, of which a third was in the form of stock subscriptions by private investors, and the remaining $6 million came from the state government. Stephen Salisbury, author of *The State, the Investor, and the Railroad*, says that "On the surface the figures seem to provide a demonstration of the primacy of government support."[18] But Salisbury goes on to contend that government played no part at all in initiating the Boston and Albany. In the important first stages of planning and construction, government's role was next to nothing; the Massachusetts legislature in the early 1830s considered canals and railroads "too novel, too untried, and financially risky to merit aid."[19] The conclusion of the Salisbury study is a strong response to those who celebrate government investment as a stimulant of railroad construction during the 1830s and 1840s:

> Only after the Boston and Worcester and its two sister systems, the Boston & Lowell and the Boston & Providence, private corporations financed entirely by private capital, conclusively demonstrated that railroads were both practical and profitable did Massachusetts finally agree to aid an Albany railroad.[20]

In the case of the Boston and Albany, government entered the picture in time to assume only the first goal of promotion—material expansion. Moreover, while the Massachusetts legislature viewed the Boston and Albany as the major link between Boston, the capital, and the western end of the state, Salisbury further contends that the stronger motive for construction was the desire of businessmen to open the interior of the state to industry. Even though final consolidation of the rails fit a comprehensive policy, this was more accident than deliberate plan. There is little evidence that Massachusetts really wished to coordinate its system through investment.

As railroad construction increased during the 1850s, the number of investment decisions government had to make swelled correspondingly. Whether to facilitate commerce or improve communication, or both, all levels of government began either cooperating with private entrepreneurs who had already begun construction, or stimulating others to take the risk. For a long time, historians have argued that during the 1850s, government units stimulated entrepreneurs who were not originally willing to risk money in railroad building. According to this traditional theory, government inspired a new demand for the rails. However, a more careful analysis shows that the effects of government assistance on railroad construction varied according to the level of government involved. Albert Fishlow argues that during this second period of railroad development, local aid was "passive," rather than active. Local aid was "offered subsequent to individual promotion and often as much extorted by threat as voluntarily given."[21]

Fishlow and others generally view state aid during the 1850s as "active incentive to initiate railroad construction." For example, Milton Heath observes in his publication *Constructive Liberalism* that there were two theories in the pre-war South concerning state support of railroad construction:

> One was that the states should assist all projects in some more or less uniform fashion, a policy exemplified most fully in Virginia and Tennessee. The other theory was the one developed in Georgia, that the state should confine its efforts to a single project that was designed to confer a general benefit upon the entire state and to stimulate efforts widely in private and local construction of complementary railroad lines; and furthermore, that the state should embark a sufficiently large sum—preferably the entire cost—to assure reasonably prompt completion of the work.[22]

Georgia's philosophy of government investment, with its emphasis on the one major project, rested on the premise of significant indirect returns from an investment in *social overhead capital* (the economist's phrase designating the components of the economy's infrastructure—transport systems, communications systems, and the like). Although the general tone of federal policy toward railroad assistance was active rather than passive during the decade before the Civil War, this active investment did not really have a great effect on actual construction. Fishlow notes that during the 1850s "only two western railroads were completed through the assistance of land grants, the Illinois Central and the Hannibal and St. Joseph. None of the land voted to Wisconsin and Iowa came into significant play before 1860. Not much of the 1850 western railroad boom is thus explained by Federal intervention."[23]

During the Civil War, the country experienced the first significant transfer of power from local and state to the federal government. A successful war effort demanded strong national leaders with sufficient power to mobilize the resources of all the states. After the war, many of these newly acquired federal powers had to remain within the federal domain. Transportation was naturally affected by this shift in power; the federal government assumed the crucial "active" role in railroad construction.

The building of the transcontinental railroad was supported by various federal investment tools, including the land grant. Although the road probably would have progressed without federal land, the influence of grants on individual private entrepreneurs cannot be denied. When considering investing in the railroad, businessmen undoubtedly considered land grants along with other monetary factors. Based on government's desire to have a specific project complete, the grants constitute the first major attempt to sway private investors through a form of subsidy.

In addition to the land grants, the federal government developed a whole program of financial incentives to help unify the continental rail system. Government funds would be given to a company only after the completion of a twenty-mile section. The federal government also forbade the Union Pacific to release bonds for public sale until the U.P. had completed certain sections.

Unfortunately, the federal policies concerning the first transcontinental railroad were seriously undermined by the Credit Mobilier scandals. Huge amounts of federal money were absconded with, wasted, and even given away as graft, and corruption ran rampant. Although federal officials still had some legal control over public funds, enforcement was so lax that this concept was not nearly realized.

Not all federal investment was handed out with no strings attached. As the Union Pacific moved from its period of initial construction and expansion to the era of consolidation (1870-1890), the government forced the company to repay loans, compelling the U.P. to adopt an investment strategy that limited possible expansion.[24] Although government originally gave loans to aid the road in the initial stage of its development, this aid later turned out to be a liability. Perhaps Washington did not foresee the destabilizing effect loan repayment would have on the Union Pacific, but the damage was done.

With the end of the active railroad construction period in the late nineteenth century came the termination of active government subsidies to the rails. The main form of railroad investment by government in the twentieth century has been regulation of rates, entry, and service requirements. Some notable exceptions came during the world wars and depression periods, when the government invested entrepreneurial ability in the railroads, but for the most part the pattern has remained consistent.

When the United States entered World War I, railroad service was inefficient and clumsy because connecting railroads often failed to integrate their services properly. President Wilson nationalized the railroads and appointed a federal administration to run the nation's entire system and facilitate and coordinate service. The federal coordinator, General MacAdoo, was responsible for many innovations and improvements in railroading—for example, some duplicate facilities were eliminated and the exchange of equipment between connecting lines improved.

The Depression brought chaos to transportation. Without an effective national railroad system, Franklin Roosevelt knew that the country could not recover, so he appointed an Emergency Coordinator of Transportation, who, while not operating the roads directly, attempted to speed up railroad service. The measure also required the coordinator to submit recommendations for a better rail system after the Depression. Although many of his suggestions were ignored, he provided a base for legislative action.

In 1933, Roosevelt gave railroads further consideration. The Bankruptcy Act of 1933 awarded the rails permission to continue operations in spite of bankruptcy, unlike other businesses. If a railroad company went bankrupt, the court would appoint trustees who were responsible for putting the road back on a moneymaking basis. Meanwhile, all debts were suspended.

In the late 1940s and early 1950s, after a series of national strikes and strike threats, the government seized and operated the nation's railroads. President Truman justified the seizure by citing his general power as Commander-in-Chief of the Armed Forces and, more specifically, legislation passed by Congress designated to prevent strikes during World War II. The government controlled the railroads from August 1950 to May 1952, ending the strike threat but pleasing neither labor nor management in the process.

The 1950s and 1960s found many of the nation's railroads in financial trouble as freight and passengers turned to other modes. After World War II, railroad management failed to innovate and effectively meet the competition of other modes. The railroads initially reacted to the truck and airline threat by raising rates and reducing capital expenditures. These actions succeeded only in driving more patrons away.

Not until the late 1950s and early 1960s did railroad management come up with ideas to generate more freight business. Passenger business was still ignored since railroad management did not believe there was any way to make it profitable. The concept of riding truck trailers on flatbed railroad cars (piggyback), introduced in 1957, combined the inherent advantages of railroad and truck services. Railroads offer less expensive long-haul carriage of freight while trucks excel in door-to-door service. The railroads calculated, apparently correctly, that many long-haul truck shippers would find the rails attractive for at least part of the trip.

In 1961, the railroads began experimenting with the "unit train" idea, specialized cars designed to carry cargo, e.g., a shipment of coal, a shipment of automobiles, or a shipment of grain. The unit train offers valuable service advantages. It loses no time in interchange or in waiting for a certain number of cars to accumulate before a shipment may proceed. Perhaps the railroads received their greatest payoff from new ideas when they introduced a special car for handling automobiles, a field which, until the early 1960s, was truck dominated. The new railroad cars, plus technological improvements in yard equipment, put the highly profitable auto transport business on rails.

In the late 1960s, the railroads joined the computer age by introducing the Automatic Car Identification System (ACIS) to maximize the use of equipment. The purpose of the system is to allow each railroad to know at any moment the exact location of its entire rolling stock and thus to meet accurately and promptly the specific car needs of potential shippers. The Union Pacific Railroad, which has ACIS in operation, estimates a 5 percent improvement in overall car utilization. The system is built around reflecting weatherproof labels, fixed on all railroad cars, which can be automatically "read" by scanners strategically distributed throughout the country. The scanners connect by wire or microwave to local or distant teletype machines which are, in turn, hooked up to computers.

In 1969, major railroads began seriously studying the minitrain concept, partly in the hope of picking up business in the highly profitable short-haul grain market. But rail transportation of grain was limited by work rules which require crew changes as trains cross seniority districts. Unions and carriers have agreed that some rule changes are needed to make the minitrain practical and competitive. Both foresee a time when trains pulling ten to thirty 100-ton covered hopper cars will provide efficient and economical single-day service to farmers coast to coast and lure many shippers back to the railroads.

These innovations, undertaken largely by the railroads themselves without government aid or guidance, are viewed as very important, but they obviously were not sufficiently profitable to forestall the vicious cash squeeze which engulfed the railroads in the late 1960s. For the industry as a whole, net operating income dropped 37 percent between 1966 and 1969, as expenses rose 14 percent and revenues only 7.5 percent. In 1969, revenues for railroads were up 5.4 percent—to a record $11.5 billion. But in that same year, expenses rose 5.6 percent—to $9.1 billion, also a record. As a result, net income dropped $24 million from 1968. Net working capital, perhaps the best single indicator of financial health, declined steadily, from $828 million in 1963 to $58.4 million on December 1, 1969. The trend continued well into 1970, when net railroad income for the first quarter was $20 million below the comparable 1969 figure. The railroads suffered a 22.1 percent decline in operating income as well as a 7.7 percent increase in operating expenses. Twenty-three of the nation's Class I railroads marked up deficits in the first quarter of 1970. The depression has been most serious in the eastern district, where more than half of the railroads showing net income deficits were located.[25]

The federal government responded slowly. For years, economists had warned that the financial plight of the railroads required prompt remedial programs. The warnings were largely ignored until June 1970, when the federal government and the public were jolted by the announcement that the Penn Central had gone bankrupt. Penn Central, product of a 1968 merger between the Pennsylvania Railroad and the New York Central Railroad and the nation's largest railroad, loads 21 percent of all freight cars in the United States, operates 20 percent of the track, and has 94,000 employees. Moreover, 70 percent of Penn Central's traffic involves other railroads.[26] The exact reasons for the failure of the merger to provide a profitable railroad will be discussed later, in the chapter on regulation, which covers ICC policy toward mergers.

The important point here is that the bankruptcy of the Penn Central raised the possibility of government capital assistance to the financially troubled railroads and even revived long-dormant talk of nationalization. The Nixon administration, in the summer of 1970, proposed that the Department of Transportation guarantee up to $750 million in loans to railroads. The program ran into opposition in Congress and was not approved by the 91st Congress. However, in December 1970, the 91st Congress approved a measure which gave the Secretary of Transportation the authority to guarantee loans of up to $125 million to railroads which are undergoing reorganization under the Bankruptcy Act. The loan-guarantee legislation was in response to a congressionally authorized pay hike to the nation's rail workers passed during December 1970. The pay raise represented a cost hike to the Penn Central railroad, whose court-appointed managers told Congress that operations would have to shut down unless loan provisions were passed. On January 13, 1971, the Penn Central received permission from the district court overseeing the reorganization of the road to issue $100 million in trustee certificates which the Department of Transportation had agreed to guarantee. The question which remains in many people's minds is how much more Penn Central will need in federal aid to keep functioning. Some argue that, rather than to continue pouring public funds into a bankrupt system, the federal government should take over the entire system.

The establishment of the National Railroad Passenger Corporation, a semi-public, for-profit operation, to take control of the nation's railroad passenger service, represents perhaps the first step in the direction of nationalization of our entire rail network.

The railroads have moved through the full spectrum of government investment since their inception. The process began with heavy government investment during the construction and expansion period until and beyond the shutting off of all direct aid after 1900, when railroads began to have problems paying back the loans. As government devoted its attention to other developing modes during the twentieth century, the condition of American railroads worsened steadily.

Motor Vehicle Transportation

Unlike its investment in railroads, which assumed all forms and was directed at all four mode components, government's motor vehicle investment has been remarkably uneven. True, government research and development encouraged improvements in trucks, buses, and cars, and more particularly, the indirect benefits of government-financed military research spread into private industry and improved the quality of the vehicles.

The structure of government regulation has particularly affected this mode. But for the most part, government investment has supported only one component of the mode—highway right-of-way. Strictly speaking then, government highway legislation and appropriations are not direct government promotion of the entire mode, but only of highways, the development of which did not directly advance the other components. By lending a hand to one aspect of motor vehicle transportation, government thought it could establish a pattern of development for the whole mode but, needless to say, it has failed, as any rush-hour commuter can verify.

In 1956, Congress decided to build a network of interstate highways for defense. The alleged urgency of the defense situation prompted government to adhere to a policy of immediate construction, no matter what the social and economic costs. The need to develop an equitable financing plan and to plan the construction in a way to minimize disruption of communities were pushed into the background. Congress sought the least cumbersome method of revenue collection (the universal gasoline tax and an excise tax on tires and other components of motor vehicles) and the least cumbersome method of administration in an all-out drive to lay 42,500 miles of concrete.

The relationship between vehicle and right-of-way presented one financing problem which the 1956 act barely touched upon. Ideally, vehicles using the public highways should pay for their construction and the government recognized this general principle in the highway act.

To accommodate buses and trucks, however, engineers had to design the interstate system for greater roadway strength, more bridge capacity, and easier curves than ordinary private automobiles require. Yet, many railroad officials and some transportation experts contend that the federal government does not make truck and bus companies pay a share of road-user taxes which would account for these expenses.

A second problem in the relationship between cost and benefits arose when Congress decided to construct the interstate system according to an overall national plan, to be financed from one national fund. The individual states would contribute whatever they received in user taxes, a sum which varied, of course, from state to state. With the national plan, costly highway construction in a state which has contributed relatively little to the national trust fund could progress with money from the other states. Thus, New York may be contributing to the building of a highway in Arizona. The state of Arizona gains all the advantages of improved transportation—more industrial growth, more residents, etc.—and the citizens themselves get to use a road they may hardly have paid for. In the words of transportation professor Robert W. Harbeson:

> There is a conflict between the present basis of allocation, which is designated to accomplish completion of the entire system by the same date, and the allocations which would be proportional to the contributions of the Highway Trust Fund made by users in the respective states.[27]

The lack of correlation between the rate of urbanization in the United States and the thrust of federal Highway Trust Fund legislation has also prevented proper distribution of highway funds. Since 1920, motor vehicles have traveled half their mileage in urban areas. Although many urban routes already are completed, they still need much expansion and improvement.

But urban highways still do not receive anywhere near half of the total federal and state funds for highway aid.

The large number of rural congressmen succeeded in capturing a major part of trust fund money for rural roads. The *1968 National Highway Needs Report* stressed the marked tendency by government to "allow deficiencies in the urban highway plant to accumulate more rapidly than in rural areas . . ."[28]

Also neglected by the 1956 Interstate Highway Act are the problems of overall area planning. The act authorized a system of roads for defense only. Any comprehensive plan for highways which did not concern defense was set aside: badly needed roads to serve the residents of depressed areas were not built unless they had military value and the already saturated East Coast would be clogged by still more roads if Congress deemed them necessary for the nation's defense.

The planned urban routes that were built through inner-city neighborhoods did not serve the needs of their residents. Instead, they threatened whatever stability existed there, while serving only suburbanites and industries. The 1956 act made no provision for rerouting or tunneling to preserve cohesiveness, nor did it allow government to help relocate displaced residents whose dwellings were razed in the highway construction. Equally ignored by the act were questions of aesthetics and the personal safety of residents.

Congress also missed a potential benefit in drafting the 1956 act. Properly planned roads can draw people and industry from one locality to another, encourage some to leave overcrowded regions, and thus promote a more even population dispersal. Not until 1962 did protests against strictly military highway planning prove effective. The Highway Act of 1962 made comprehensive planning of highway land-use relationships a prerequisite for federal aid. In June 1968, Secretary of Transportation Alan Boyd announced that new highways would no longer necessarily follow the shortest and cheapest routes.[29] Boyd was reacting to the strong complaints of urban dwellers that highway construction resulted in the destruction of their neighborhoods for the convenience of suburban dwellers. Although Boyd's stated policy was a step in the right direction, government still appeared to be a long way from solving the problems of inner-city highways and balancing the promotion of all modes and their components.

Pipelines

Government investment in pipelines has done more to improve the general economic climate than to aid specific projects. Two important direct, tangible investments do stand out, however.

Wartime pipelines, built by the federal government, represent a full investment package of capital, labor, and management. Of these, the most important was the "Little Big Inch," which runs almost parallel to the "Big Inch" and connects the Gulf Coast refineries with the New York area. The federal government spent $67.3 million on this pipeline, operated it during 1944 and 1945, and sold it to the Texas Eastern Transmission Company.[30] This investment is a fine illustration of government's planning-financing goal, for government tied its investment to a policy of meeting essential military needs.

In addition to its wartime investment, the government has activated research and development projects that have advanced pipeline technology. The extent of research and development outlays are impossible to measure, but some results are clear. Recent developments include the use of large diameter pipes, automated pipeline controls, and pipelines capable of moving solids.

Despite these substantial investment aids, pipelines are, for the most part, a laissez-faire mode. Although the pipeline obviously cannot vie for importance with railroads, water carriers, motor vehicles, or airlines, its relatively specialized role probably merits a higher priority in government's investment portfolio. In its beginning and maturing stages, the mode thrived almost completely on private finance. The construction of vehicle service facilities and the purchase of right-of-way were cheap enough for private business to handle without government help, and since pipelines are one necessary suboperation of the private petroleum industries, it is hard to find any justification for extensive government aid.

Airlines

Government investment in airlines has been generally in the form of capital, labor, research, and development. Since its creation in 1938, the Civil Aeronautics Board has had the responsibility for dispensing government subsidies which have two distinct forms. First, the board is authorized to make direct cash payments supporting certain airline services. These cash payments have been justified by Congress as a means of bringing about the sound development and expansion of air service. Second, the Civil Aeronautics Board allocates route patterns to the various airlines. The manner in which these routes are divided is of crucial importance to the airlines. The economics of airline operation make the cost per-seat-mile for a short distance much greater than for a long distance. This is due to the high fixed cost which must be met in putting a plane into the air, no matter how distant its destination. The cost includes landing fees, fuel consumed in takeoff and landing, plus the general operating and management overhead. Consequently, as the length of the flight increases, significant economies of scale are realized. The Senior Vice-President of Economics and Planning at United Air Lines, Andrew M. DeVoursney, has estimated that the per-seat-mile cost for a two-hundred-mile trip is about twice that for a nine-hundred-mile trip; the cost for a hundred-mile trip is twice as much per-seat-mile as for the four-hundred-mile trip.[31] Thus, each of the airlines hopes that the CAB will certify it to serve the profitable long-distance routes. The gains received from long-distance flights are, of course, expected to exceed any losses incurred in servicing shorter routes.

During the 1940s and early 1950s, the direct cash payments of the CAB went to the "trunk" or "long-haul" airlines (such as United, TWA, American, and Eastern) to help them through growth stages. Satisfied that the trunk lines had matured, CAB phased out the subsidy program in the 1950s. In its place, CAB initiated a program of subsidies to the regional or "local service" airlines. In 1970, nine such carriers—Air West, Allegheny, Frontier, Mohawk, North Central, Ozark, Piedmont, Southern, and Texas International—were serving 544 cities in the United States.[32] The CAB in the early 1960s based its subsidy program on the financial needs of the regional air carriers and disbursed an average of $80 million a year. Service was introduced for many small cities which had never had airports, let alone scheduled air service. The CAB made no effort to coordinate its new air service policy with the ICC's terminating of rail passenger service to many small cities during the early 1960s. This lack of policy coordination drew heavy criticism and a demand for subsidization of some type of transport service to small communities in the interest of overall regional growth. But such issues may be formulated and dealt with in an overall policy rather than on a case-by-case basis.

The CAB did not want to maintain a flow of $80 million a year to the regional air carriers and, in 1965, it announced a dual program to reduce drastically the subsidy payments. First, the board decided that the service would be cut off from any small community which did not use the scheduled service of a regional carrier. Second, the board began utilizing the second method of subsidization—dispensing air routes. The CAB began granting regional carriers longer and supposedly more profitable routes. Profits from the long routes, it was felt, would offset losses sustained in short-haul service. The regional carriers began buying new, expensive jets for the new routes, and their collective debt rose from $110 million in 1965 to $550 million in 1970. Between 1966 and 1970, the CAB carried through on its subsidy-reduction policy, cutting back from $74 million in 1966 to $37 million in fiscal 1970. However, with the loss of federal subsidies, regional airlines found that the long-haul routes did not compensate them for the short-haul losses. In 1969, the local service airlines reported that in spite of government subsidy, they lost $55.6 million. Furthermore, between 1965 and 1970, the regional airlines stopped serving sixty-six small communities. In forty-four of the sixty-six, the CAB allowed only the regional carriers to suspend service because air-taxi lines agreed to provide transportation to established airports. This, however, has not satisfied communities which lost the scheduled service of regional carriers. They complain that air-taxi is expensive, unreliable, and accident-prone. The CAB, caught between pressures from communities which want scheduled service either restored or maintained and airlines facing substantial losses, requested more subsidy aid for regional carriers, and thus abandoned its five-year subsidy reduction plan.

Two CAB decisions have been widely criticized: (1) the introduction of air service on a large scale to very small communities without consulting other government transportation agencies, and (2) the granting of long-haul routes to regional carriers, thus forcing them to incur large capital expenses without real assurance that such routes would solve the small town problems.

Common-carrier transportation service to small communities has proven unprofitable, and airlines serving them have performed no better than railroads. Government has made a major investment in airports, including both terminal facilities and runways. This investment in airline right-of-way is followed by forceful government guidelines as well as by material assistance. The Federal Aviation Agency not only formulates a national airport plan, but also sets and polices standards of design and construction. Many believe the federal government has failed in its role as airport planner and they cite air-terminal congestion as evidence that FAA badly underestimated the need.[33] Others contend that FAA should not have planned the construction of more airports, but should have taken one of two courses to accommodate the growth of air travel: (1) calling public attention to the necessity for alternatives such as high-speed rail transportation in corridor areas, or (2) influencing the pattern of air traffic to relieve congestion at major population centers such as New York, Chicago, and Los Angeles, perhaps by rerouting overseas flights and expanding existing facilities.

For many years the government paid for 50 percent of all authorized airport construction. The federal share came from the general tax revenues of the Treasury Department, but every year since 1947, state and local contributions for construction and maintenance have surpassed the federal contributions. State and local agencies raise funds in a variety of ways: revenues from parking, as well as a whole host of other concessions at airports —restaurants, gift shops, and drugstores—and from landing-fee levies on the airlines.

A rash of passenger tie-ups at major airports in the summer of 1969 and the spring of 1970 led to congressional concern for the course of airport development. Many believed that a greater injection of federal capital funds was needed for new airport construction. That kind of federal capital could not come from the general Treasury Department revenues in view of a tightening economic situation. Therefore, Congress decided to apply the trust fund concept—the basis for highway construction—to airport construction. On July 1, 1970, the Airport and Airway Trust Fund was established and scheduled to raise $16 billion in ten years for airport and airway development through a variety of user taxes.[34] An increase from 5 to 8 percent in the tax on each passenger ticket is expected to raise $540 million a year. An extra three-dollar departure fee charged to every passenger departing from a U.S. airport probably will raise $30 million a year. Tax on jet fuel used by privately owned and operated airplanes will be raised from four to seven cents a gallon, bringing in $47 million a year. Also included are taxes for registration of airplanes, a takeoff charge based on weight of aircraft, and taxes on aviation tires and tubes. Finally, the bill includes a 5 percent tax, designed to yield $38 million, on all air cargo waybills. Congress included a provision in the bill which makes it a penalty for any airline employee to indicate to a customer how much of the total fare is federal tax. Furthermore, the airline ticket "shall not show separately the amount paid for such transportation nor the amount of such taxes."

Thus, Congress attempts to apply the cost-benefit prin҉ e to transport development, i.e., those who benefit from tra҉port facilities should pay the bill. But, like the predecessor Interstate Highway Trust Fund, the Airport and Airways Development Fund provides for only one mode of transportation. Congress did seem to recognize the inherent danger in a single-mode approach. However, by including in the airport bill a provision which directs the Secretary of Transportation to formulate, within a year, a national transportation policy which will consider "the coordinated development and improvement of all modes of transportation, together with the priority which shall be assigned to the development and improvement of each mode of transportation," Congress recognized its responsibility for an intermodal approach to transportation development. Meanwhile, the act itself represents a ten-year commitment to airport development which limits policy-makers who may wish to draft a flexible transportation plan.

A possible shortcoming of the Airport and Airways Trust Fund bill is its failure to accept a comprehensive definition of an airport. As indicated in this section's introductory remarks, the definition of an airport should include access roads and adequate parking facilities. Planners generally contend that no airport should be constructed without considering access to major industrial centers. In spite of this, Governor William T. Cahill of New Jersey stated that the 1970 expansion of the Newark Airport was undertaken without serious consideration of available mass-transit facilities. He said the omission could create "one of the most chaotic transportation messes in the world unless something is done about it."[35]

A very important form of government investment in the airlines is the funding of research and development, a spinoff from military research. Every major commercial aircraft design can be traced directly to research performed by the armed services.[36] The Boeing 707, for example, is a slightly redesigned version of the KC-135 tanker which Boeing developed to provide for the in-flight fueling of Air Force jet bombers. The federal government itself, as it moves away from the construction of heavy bombers to the deployment of missiles, has recognized its key role in accelerating the rate of technological change in aviation, and has accordingly planned for the future improvement of air technology. One example is the supersonic transport (SST) research program to which the FAA has contributed large amounts of seed capital for research work since 1963. In the late 1960s, criticism of the SST project became intense, with many contending it was simply not needed. At best, critics argued, the big plane could reduce trans-Atlantic flight by one or two hours, a gain outweighed by the noise factor, added air pollution, and other potential atmospheric disruptions. These arguments influenced the cost-aware Congress which in 1971 decided to terminate government funding for the SST development project. Indications are that the American supersonic transport may well die without government funding since private industry is not willing to invest large sums of its own money in the research aspects of the program.

The reaction to government investment in the SST has touched off a more general criticism of federally funded transportation research. While research and development for the airlines is comprehensive, government research and development for water transport is notable but not crucial, and negligible for the railroads and motor carriers. The Northeast Corridor project—the government's major venture into railroad research—is considered too limited to yield impressive results. The government has devoted almost no research to the development of a pollution-free motor carrier engine.

Government influence for improvement in transportation apparently is not always in response to the needs of the overall transportation system. The airline industries benefited from military requirements while, in a sense, the railroads suffered because airplanes became more important for military reasons throughout the 1940s, 1950s, and 1960s. This uneven distribution of government weight is seen as a major obstacle to the rising demand for a balanced system of transportation.

Government promotional investment has also influenced regulatory procedures. The ICC's attitude toward rail rates may have as much effect on water transportation as direct payments by the Army Corps of Engineers for waterway improvements.

In the same manner, government regulatory policy is affected by government promotion policies.. All three levels of government have contributed large sums to the development of a fast, efficient highway system which substantially subsidizes motor carriers. Railroads, on the other hand, own and maintain their right-of-way facilities in addition to paying taxes on them. Their prices, by necessity, reflect these costs. The ICC is instructed to regulate each sector "fairly and impartially," but this may be impossible without a common cost determination structure. In this case, promotion has prevented an equitable regulatory system.

Promotion and regulation may be combined into one policy. The CAB is commissioned to promote adequate, efficient, and economical air service. The commission is also required to regulate air transportation. Thus, the CAB, while regulating the airlines, is at the same time greatly concerned with promoting their growth and development. The board, therefore, will avoid any regulatory action which would handicap the airlines in their competition with other modes.

CHAPTER 3

REGULATION

American transportation can be decartelized only by abolishing the ICC and subjecting the industry to the usual policy of prohibition of collusive pricing and predatory behavior embodied in the Sherman Act. Such an act would entail the usual transitional problems of decartelization as resources flowed out of the industry, but the economy would secure its freight transportation with fewer resources and an annual saving in the national freight bill probably of several billion dollars.   —George W. Hilton[1]

Economic regulation of transportation is in the national public interest and should be retained. It involves regulation of pricing, structure, and service. Since the needs and desires of transportation users, non-transportation factors such as location of population, industry and markets, and the technology and cost characteristics are constantly changing, regulatory law should be flexible and frequently subjected to review.   —Major General John Doyle[2]

The statements of these two transportation experts indicate the intense controversy that has developed over the role that regulation should assume in government policy. The Interstate Commerce Commission has been regulating rates for railroads since 1887, pipelines since 1906, motor carriers since 1935, and water carriers since 1940. The Civil Aeronautics Board has had regulatory responsibility for airlines since 1935. Pipeline regulation (like safety regulation) is not a hotly debated topic, but the intermodal rate relationships among the other four modes are controversial, to say the least, and the bulk of this chapter will center on them.

Control of entry into the transportation market is closely allied to rate regulation. The theoretical purposes of entry control are described by Professor James C. Nelson of Washington State University:

> First, essential common carrier services can be required of carriers given certificates (of public convenience and necessity). . . . The reduced competition due to entry restrictions can encourage adequate investment and technological change by assuring profitable returns. . . . Standards of service can be improved by encouraging able and responsible carriers, by discouraging "fly-by-night" firms, and by imposing high standards of saftey. . . . Duplicating fixed investments can be avoided, excess capacity can be reduced and large firms can be encouraged. Finally, greater coordination can result from through services and joint rates.[3]

Regulation Rationale

The history of rate regulation begins with the railroads. The railroads had (and defenders of regulation like to point out that they still have) many "natural monopoly" characteristics which, for this industry, make the forces of ordinary market competition ineffective.[4]

Railroads were thought to be noncompetitive because their construction required a huge investment in land for right-of-way, in labor to prepare roadbed and lay track, in construction materials, in rolling stock, and in terminal facilities. All of these investments are irrecoverable and so expensive that a number of localities could not be served efficiently by more than one railroad. This gave rise to the argument that railroads charging monopoly rates could take unfair advantage of the powerless shippers and that regulation was needed to protect the public.

Yet, in the latter part of the nineteenth century, the railroads by and large did not have a monopoly situation. By 1875, most large cities of the United States were served by more than one railroad.[5] At other points, canals and lake steamers provided alternative service. The railroad companies engaged in rate-slashing wars. With their high fixed costs behind them,[6] the railroads worked on competitive pricing policies geared to their relatively low variable or marginal costs. Marginal costs (which tend to vary more or less proportionately with traffic volume) include payment to train crew and other ancillary services, fuel consumption, track maintenance, and equipment depreciation. Ignored in the frenzy of competition, however, was the all-important "average cost," which is composed of the variable costs and a certain proportion of fixed costs, and, therefore, is greater than its variable or marginal components. Wherever competition existed, the railroads, basing rates on marginal costs, frequently failed to cover their average costs. According to John Meyer:

> Prices could be cut well below average total costs and be still greater than short-run marginal costs. In competitive situations where one road faced competition from other railroads or water transportation, extensive price-cutting to the level of the short-run marginal cost almost inevitably followed. As long as the marginal costs could be covered, the railroads figured it would be to their advantage to slash rates to attract as much traffic as possible.[7]

This practice became officially known as "discrimination," differences in rates which cannot be explained by differences in the actual cost of providing service.

Roots of Regulation

Before 1887. Although the railroads did not by and large have a monopoly situation in the late nineteenth century, a single railroad in certain areas, primarily the western agricultural regions, provided the only feasible transport. Small shippers in such areas had to pay whatever the railroad charged, and rates were often exorbitant. The farmers set up Grange (or Patrons of Husbandry) organizations which agitated for state control of rail abuses.[8] The Grange movement was successful in getting regulatory legislation passed in four states.[9]

Many commentators point out that the federal government first became involved in regulation of railroads engaged in interstate commerce only after the Supreme Court had ruled in the famous

Wabash Case of 1886 that only the federal government, not the states, had the right to regulate interstate commerce. Congress then acted hurriedly, many contend, to fill the vacuum left by the Wabash decision.[10]

Yet this interpretation fails to emphasize that the railroads had been working in Congress for a number of years previous to the *Wabash Case* to obtain some type of federal regulation. Nine months before the Wabash decision, the Senate Interstate Commerce Committee released this statement:

> The committee has found among the leading representatives of the railroad interests an increasing readiness to accept the aid of Congress in working out the solution of the railroad problem which has obstinately baffled all their efforts, and not a few of the ablest railroad men of the country seem disposed to look to the intervention of Congress as promising to afford the best means of ultimately securing a more equitable and satisfactory adjustment of the relations of the transportation interests to the community than they themselves have been able to bring about.[11]

Many railroad leaders wanted federal regulation for a number of reasons.[12] They wanted relief from the tough competition at major terminal areas, competition which forced the railroads into rate wars, and the granting of rebates to large shippers. The railroads themselves attempted to correct this situation by entering into traffic pools whose members agreed to adhere to the prepublished rates (which were high enough to allow each road to make a healthy return on investment). But outside of a few brief-lived exceptions, all efforts to establish voluntary pooling agreements failed. The railroads began to recognize that a federal regulatory body could legalize and enforce the unsuccessful voluntary arrangements which were constantly disrupted by overeager carriers in the heat of competition. Regulation would give the weight of law to rate structures which they, in loose-drawn contracts, were powerless to enforce. Regulation outlawed the rebate, and with greater revenues from the transport of high-valued commodities, the roads could afford to maintain low rates on the politically more delicate agricultural freight. The railroads discovered early that industries whose transportation costs do not greatly affect their retail price are not likely to object to rate increases. These industries could easily meet increased transport costs with modest price boosts. This led to what has been aptly named the "value-of-service" method of rate discrimination.[13]

A second variable which motivated major railroad interests to seek protection from the federal government was the clear partnership they had been developing over the years with the government in other matters. The federal government had given huge land grants to railroads as well as direct cash subsidies for the construction of the first transcontinental railroad finished in 1869. During the administrations of Hays and Cleveland, the federal government also protected the vested interests of railroads by using troops and court injunctions to thwart attempts by railroad workers to organize and bargain. Furthermore, railroads, being among the largest businesses in the country, wielded tremendous political power. It is often said that Tom Scott of the Pennsylvania Railroad helped to engineer the compromise of 1876, which resulted in the election of Hays over Tilden. As a result of these close ties with the federal government, it was natural for the railroads to get federal help in establishing a firm pricing policy for their industry.

A third variable which drove the railroads to seek federal regulatory laws was the growing demand by Grangers and even more radical groups for tight public control. State regulation, spurred on by the Grangers, was not only restricting, but confusing and inconsistent as well. An accurate prophecy of the effect of federal regulation on railroads was given by Attorney General Richard Olney in 1892:

> The ICC, as its functions have now been limited by the courts, is, or can be made of great use to the railroads. It satisfies the popular clamor for a government supervision of railroads, at the same time the supervision is entirely nominal. Further, the older such a commission gets to be, the more inclined it will be found to take the business and the railroad view of things. It thus becomes sort of the barrier between the railroad corporations and the people and sort of protection against hasty and crude legislation hostile to the railroad interest.[14]

In 1887, not all railroad officials were in favor of federal regulation. The many who did favor regulation, however, did not want the type of controls demanded by the farmers in the West. The railroads wanted a regulatory body responsive to their needs, including the immediate need for a solid rate structure.

A final factor in the agitation for railroad regulation was the small shipper. The large shippers, with their great bargaining power, were prime beneficiaries of the rate wars, even where the railroads had a monopoly on transportation. The railroads were forced to give rebates to powerful steel, coal, and petroleum shippers on whose business they heavily depended. Sometimes a practical monopoly was given to certain individuals or corporations for supplying wood or coal to particular cities. These dealers received preferential rates, while the railroads raised their rates to others. Smaller shippers, feeling that regulation could help end the large-shipper abuses, allied themselves with the Grangers.[15]

1887-1920. The regulatory legislation which passed Congress in 1887 provided no real threat to railroad interests. The legislation, as Gabriel Kolko adequately shows in his excellent work, was not exactly a populist effort to control railroad excesses. The first chairman of the ICC, Mr. Cooley, a man with strong past railroad associations, sought to obtain for the railroads authority to legalize pooling arrangements for rate determination, freely granted exemptions to railroads allowing them to discriminate in terms of rates between long and short hauls whenever it was to their advantage to do so, and gave informal decisions to railroads but not to shipping groups. Commissioner Cooley also sought to institutionalize railroad rate practices which were based on discriminatory techniques—high rates for high-valued goods and lower rates for low-valued goods.

The law was vague enough to allow the commissioner of the ICC to determine policy as he saw fit. It did not forbid geographical or commodity preferences outright but only those which were "undue." The legislation stipulated that the commission would prevent rates which were "unjust and unreasonable." Yet Congress did not define these crucial terms or attempt to advise the ICC on how to make its own definitions. Discrepancies in rates between long-haul and short-haul traffic were curbed only if they were "unjustified discrepancies." Again, the Congress failed to define another term and vast power fell into the hands of the ICC.

The Act to Regulate Commerce did not provide machinery for nonrailroad interests to present an effective case. Small shippers and farmers could hardly pay the excessive fees necessary to bring a case before the ICC. Furthermore, as Kolko noted, the average length of a case before the ICC until 1900 was four years, and small shippers did not have the resources to fight drawn-out legal battles. Large shippers, who had both time and money to take cases before the ICC, were not motivated to do so, since they either had enough power to negotiate lower rates from the railroads, or could pass on shipping cost increases to their customers. As a consequence, very few cases were brought before the ICC for formal decision between 1890 and 1900. Kolko summarizes the nonrepresentative nature of proceedings before the ICC:

> During 1890 and 1900, only 180 cases were formally decided by the Commission—of the many thousands brought to its attention. In this context, railroad regulation essentially represented an internal class affair. The vast majority of farmers and the consumers were powerless and forgotten. It did not occur to the authors of the Collom or Reagan Bills to create some formal mechanism for representing the "public interest" in railroad regulation, since it appeared almost axiomatic that shippers would eliminate any injustices through their appeals. Nor did it impress many politicians that the larger shippers and railroads might have more in common with one another than an amorphous, unorganized mass of poorer farmers and workers.[16]

The initial working relationships established between the ICC and the railroads were disrupted when the Supreme Court challenged many of the existing practices of the Commission. As Kolko maintains, the majority of justices on the Supreme Court were dedicated to the principles of laissez faire. The Supreme Court's anti-ICC decisions during this period have been viewed by some as an effort to restrict a body which was defending the public against big business. But this view assumes that the ICC was acting in the interest of the public before the Supreme Court handed down its decisions.[17] The decisions actually caused as much disruption for the railroads as they did for the ICC. Decisions which restricted the ICC's ability to head off expensive competition forced the railroads back to where they had been before 1887—with unstable earnings and rate wars. The decisions of 1897 and 1898 led the railroads to seek congressional legislation which would secure an environment in which they could prosper. The effect of the additional legislation—the Hepburn Act of 1906, the Mann-Elkins Act of 1910, and the Transportation Act of 1920—was to limit the forces of competition and to legalize the railroad cartel with government protection guaranteed.

In 1896, in the *Maximum Freight Rate Case* and in the *Social Circle Case*, the Supreme Court stated that the Act to Regulate

Commerce did not "expressly, or by necessary implication" give the commission the power to fix rates. The Court ruled that the legislation stipulated that the Commission could only declare a rate unreasonable but had no power to change that rate. The Commission, as Kolko demonstrates, never really asserted the right to fix maximum and minimum rates and certainly was not actively doing so in a number of cases.[18] The ICC had developed only a vague notion of which rates were reasonable and which were unreasonable, let alone a formula for determining instances of unreasonable rates. If anything, the Commission, Kolko says, sought the ability to prescribe maximum rates and thus to protect railroad interests from the competitive effects of rate variations. The Hepburn Act of 1906 gave the ICC unequivocal power to set maximum railroad rates.[19]

The long-haul, short-haul stipulation in the 1887 Act to Regulate Commerce forbade a carrier to charge more for a shorter haul than a longer haul over the same line, in the same direction, and under substantially similar circumstances. However, the Supreme Court held in the *Alabama-Midland Case* in 1897 that the noncompetitive nature of stations serviced by only one railroad did create a "dissimilarity of circumstances and conditions such that ICC prohibitions did not apply." Yet, if the long-haul, short-haul clause were to correct any injustices, it would have to prevent discriminatory rates due merely to the fact that one area had competition and another did not. The decision by the Supreme Court did not hamper the ICC, since the Commission, Kolko states, did not apply the long-haul, short-haul clause until 1893, and only loosely thereafter.[20] The Mann-Elkins Act in 1910 amended the clause by prohibiting any party from justifying rate discrimination on the basis of dissimilar circumstances between main terminal and intermediate points.[21]

The *Trans-Missouri Freight Association* decision (166 U.S. 290) of 1897 and the *Joint Traffic Association* decision (171 U.S. 505) of 1898 demonstrate the effect of Supreme Court decisions on ICC policy. These two decisions declared that traffic pools, rate associations, and voluntary efforts at self-regulation, all of which the ICC had sponsored, were restraints of free trade and violations of the Sherman Anti-Trust Act. The railroad-conscious ICC reacted to the decision in a predictable fashion. "Certainly it ought not to be unlawful for carriers to confer and agree for the purpose of doing what the law enjoins."[22]

The legislation with which Congress nullified the effects of some of the Supreme Court decisions restored the working relationship between the Commission and the railroad industry. In 1888 only 39 percent of the railroad stock was paying dividends. By 1910 this figure had risen to over 67 percent. During the same period the average rate of dividends on all stock rose from 2.1 percent to 5 percent.[23]

The Transportation Act of 1920 eliminated once and for all competitive pricing among the railroads by giving the ICC the power to control minimum rates in addition to maximum rates. The clear concern of Congress with railroad economics is indicated by the legislative prescriptive to the ICC to set railroad rates which would enable the companies to earn a "fair return" on their investment.[24] The practice of determining rates by the value of goods shipped rather than by the cost of shipment was approved by Congress. This meant lower rates for bulk agricultural freight (and hence appealed to the Midwest and South) and higher rates for high-valued manufactured goods.[25]

In 1906, Congress also placed pipelines under ICC jurisdiction. The ICC determination of the reasonableness of rates was based on its experience with railroads.

1920-1935. Truck transportation developed into a serious competitor to the railroads during the 1920s by diverting much of the high-value traffic from the rails and threatening the value-of-service rate-making system. The railroads sought to make up their losses by increasing rates on agricultural goods, but met with strong opposition from Congress.[26] As a stopgap measure, the Emergency Transportation Act of 1933 directed the ICC to regulate rates so that traffic would move freely at the "lowest charges consistent with the cost of providing the service. The revenue needs of the carriers were to be considered only to the extent necessary to insure the maintenance of adequate transportation service. Fair return, based on plant value, was abandoned as the prime objective of ratemaking. Under the new rule, the public need for cheap and adequate transportation was the prime consideration and the revenue need of the carriers was made subsidiary."[27]

The measure obviously did not solve the revenue problems of the railroads, which, while still losing their high-valued traffic to the motor carriers, were prohibited from raising rates on bulk commodities. In order to preserve value-of-service rate-making, Congress in 1935 brought motor carriers under the ICC.[28] Many feared that regulation of motor carriers would raise their rates, and in order to allay some of these fears, Congress exempted agricultural goods from regulation. Private carriers were likewise exempted.

An important point about the extension of regulation to motor carriers is that it was done without any long-range view. It had to solve immediate problems: a declining railroad industry whose rate structure was endangered by competition and a motor industry with extremely low rates and excessive intramodal competition in a temporarily disorganized state because of the Depression.[29]

Most economists agree that there is no economic justification for motor-carrier regulation. David Boies, a member of the New York Bar Association, is only one of many who believe that the industry is differentiated

> by easy entry, few important economics of scale, mobility of resources and the division of the market among a comparatively large number of firms. It seems an almost ideal industry for the effective operation of competition. In the absence of administrative controls of entry, the accumulation of substantial monopoly power would be almost impossible—and maximum rate regulation unnecessary.[30]

But the railroads saw motor carriers only as a competitor and lobbied vigorously for control. The motor carriers supported regulation to restore order in the topsy-turvy situation caused by the Depression. Many shippers pressured for regulation in order to preserve value-of-service benefits.

Water carriers also continued to give problems to the railroads and after a tediously long debate, they too were brought under ICC control with the passage of the Transportation Act of 1940.

1935-1958. There is no question that the ICC intended to perpetuate value-of-service rate-making once it regulated motor carriers. As Robert Nelson and his colleague, William Griener, suggest:

> The ICC did not misunderstand the significance of the Motor Carrier Act. It gave immediate approval to truck rates and classifications which are almost exact duplicates of rail rates and classifications. Moreover, in the early days of 1935, the Commission made use of the minimum rate power to level up the truck rates.[31]

Thus, the Commission embarked upon a philosophy which kept the rates of railroads and motor carriers essentially at parity, which would put both modes in the same position as when motor carrier regulation was first introduced. David Boies describes the situation:

> With respect to the relationship of rail to motor carrier rates the Commission seemingly has been moved by a desire to preserve both types of transportation in virtually the whole range of service they had come to occupy at the time its jurisdiction was broadened. Consequently it has given large emphasis to the preservation of the opportunity to compete and to secure a "fair share of the traffic."[32]

The policy of rate parity between modes obviously favored the motor carriers; their service was more specialized and door-to-door. The railroads' biggest potential competitive weapon was economic in longer hauls, made possible by their traditional high-fixed-cost, low-variable-cost structure. This weapon, however, was neutralized by the ICC.

The ICC justified its apportioning of traffic through parity rate-making in the Transportation Act of 1933 which directed the Commission, in determining the reasonableness of a proposed rate, to give consideration to the "effect of rates on the movement of traffic."[33] The Transportation Act of 1940 tried to force the ICC to abandon this policy, directing it to consider only "the effect of rates on the movement of traffic by the carrier or carriers for which the rates are prescribed." Ostensibly, no longer could the ICC make rates for the railroad by taking into account what the effects of those rates would be on the motor carriers' business. However, this directive was shrouded in the ambiguity of other legislative directives set forth in the national transportation policy for regulation. David Boies puts together all the factors (which are by no means entirely consistent) that the ICC considered in changing rates:

1. the effect of rates on the movement of traffic by the carrier or carriers for which the rates are prescribed;
2. the need, in the public interest, of adequate and efficient . . . service at the lowest cost consistent with the furnishing of such service;
3. the need of revenues sufficient to enable the carriers, under honest, economical, and efficient management to provide such service;
4. the "inherent advantages" of each mode of transportation.[34]

The ICC continued to protect motor-carrier traffic by forcing the railroads to maintain their high rates on high-value goods. The railroads could not reduce their rates to reflect any costs other than value-of-service.

A summary of the 1935-1958 period is provided by Ernest Williams, professor of transportation at Columbia University:

> The railroads, with exceptions, are not permitted to go below the level thus looked upon with approval for motor carriers, even when a showing of costs upon any of the accepted bases would indicate rate costs below the motor carrier level. Yet this is often the case, especially in view of the fact that the traffic for which the competition is most strenuous is often high grade traffic which has been required to bear considerably more than a proportionate burden of overheads because of the comparatively high value of the service. Elements of the value-of-service structure are thus preserved and the motor carriers are retained and encouraged further to develop a service for which they have an apparent cost disadvantage. At the same time, since important segments of the rail structure are governed by outstanding Commission maximum rate orders governed by traditional value-of-service concepts, considerable traffic is forced upon the railroads by below cost rates which motor carriers could handle more economically were rates free to adjust to a more natural level.[35]

The ICC also protected the barge lines by canceling compensatory rail rates, settling on a policy to permit no rate decrease which would eliminate competitors. "Wherever the question of survival of competing carriers has been severely posed, the ICC consistently favored protection of the high-cost competitor regardless of whether the proposed tariff was compensatory," Boies said.[36]

In 1938, the Civil Aeronautics Board was created to regulate airline rates. The CAB followed practically the same criteria as the ICC, determining rates by:

1. the effect of such rates upon the movement of traffic;
2. the need in the public interest of adequate and efficient transportation of persons and property by air carriers at the lowest cost consistent with the furnishing of such service;
3. such standards respecting the character and quality of service to be rendered by air carriers . . .

   4. the inherent advantages of transportation by aircraft;

   5. the need of each air carrier for revenue sufficient to enable such carrier, under honest, economical and efficient management to provide adequate and efficient air carrier service.[37]

1958-1963. Recognizing the problems to which Professor Williams referred, the Report of the Presidential Advisory Committee on Transport Policy and Organization (1955) sought to redirect ICC rate-making philosophy. Briefly, the report requested that the ICC no longer consider the effects of rate changes on other modes, or whether the new charge would be lower than necessary to meet competition. The railroads also joined in the clamor, seeking to end the Commission's policy of competitor protection. Railroad executives now realized that it would be more profitable for them to lower rates in an attempt to attract new business and regain old. Their support for competitive pricing restriction evaporated.[38]

These and other protests showed the need for new legislation. The Transportation Act of 1958 developed a new rule for ICC rate-making:

> In a proceeding involving competition between carriers of different modes . . . the Commission in determining whether a rate is lower than a reasonable minimum rate, shall consider the facts and circumstances attending the movement of the traffic by the carrier or carriers to which the rate is applicable. Rates of a carrier shall not be held up to a particular level to protect the traffic of any other mode of transportation, giving due consideration to the objectives of the National Transportation Policy.[39]

Although the act seemed a clear directive to the ICC to desist from its policy of rate parity, the reference to national transportation policy obscured the situation.

The policy told the ICC to prevent "destructive competition." As already seen, the ICC interpreted "destructive competition" as that in which a rate reduction by one mode would drive another out of business. ICC was instructed to develop, coordinate, and preserve a national transportation system by water, highway, and rail. Thus, the Commission did not substantially change the policies it employed in the previous period. Robert W. Harbeson, professor of economics at the University of Illinois, after an exhaustive study of all ICC cases dealing with rail-motor rate competition through mid-1961, declared that there had been no significant changes from the situation that Professor Williams described.[40] The ICC was still protecting the motor and water carriers by preventing lower railroad tariffs. The classic case of this period was the *Commodities-Pan-Atlantic Steamship Corporation* case.

> Reduced rail trailer-on-flatcar rates were resisted by water carriers. . . . The Commission [found] . . . that the proposed railroad tariffs "can fairly be said to threaten the continued operation and thus the continued existence" of the protestant water carriers. Relying on the national transportation policy's prescription of destructive competition and on the assertion that the continued existence of water carriers was necessary to the national defense, the ICC held that trailer-on-flatcar rail rates must "be maintained on a level of not lower than 6% above" the then existing water rates in order to compensate for the railroad's service advantage.[41]

1963-1968. The railroads protested this decision and carried the *New Haven* case to the Supreme Court. Affirming a district court decision, the Court lashed out at the ICC for its policy of protecting competition by forcing modes to keep their rates excessively high. The Court said that

> if there is one fact that stands out in bold relief in the legislative history of the rule of ratemaking, it is that Congress did not regard the setting of a rate at a particular level as constituting an unfair or destructive competitive practice simply because that rate would divert some or all of the traffic from a competing mode.[42]

However, the Supreme Court realized that the ICC could use its minimum-rate power to prevent rate decreases if such cuts threatened to injure a carrier with "inherent advantage." The Court stated that

> the purpose of the amendment to the rule of ratemaking in 1958 was to permit the railroads to respond to competition by asserting whatever inherent advantages of cost and service they possessed. The Commission, in the view of the proponents of the bill, had thwarted effective competition by insisting that each form of transportation subject to its jurisdiction must remain viable at all costs and must therefore receive a significant share of the market. It had, in the words of one Congressman, become a giant handicapper. Moreover, it is clear that Congress did not unconsciously

or inadvertently defeat this purpose when it included in the rule of ratemaking a reference to the National Transportation Policy. The principle reason for this reference, as the hearings show, was to prevent the railroads from destroying or impairing the inherent advantages of other modes.[43]

The major weakness of this decision is that it gave the ICC no explicit definition of which carrier had the "inherent advantage." The Court said only that when the average total (or fully distributed) cost of the railroads was below the average total (or fully distributed) cost of the water carriers, the ICC should not force the railroads to inflate their rates. The decision made no judgment as to whether or not marginal (or out-of-pocket) costs could be considered in the determination of "inherent advantages." It also offered no rules to guide the ICC when the railroads want to cut their rates below average total (or fully distributed) costs.[44]

The ICC's intermodal rate decisions since the *New Haven* case indicate a consistent refusal to allow the railroads to reduce rates below fully distributed costs, if these costs exceed the fully distributed costs of a competing regulated mode.[45] Thus, the ICC maintains that fully distributed cost, and not out-of-pocket cost, is the basis for "inherent advantages." The ICC contends that railroads would destroy the "inherent advantages" of other regulated modes by reducing their rates below fully distributed costs (if these costs exceed the fully distributed costs of other modes). This policy has drawn sharp criticism from economists and railroad officials who believe that pricing based upon marginal or out-of-pocket costs is the only efficient method of allocating transportation resources. They see the ICC policy as harmful to the economy.[46]

A more recent Supreme Court decision on intermodal rate competition, however, affirmed the ICC's right to refuse reduction of railroad rates below fully distributed costs when these costs exceed the fully distributed costs of competing modes. In 1963, the Pennsylvania Railroad and the Louisville & Nashville lowered their rate on ingot molds from Neville Island and Pittsburgh, Pennsylvania, to Steelton, Kentucky. The new rate, set below the fully distributed cost but above the out-of-pocket cost, equaled the rate of the combined barge-truck service. Before the new rate was put into effect, virtually all ingot molds were moved by barge-truck service. But equal railroad rates would divert almost all of that traffic. The competing barge and truck lines protested that their "inherent advantage" was being destroyed, and the ICC agreed, forbidding the proposed rate reductions. A district court reversed the ICC upon appeal by the railroads. The matter was finally settled in favor of the barge and truck lines when the Supreme Court, on June 17, 1968, ruled that it was up to the ICC to evaluate cost factors in defining "inherent advantage." The Court stated that, if the ICC uses fully distributed costs as its criterion, there can be no contest. If a change is desired in the costs which are used to determine "inherent advantages," said the Court, new legislation should be passed to effect such change. The decision maintained that the Supreme Court is not properly qualified to make basic judgments about economic policy.[47] Thus, the burden fell to Congress to formulate whatever new ICC guidelines may be desired.

Piggyback Service

The use of rail-carrier flatcars to transport motor-carrier trailers has steadily expanded. This service is often referred to as "trailer-on-flatcar" (TOFC), or "piggyback" service. Piggyback has enabled the railroads to retain and develop a large volume of traffic which they might have lost to motor carriers. The Interstate Commerce Commission has stated that the

rapid growth of piggyback has been largely the result of its effectiveness in meeting the need for co-ordinated rail and motor services. Piggyback combines the advantages of movement by truck with the long-haul economies of rail or water transport, under conditions which hold total expense to a minimum.[48]

Since all transportation acts of Congress had been passed before the development of piggyback service, regulatory guidelines were clearly lacking. As a result, the railroads deprived some motor carriers of access to this most efficient system by providing the service arbitrarily and by charging discriminatory rates. In 1964, therefore, the ICC promulgated rules to govern piggyback service, including one which declared that the railroads had to make the service available to all carriers seeking it at reasonable, nondiscriminatory rates:

TOFC service, if offered by a rail carrier through its open-tariff publications, shall be made available to any person at a charge no greater and no less than that received from any other person or persons for doing for him or them a like and contemporaneous service to the transportation of a like kind of traffic under substantially similar circumstances.[49]

Exemptions

Complicating the ICC's ability to set rates is the fact that Congress has granted exemptions from regulation to certain water and motor carriers. The Transportation Act of 1940 granted exemption to water carriers for bulk commodities. Locklin is one of the many experts who believe that this exemption has turned out to be a mistake and severely hampers regulated carriers:

> The exemption of bulk cargoes was based in part on the belief that such transportation was not competitive with railroads or motor carriers. As a matter of fact, much of the bulk commodity movement by water is competitive with railroads. The latter are at a serious disadvantage in competing for it, since they must adhere to published rates while the exempt carriers are free to make whatever rates are necessary to obtain the traffic. For this reason considerable sentiment has developed for repeal of the bulk cargo exemption. For many years the ICC recommended such action. These recommendations were strongly seconded by the Doyle Report.[50]

Similarly the exemptions for private motor carriers, and for motor carriers of agricultural commodities, have caused problems for regulated carriers:

> The ICC has estimated the number of exempt for-hire truckers subject to its safety rules. In Gray Area of Transportation Operations, published in June 1960, the Commission estimated the number of such truckers at 30,666. . . . The recent Doyle Report stated that exempt commodities were trucked by more than 9,000 commercial carriers which generally operated large equipment but not a large number of trucks per firm. Their principal operations were described as "subsequent to the initial farm to market movement, between commercial establishments, and often for long distances in intercity movement."[51]

Pipelines

Although pipeline rates have been under ICC control since 1906, there has been no legislation to control market entry or consolidation or merger. Pipelines are free from much of the other regulation that other modes are subjected to:

There is no control over the construction of new lines or of extension of existing lines; there is no control over abandonment of pipelines; there is no control over the security issues of pipeline companies; and there is no regulation of consolidations and acquisitions of control, although the pipelines are subject to the anti-pooling provisions of the law.[52]

The nature of the industry has made entry regulation unnecessary. Huge minimum investments and marked economies of scale and utilization have limited the number of firms in the field to one per route, or to not more than four firms for large markets.

Entry Control

Railroads. As mentioned earlier, railroads in the late nineteenth and early twentieth centuries faced severe competition in certain areas and low earnings, partly as a result of overcapacity. During the unrestricted railroad building era, there was simply too much right-of-way constructed for maximum efficiency. Before 1920, the ICC had no power to rationalize the railroad system in this area by encouraging merger or consolidation. However, the Transportation Act of 1920 gave the ICC power to limit the establishment of new railroads and to control the extension or abandonment of railway lines through the granting or denial of certificates of public convenience and necessity. Congress directed the ICC to develop an overall plan for mergers and consolidations for the entire country. This plan would contain the criteria for the Commission in all merger cases. Any railroad proposal which did not fit into the ICC plan would be denied by the Commission. Congress wanted the ICC's consolidation plan to bring about a merger of some weaker railroads with some of the stronger:

The Transportation Act of 1920 relaxed and eased the previously existing policy on competition. It sought to encourage the consolidation of railroads into a limited number of systems, but under the comprehensive plan for the consolidation of railway properties embodied in the act, competition was to be preserved as fully as possible and existing routes and channels of trade and commerce were to be maintained wherever practical.[53]

The ICC, in accordance with the Transportation Act of 1920, asked Professor William Z. Ripley of Harvard University to draw up the national plan. In 1921, Ripley released proposals which touched off two years of debate among the members of the ICC. Finally, in 1925, the ICC asked Congress to repeal the legislation provision which required it to draw up a national railroad map. The ICC request was repeated over the next three years. Not until 1929 did the ICC submit its plan for a feasible railroad system.

Between 1920 and 1929, merger discussions were deferred as railroad management waited for the ICC to release its plan. Shortly after the plan was released, the stock market collapsed and the Great Depression set in. Throughout the Depression, railroads were in no financial position to even consider merger, and the ICC plan lay moribund.[54]

The ICC got relief from the requirement of developing a railroad master plan in the Transportation Act of 1940. In that legislation, however, Congress gave the Commission authority to approve mergers initiated by individual railroads only after considering:

1. the effect of the proposed transaction upon adequate transportation service to the public;

2. the effect upon the public interest of the inclusion, or failure to include, other railroads in the territory involved in the proposed transactions;

3. the total fixed charges resulting from the proposed transaction;

4. the interests of carrier employees.[55]

Obviously, the idea of developing a master plan and approving only mergers which complied with its provisions never had a chance to function. Both the attitude of the ICC and the Great Depression ruined any chance that the plan might have had. Yet, ICC commissioners continued to contend that experience with the ICC plan adopted in 1929 proved beyond a doubt that a master plan for railroad mergers will not work. In testimony before the Senate Subcommittee on Surface Transportation in June 1969, Commissioner Tuggle of the ICC stated:

Some of the regional proposals for railroad mergers were tried back in the 1920's, and they failed. The Congress directed the Commission to make a study of all railroads in the United States and set up regional railroad networks or systems. . . . After a few years Congress relieved us of that responsibility. . . . They repealed that law. . . . I see no reason to change the legislation now. . . . I don't think you can get together any 11 men in the United States who can sit up here in Washington and draw lines on a map and make a viable, practical, efficient, economical national railroad network. It just couldn't be done. There is not that kind of knowledge.[56]

Abandoning the national or regional systems philosophies, the ICC began approaching railroad-merger proposals on a case-by-case basis. The new movement began in the late fifties with the merger of the Norfolk & Western and the Virginian, and has included a vast number of railroads since then. All merger proposals are viewed case by case despite the fact that one may seriously affect the distribution of traffic in an entire region or may not be in the best interests of maximum transportation effectiveness. Commissioner Tuggle stated in 1969:

We can't give a single merger case national consideration. As the law is now, a merger proposal has to be started by the carriers. We have no authority to start that. Until something comes before us there is nothing we can do.[57]

Thus, according to Tuggle's statement, if eastern railroads A and B with parallel tracks initiate merger discussions, the ICC will docket the case and assign a hearing examiner with exclusive jurisdiction. If shortly after the first case is underway, two more eastern railroads (C and D, with parallel tracks) adjacent to the first pair initiate merger discussion, the ICC will docket this case and assign to it a second hearing examiner, also with exclusive jurisdiction. The hearing examiners have no responsibility to coordinate their efforts. For example, the best interest of effective transportation may be served by mergers of A with C and of B with D, but these possibilities cannot be considered because they are not proposed by the railroad.

Companies proposing to merge usually build their case around two main points—great economies in operation and the opportunity for improved service. Commissioner Tuggle has stated: "Mergers are supposed to render better service, and one of the main reasons for permitting these consolidations is to improve the service."[58] For example, on April 6, 1966, the ICC issued an initial approval for the proposed merger between the Pennsylvania Railroad and the New York Central Railroad because the merged railroad could offer improved, modern, and efficient service to the public. The ICC report concluded:

Shippers may expect numerous service advantages as a result of the merger. There will be single-line service between more points, with less route-circuity, less handling of freight, less switching of cars, and consequently less likelihood of damage, less time in transit and terminal, and easier tracing of shipment. . . . There is no question but that the transaction will permit more economical and efficient use of the applicants' transportation facilities. The economies realized through the merger operation will rebound in large part to the benefit of shippers, and thus to the general public, either through the improved service thereby made possible or through lower rates. For this reason the merger has met with the almost unanimous approval, in principal, of shippers throughout the nation.[59]

The ICC also accepted the estimate, made by the Penn and Central attorneys, that through the changes in operation brought about by the merger, annual savings would reach $81.2 million by the eighth year the merger was in effect. The breakdown of savings was listed as follows:

Item	Savings in Millions
Freight service—road	$14.5
Freight service—yard	42.1
Passenger service	6.8
Maintenance of equipment	6.4
General and traffic expenses	11.7
Joint facilities	(0.3)
	$81.2[60]

The railroad attorneys also gave the ICC their word that under the proposed merger, Penn Central would make capital improvement costing an estimated $74.6 million over a four-year period. The Penn Central promised to undertake extensive construction at major terminal areas in Selkirk, Cleveland, Cincinnati, Toledo, and Chicago.

The rationale behind the greater efficiency and enormous savings from railroad mergers is that the cost structure of the industry lends itself to achievement of economies of scale. The larger a railroad company is, the theory goes, the greater the chances for curbing expenses and wasteful practices. The ICC apparently accepted this philosophy.

The merger of the Pennsylvania and the New York Central became effective in February 1, 1968. Just a little more than two years after the merger was consummated, the Penn Central Transportation Company filed for bankruptcy in the federal courts. The great "cost savings" projections set forth by the company and accepted by the ICC were not realized.

Basically, the ICC rationale for mergers does not distinguish between railroad mergers which serve only to increase size and those which are truly conducive to greater efficiency. A study conducted by the Department of Transportation on the problem of railroad mergers makes this distinction:

> Density (or the amount of traffic over a given portion of track) in railroading is the most certain area of economies of scale. Confusion often exists between economies of scale, meaning system-wide size of the railroad company, and economies of density on given segments of the route. The general presumption that the technology of railroading should produce economies of density has often been misread as a presumption that there should also be system-wide economies of scale in railroading. . . . The important task for analysis and regulatory policy is to distinguish between mergers that are conducive to greater density, as opposed to those which will merely produce large size. Greater density depends upon (1) new traffic, (2) consolidation of existing routes and reduction of parallel trackage or (3) abandonment of branch lines. New traffic can be a result of various kinds of mergers, particularly end-to-end mergers that divert traffic.[61]

The fact is that greater size alone may produce dis-economies of scale and lesser efficiency, as happened in the case of the Penn Central. The merged railroad suffered severely from incompatible management philosophies. Professor Kent Healy has estimated that managerial dis-economies begin to set in when a railroad has more than twenty thousand employees.[62] The Penn Central has at least three times that number. Alfred E. Perlman, initially the president and chief administrative officer of the merged road and later the vice-chairman, successfully ran the New York Central Railroad before the merger was consummated. Perlman conducted the classic rebuilding of the four-time bankrupt

Denver and Rio Grande Western Railroad. In the year before the merger, Perlman led the New York Central to one of its most profitable years in the post-World War II period. Stuart Saunders, who ran the Pennsylvania Railroad before the merger, was board chairman of the merged road. Saunders had a relatively undistinguished railroad record, but Pennsy management seemingly felt that their railroad had effectively "acquired" the New York Central instead of merging with it as a coequal. Each top management position in the new company had two executives—one a former New York Central manager and the other a former Pennsy manager. The man from the Pennsy always was above the New York Central man. As a result of this arrangement, many Central managers (who had been carefully selected by Perlman for their skills as railroad operators) left the Penn Central.

Perlman reportedly wanted to make large investments (as he had previously done on the Rio Grande) in order to develop a modern, efficient, and profitable system. The Saunders team, however, proceeded on the theory that, since the rate of return on railroad investments was generally low, more of the liquid assets of the railroad should be invested in nonrailroad activities in order to increase the overall rate of return. As a result, Saunders began an extensive diversification program, the effect of which will be discussed later in this chapter. Meanwhile, it should be kept in mind that the merged railroad developed diseconomies resulting from management conflicts.

Penn Central never offered the shippers better service as promised. Even though merger negotiations between the Pennsy and Central began approximately nine years before official approval, the electronic data-processing systems of the two railroads were incompatible. Information concerning car location and availability could not be transferred between the computers. As a result, whole freight cars and shipments were lost. Perishable goods were frequently spoiled before they could be located. Once the initial computer problem was adjusted, service still did not improve markedly. The list of complaints from shippers included: inability of the road to meet car requests, lengthy delays, terminal tie-ups, and misdirected cars. Anywhere from seventy to eighty freight trains a day were held up for want of engines to pull them. According to the *Wall Street Journal* (June 12, 1970), one shipper reported that several of his loaded cars left the plant only to return several weeks later still fully loaded. This record indicates that the proposed annual merger savings of $80 million was due primarily to curtailment of services rather than true economies of scale. In fact, one year after the merger, Penn Central complained that the entire $80 million savings would be wiped out by higher labor costs and the costs of capitalization.[63]

Experts trying to draw lessons from the Penn-Central collapse are often directed to the way in which ICC handled the original merger proposals. The ICC hearing examiner who approved the merger accepted without question the evidence presented by railroad attorneys concerning projected cost savings. He saw no reason for an independent study of the figures submitted by the company lawyers. By accepting railroad claims at face value, the ICC left itself open to the many questions that inevitably followed about its public responsibility. One question often raised is whether the Penn-Central miscalculations were an isolated occurrence. The ICC has approved thirty of the thirty-four merger proposals initiated by the railroads since 1959.[64] In almost all cases, the railroad attorneys submitted claims concerning projected savings. In almost all cases, the ICC hearing examiner accepted these claims at face value. Robert Gallamore, after studying the operations of a number of merged railroads, has concluded that the cost savings projected by railroad attorneys were never fully realized:

> In most circumstances there have been difficulties in achieving merger savings. Merger is not a panacea. The summary picture is that the larger, more recent, and more complex mergers have produced the least favorable results. The particular configuration of routes involved does not seem to make as much difference as the overall size of the consolidation. Financial control short of merger may be a factor, since those cases which performed best were those where integration was probably most swift and thorough. But the overwhelming evidence is that size and complexity of a merger plan are the qualities that can lead to extra costs, rather than savings, in the wake of consolidation.[65]

In the recent Northern Lines case, the Department of Justice took the extremely unusual position of arguing publicly that the ICC hearing examiner was biased in favor of the railroads. A report by the Center for the Study of Responsive Law entitled *Surface Transportation, the Public Interest, and the ICC* sums up the arguments of the Department of Justice:

> In the "Northern Lines" merger, the Justice Department

criticized the handling of the arguments in opposition to the merger. In its exceptions to the examiner's report, Justice stated that "the affidavits disclose a shocking, extreme, and undisciplined personal bias in favor of the merger. It is a bias which resulted in an unfair hearing and an unreliable report to the Commission." Justice continued that the remarks of the examiner during the hearing "betrayed a dismaying gullibility" to the applicants' presentation. The examiner's attitude towards the public was "clearly hostile and impatient." Further, "this basic attitude—that industry-sponsored witnesses are all-knowing and wise and that others are naive or ill-informed—must certainly account for the Examiner's unfair conduct during the Hearing." Finally, the Justice Department admonished the ICC that "the public trust was not given to the Commission to be handed over bodily to the carriers."[66]

The ICC apparently has learned little from its experiences. As this is written, many merger proposals are before the ICC, all to be handled on a case-by-case basis through adversary proceedings. The approach gives decisive weight to the pleadings of railroad attorneys and the colored charts prepared by railroad advertising experts to impress ICC hearing examiners. The ICC contends, of course, that it cannot develop an overall merger plan without a congressional directive to do so. In a recent decision, Supreme Court Justice Brennan chided the ICC for taking such a position:

> That the ICC is no longer told to plan does not mean it is unable to do so when planning is necessary to fulfill its duties. . . . The agency has wide latitude in fashioning procedures, and a broad power to condition its approval of proposals. In other words, the ICC is not the prisoner of the parties' submissions. Rather, the agency's duty is to weigh alternatives and make its choice according to the judgment how best to achieve and advance the goals of the National Transportation Policy.[67]

Airlines. Like the ICC, the CAB controls entry, consolidation, and merger in its domain. The CAB's philosophy of entry into the market is one of promotion of the airline industry while simultaneously regulating it. This dual role stems from the Civil Aeronautics Act of 1938, which established the CAB with both regulation and promotion functions, despite the inherent possibility that the two roles can come into conflict. Competition in rates and service, which might benefit the public, is not always consistent with the industry's financial objectives. The history of CAB entry-control policy is a history of the struggle between these conflicting goals. On a practical level, the CAB has tended to allow more firms to compete when the earnings of the existing airlines are favorable and to close entry when the competitors in the field are experiencing financial difficulty. The Civil Aeronautics Act, which set down the rules for granting market entry, is ambiguous enough to permit shifts in CAB policy. The CAB is directed to consider—when granting certificates of public convenience and necessity—"competition to the extent necessary to assure the sound development of an air transportation system properly adapted to the needs of the foreign and domestic commerce of the U.S. . . (and) the promotion of adequate service by air carriers . . . without . . . unfair or destructive competitive practices."[68]

CAB history has been well analyzed:

> From 1938 to 1944, for example, it invoked a "strong, although not conclusive, presumption in favor of competition on any route which offered sufficient traffic to support competing services without unreasonable increase of total operating cost" . . . it seemed favorably disposed to more competition as a factor which assists in the fullest development of the national air transportation system. Beginning about 1944, however, the Board abandoned the presumption of doctrine. If existing services were deemed adequate, new awards were rarely made, the Board majority cynically disowning the competition under such circumstances as amounting to no more than "competition for competition's sake." In 1955, under the guidance of its new chairman, Ross Rizley, the Board once more swung back to a policy of favoring competition wherever there was sufficient traffic. Not only did it feel that competition was conducive to the vigorous development of air transportation, but it felt it might offer other advantages—such as eliminating airline subsidy by permitting weaker carriers to tap richer markets.[69]

Thus, the 1955 policy change was due not so much to the CAB's desire to give the consumer better, less costly air service, as to its desire to reduce government promotion subsidies. Nevertheless, between 1955 and 1970, the CAB made a conscious effort to increase airline competition between cities. Some proponents of deregulation argued that this policy still limited competition in certain markets, that the advantages from competitive pricing were being withheld from the consumer by the CAB.[70]

By 1970, the CAB gave some hints that it would return to the more restrictive entry approach. Airline officials, facing the prospect of significant net revenue losses, were complaining of the ruinous effects of competition. "Overcompetition" on selected major city routes was the lament of some firms that blamed the CAB policy of allowing greater competition for their financial problems.[71]

In sum, the CAB decisions with respect to certificate or operating authority are based on the financial needs of the carriers rather than on the needs of the public.

The CAB has control over the consolidations and mergers of air carriers as well as over the purchase, acquisition of control, and lease of air carriers by other air carriers. Consolidation and other forms of unification are again governed by the omnipresent "public interest." The CAB may not approve any unification which would result in monopoly, restraining competition, or jeopardizing another air carrier. Generally, the CAB has resisted proposed acquisition by any of the Big Four (American, Eastern, TWA, and United) which would enhance their size and extend their market power to the disadvantage of other lines. The last major merger was between Capital and United which, even though it eliminated competition, was considered unavoidable if Capital's system was to be saved.[72] Up to 1970, there was little pressure for mergers between airlines. However, when financial difficulties began to plague some major lines, the merger idea suddenly became attractive. As this is written, however, the exact nature and extent of the merger movement had not taken shape. -

Finally, the CAB can require an airline to serve certain low-density routes which quite probably will be "unprofitable." The CAB tries to offset the losses by allowing the carrier at the same time to serve areas with a higher traffic density and greater profit potential. For areas which generate little traffic, rather than burdening the major airlines with responsibility for service to them, the CAB has adopted a policy of creating local and feeder service, subsidized by government airmail business. After President Kennedy's call upon the CAB to present a plan for the reduction of subsidies to airlines over a period of years, the CAB became much more restrictive in granting operating rights to feeder airlines. Present CAB policy is characterized by:

1. a reduction in the number of flights that the board considers eligible for subsidy;

2. a consolidation of service to single regional airports where possible, instead of to an airport in individual cities in an area;

3. elimination of unremunerative stops and route segments through enforcement of the "use it or lose it" policy.[73]

Motor Carriers. The ICC was given jurisdiction in 1935 to require that all common and contract motor carriers obtain certificates of public convenience and necessity before beginning operations. A common carrier must serve anyone in his area who is willing to pay for the service; a contract carrier is, as the name implies, under contract to only certain shippers. The contract carriers usually perform more specialized services, such as hauling goods in refrigerated trucks.

The certificates issued by the ICC, says James C. Nelson, are extremely detailed, "specifying whether the carrier is common or contract, the routes or territories where the carrier may operate, the points to or from which the carrier may service, the commodities or classes of commodities which may be carried, and the extent to which the authorized physical movement of trucks is tied to specific highway routes and gateways."[74]

Generally, the ICC has attempted to restrict the growth of contract carriers in order to protect common carriers.

Contract carriers have . . . been restricted to a highly specialized service for one or a few shippers. Where it is necessary to grant a wide range of commodities, the opportunity to add or substitute contracts has been limited to shippers of a certain type, such as meat packers or chain grocers. In other cases, contract carriers have been restricted to one or a few commodity classes. In an early leading case . . . the Commission justified a restrictive entry policy for contract carriers . . . in terms of an inferred need to protect common carrier service from "cut-throat competition."[75]

In addition, the ICC has sought to assist the common carrier by restricting entry into his field. Before issuing a certificate to a common carrier, the ICC tries to find out whether the applicant would provide a useful public service and fill a genuine need. The "public need" criterion, some would-be competitors contend, may be used as a screen behind which the ICC can justify protective policies. The ICC does maintain, for example, that if the existing common carriers can deliver the services the new carrier proposes, then the new certificate application will be denied. Furthermore, if the service by the new carrier would cause serious loss of income to the existing common carriers, the certificate will be denied. In short, successful applicants must clearly and unmistakably show that existing facilities are physically inadequate.[76]

Some abuses are inevitable when carriers feel a public agency is shielding them from competition. Existing common carriers in such a setting can set rates at levels which would not be wise in a competitive situation. James C. Nelson has documented well the decline in competition which stems directly from ICC policies. He points out that the total number of ICC-regulated common carriers has fallen from 26,167 in 1939 to 14,120 in 1970, despite enormous increases in total traffic and revenues. Nelson adds:

> Numerous routes of light traffic are served by only two or three regulated carriers and many routes having dense traffic flows are served by only two or three up to six to ten general commodity motor carriers authorized to give single line service. In the national aggregate, there are still large numbers of sellers, but between city-pair markets over particular routes and for particular groups of authorized commodities the typical situation has become one of oligopoly, even, in many cases, of a small number of firms.[77]

The ICC has been under great pressure from shippers and the Department of Transportation in recent years to reverse this policy and to allow a larger number of companies into the common-carrier industry. The ICC recently relaxed some restrictions on awarding certificates of operation, but made no attempt to ask Congress to amend the Interstate Commerce Act to permit a greater relaxation of restrictions. The ICC remains fundamentally unmoved by the arguments of shippers and the Department of Transportation.

The ICC policy toward mergers and consolidations in the motor common-carrier industry has been most sharply criticized. As noted earlier, there are no significant economies of scale in the motor-trucking industry. Greater size by itself will not bring about greater efficiency and superior performance. As a consequence, shippers complain loud and long that the ICC rejection of merger proposals of large trucking companies results only in the narrowing of competition. The Associated Transport Company, for example, acquired control of several large carriers in the East, even though there would be no other motor carrier company of similar size to compete with it.[78]

In sum, the effect of ICC policy toward the motor common carrier seems to encourage the growth of a limited number of large trucking concerns which have a monopoly, or at best an oligopoly, in the markets they serve. The policy has meant a great deal to trucking companies. James C. Nelson states:

> The DOT has submitted evidence to the ICC showing that Class I regulated truckers earned a return on net investment after income taxes averaging 11.78% in the 1957-1966 decade, with a range between 7.21% in 1960 and 13.86% in 1964. The ratio of net income after taxes to shareholders' and proprietors' equity for Class I motor carriers was 15.7% in 1966, placing this regulated industry among the leaders in comparison with 21 representative durable and non-durable goods industries . . .[79]

Water Carriers. The largest position of intracoastal shipping, as mentioned earlier, is unregulated under exemptions granted in the Transportation Act of 1940. The act requires all regulated water carriers to obtain permission from the ICC before beginning service. Water carriers are also subject to the same stipulation concerning consolidation and merger as are the railroads.

It seems the ICC has adopted a more liberal policy in granting operating right to prospective carriers. James Nelson regards this liberality as reflecting

> the Commission's awareness that it had gone too far in suppressing motor carrier competition. In addition, a smaller number of firms compete on water routes, entry control for water carriers was inaugurated when the economy was in an expansionist phase, and, in general, the postwar restoration of coastal water service was a national goal.[80]

However, the Commission does refuse to grant operating rights when it is obvious that there is not enough traffic to sustain more than the established number of carriers:

> In one case the Commission denied a certificate for operations that would compete with two existing carriers, pointing out that the additional service "might so diffuse the available traffic as to result in uneconomical operation detrimental to all concerned." Where the traffic will support additional services, or where there are prospects of

new traffic in the future, certificates have been granted, notwithstanding the opposition of existing carriers who might be adversely affected . . .[81]

This, of course, is consistent with the prevailing ICC position which seeks to protect established regulated concerns from competition.

Intermodal Relationships of Entry Control. Control or ownership of one mode's facilities by another mode has largely been prevented by Congress. The Panama Canal Act of 1912 prohibited railroads from owning or controlling water carriers traveling in the canal. Railroads were permitted ownership of water carriers outside the canal only if the public interest was served and competition was not hindered. The act sought to protect water carriers from the railroad.

This strict policy is still maintained, as evidenced by a recent ICC decision which ruled that the purchase by the Illinois Central and the Southern Pacific of the John I. Hay Company, a profitable Mississippi barge line, would threaten "a sharp reduction of, and possible elimination of, competition on the water routes involved."[82]

The Motor Carrier Act of 1935 and the Transportation Act of 1940 both contained provisions which restricted railroad control or ownership of motor carriers. Again "public interest" and the effect on competition are the ICC's guides. The typical certificate restrictions on railroads were initially adopted in the *Kansas Southern Case*:

First, service is limited to that which is auxiliary to, or supplemental of, rail service. Second, no point may be served that is not a station or a rail line. Third, no shipments may be transported wholly by motor vehicle between the so-called designated "key points," usually large traffic generating points. Fourth, all contractual arrangements between the motor subsidiary and the parent railroad are subject to ICC modification. Fifth, the ICC has preserved the right to impose further restrictions to preserve the supplementary character of rail motor carrier service.[83]

In recent years, the ICC has become more flexible in granting railroads the right to own and operate motor carriers under "special or unusual circumstances." "Special circumstances" may be found in areas where service by other carriers is inadequate, or where the proposed service will not materially affect competition.

The Civil Aeronautics Board may permit a railroad to acquire an airline if the board rules that "the transaction proposed will promote the public interest by enabling such carrier other than the air carrier to use aircraft to the public advantage in its operation . . ."[84] The Board must also decide whether the transaction is "consistent with the public interest" and will not "restrain competition or jeopardize another air carrier . . ." In interpreting this language, the CAB has held that "to use aircraft to public advantage in its transport operations" does not refer to consolidation of terminal facilities alone, and merely showing that a proposed acquisition will enable a railroad to coordinate facilities and better meet competition is insufficient to fulfill the railroad's burden of proof. A railroad must show that the proposed acquisition will provide carrier service which is auxiliary or supplemental to railroad. In fact, the CAB has virtually barred entry by other modes into the airline field.

Railroads face no regulatory restrictions only when they seek to purchase pipelines or trucking companies which function outside the jurisdiction of the ICC.

Water carriers desiring to engage in motor operation, on the other hand, need only show that the transaction will be "consistent with the public interest." Compared to the special conditions imposed upon railroads, this is a relatively minor restriction. The railroads see this treatment as detrimental and discriminatory.

Railroads, indeed, have responded by demanding that they be allowed to establish transportation companies consisting of air, rail, and motor facilities. They contend that the proposed multimodal companies will result in great economies for the shipping public as well as increased profits for themselves. In November 1968, Alfred Perlman, then president of the Penn Central Railroad, expressed a common railroad belief:

> A true transportation company could provide the public with tailor-made service, shaped to suit each user's particular need, and employ in the process any of the several modes or any combination of them. Today, however, to determine what service would be best suited to the needs of the particular shipment, and to arrange the service is costly, awkward, and time-consuming.[85]

In February 1969, Stuart Saunders, then chairman of the board of Penn Central, claimed that "billions of dollars can be saved through the efficiencies and the economies of integrated transportation companies."[86]

Proponents have long spoken of the efficiencies and economies of scale which would result from the integrated transportation, but they have failed to enumerate and document these efficiencies. No statistical studies have been advanced to support this position. Railroads talk about the savings shippers might enjoy with a single transportation company offering a choice of various modes. However, Merrill J. Roberts, professor at the Graduate School of Business, University of Pittsburgh, has cited some of the inefficiencies which could result from a narrowing of shippers' options:

> Common ownership might, in fact, cause efficiency aberrations by introducing distortion in the decision processes. Determination by integrated carriers of the mode or modal combination to be employed for a given mission is a major tenet of the common ownership faith. Distribution efficiency (as a facet of overall economic efficiency) contemplates that shippers will make price-quality choices among transportation alternatives which are designed to optimize their distribution systems, a goal which might be defeated by switching this function to the carriers. Furthermore, the range of choices of price-quality combinations may itself be restricted by the integrated firm.[87]

The efficiencies resulting from integrated transportation can come only if management makes an effort to continually research and modernize operations for all the modes. The danger exists, however, that management may favor only one mode. A company may put all its effort into the development of truck transportation while totally neglecting rail technology, since research and development as well as equipment are much cheaper for motor carriers than for railroads. If the integrated company begins to neglect one mode of transportation, then the shipper will be faced with a narrower rather than a wider choice of transport modes. Finally, the idea of an integrated transport company reverses the traditional idea of a consumer-determined choice. The integrated transport company, not the shipper, makes the choice concerning the optimal means of transport from point A to point B for the shipper's goods. Yet the optimal means from the perspective of the company may be determined by such variables as load capacity, equipment shortages, or convenience. Without question, these considerations may not coincide with the best interests of the shipper, who may place a higher priority on speed of delivery.

Investment in Nontransportation Activities

During the 1960s, the ICC faced essentially new problems. Many transportation companies, especially railroads, had begun to utilize available capital for nonrailroad investments. Some railroad officials argued that the nonprofitable nature of their railroad operations forced them to divert resources into nontransportation areas in order to increase return on investment which at the present rate is not high enough to attract capital. Many railroads have achieved diversification by setting up holding companies which, in turn, buy out the railroad operations through a transfer of stock. The holding company then proceeds to purchase interests in other nontransportation concerns. Fourteen holding companies presently own railroads as well as other businesses. Some major railroads are controlled by holding companies: the Illinois Central is controlled by Illinois Central Industries; Missouri-Kansas-Texas by Katy Industries; Chicago and Northwestern by Northwest Industries, Inc.; Atchison, Topeka & Santa Fe by Santa Fe Industries, Inc.; Boston & Maine by Mississippi Fuel Corp.; and Seaboard Coast Line by the Seaboard Coast Line Co.

An amazing range of operations are controlled by these holding companies. Northwest Industries controls Union Underwear Co., Universal Manufacturing Corp., Acme Boot Co., Michigan Chemical Corp., and others. Kansas City Southern Industries, Inc., in addition to the Kansas City Southern Railroad, controls a chain of broadcasting properties—two television stations and a radio station in Missouri and two television stations in Illinois. Katy Industries controls W. J. Smith Wood Preserving Co., E.J. Trum, Inc., and the American Gage and Machine Co. Illinois Central Industry has purchased controlling interest in Chandeysson Electric Co., Waukesha Foundry Co., and the Abex Corp.[88]

The ICC contends that it has no authority to prevent the establishment of holding companies. Under Section 5 (2) of the Interstate Commerce Act, the Commission has the power to authorize the purchase of more than one carrier by a noncarrier. However, if a noncarrier purchases a single carrier, such a transaction is automatically exempted from regulation. Thus, a holding company which purchases a single railroad can avoid the necessity for securing ICC approval of the transaction.[89]

Certain cases of holding-company control of railroad operations did, however, come before the ICC. In the early 1960s, the Commission adopted the railroad position that investments in nontransportation ventures were necessary to provide funds to keep the railroad healthy and modern. In the case of the control of the Missouri-Kansas-Texas Railroad Company by Katy Industries, the Commission declared:

> The proposed transaction (i.e., acquisition of the M-K-T RR. by Katy Industries—a holding company) will have no direct effect on Katy's operations, railway employees, or transportation service to the public, since Katy and its subsidiaries will continue to operate in the same manner as at present. However, the indirect benefits of additional funds for rehabilitation and modernization will accrue to Katy and the applicants believe that it will be in a better position to continue and improve its transportation services.[90]

These railroad promises, which the ICC accepted unquestioningly, have not been realized. Many argue that the holding companies, established to control railroads and to buy controlling interests in other companies, have not saved the railroad operations and have not substantially contributed to the best interests of the public. In fact, such holding companies, critics argue, have taken money out of railroads to the detriment of the national railroad system.

The ICC itself finally began to question the authenticity of railroads claims and conducted a study of railroad holding-company practices. Although the study was completed in June 1969, the ICC failed to release it until June 1970—in aftermath of the Penn Central bankruptcy. The ICC report, prepared by the agency's Bureau of Accounts, cited specific abuses by the holding companies. In some cases, the railroad subsidiary had paid special dividends to the holding company and in other instances had loaned money to the parent firm at less than prevailing interest rates. The report discovered cases in which the holding company utilized railroad rolling stock as credit for loans. On other occasions, the holding company had sold railroad assets (some of them set aside by the railroad as cushions against financial difficulty) and then kept the profits from the sales. The parent holding companies have also charged railroad subsidiaries for managerial services which apparently were never performed. The ICC found that tax credits available to the railroad were used by the holding company. Dividends from the railroad to the parent company were, in some cases, paid in cash or securities, thereby significantly draining railroad assets. Companies examined by the Bureau of Accounts were the Bangor Punta Corp., which owns the Bangor and Aroostock Railroad, Illinois Central Industries, Kansas City Southern Industries, Katy Industries, and Northwest Industries.[91]

The ICC report suggested that the Commission be given more authority to prevent such abuses. Specifically, the ICC wanted authority to force a noncarrier which owns one or more railroads to divest itself of carrier holdings in the event that the noncarrier is "bleeding" or taking funds from the carrier. The ICC also wanted more power to conduct investigations of the books of holding companies.

Congress thus faced a situation which requires immediate attention. The experiences of railroads in nontransportation activities have not achieved the desired goal of strengthening our railroad network. The contrary may, in fact, be a more accurate description of what is occurring. Few deny that the abuses must be eliminated, but if, in the process, the holding companies are rendered powerless to make investments in transportation, some carriers may face instant financial disaster. Neglect may occur at many levels. The holding company may refuse to undertake the large capital expenditures needed to maintain and upgrade both railroad right-of-way and rolling stock, and instead commit all available capital to the purchase of nontransportation operations which promise large return on investment. Capital investment in the railroad is certainly long term, unlike speculative real estate or some kinds of manufacturing. A holding company in financial difficulties is likely to concentrate on short-term investment, even at the risk of hastening the decline of privately owned railroads.

The Penn Central railroad bankruptcy has brought to light some of the dangers inherent in nontransportation investment by holding companies which own railroads. Shortly after the merger between the Pennsylvania and the New York Central was consummated, board chairman Stuart Saunders established a giant holding company (the Penn Central), whose subsidiary (the Penn Central Transportation Co.) ran the railroad (8.415 miles of track owned and 10,608 miles of track operated under lease or agreement) and owned 100 percent of the Pennsylvania Co. (an investment company with holdings in many firms). In total,

Saunders directed the spending of $150 million in cash in non-railroad ventures between February 1968 and June 1970. The assets of the entire holding company in June 1970 totaled $7 billion.[92]

In addition to its railroad, the Penn Central Transportation Co. owns trucking, warehousing, terminal, and refrigerator car companies. It owns 100 percent of Dispatch Shops, Inc., which in turn owns and operates the Barclay, Biltmore, Commodore, and Roosevelt Hotels in the heart of New York City. The Penn Central Transportation Co. also has 25 percent interest in the Madison Square Garden Corp., which owns the New York Knickerbockers basketball team, the New York Rangers hockey team, and Holiday on Ice.

The Penn Central Transportation Co. also owns 100 percent of the Pennsylvania Co.—an investment operation. The Pennsylvania Co. bought 90 percent of the stock of the Great Southwest Corp., which owns industrial and amusement parks between Dallas and Fort Worth, as well as real estate in Los Angeles, San Diego, San Francisco, and Atlanta. The Great Southwest Corp. was highly profitable in 1969 with after-tax earnings of $34.4 million but this figure dropped off sharply in the difficult year of 1970. More than 50 percent of the Arvida Corp., which operates the luxurious Boca Ratan Hotel and Club as well as properties in Miami, Fort Lauderdale, Palm Beach, and Sarasota, belongs to the Pennsylvania Co. The company also owns 100 percent of the Buckeye Pipeline Co. and 100 percent of the Clearfield Bituminous Coal Corp.

Saunders has been criticized for devoting too much attention and resources to speculative nontransportation investments. The Penn Central Railroad was caught in a critical cash shortage in the months preceeding its bankruptcy declaration. The $150 million which Saunders invested in nontransportation probably could have helped the railroad, but whether this sum would have made a significant difference to the critically sick carrier is debatable.

What Congress may have learned, meanwhile, is that the holding-company movement has contributed little in terms of more efficient transportation.

The Case Against Regulation

There are numerous arguments against regulation, some of which were covered previously. They will be clarified and expanded here, and followed by some pro-regulation points at the end of this chapter.

Stifling of Technology. Regulatory commissions, especially the ICC, are highly protective of the status quo and therefore are opposed to innovations that might benefit one mode at the expense of another. This fact, coupled with prospects for long costly hearings, are frustrating to management, which might consider investing in new methods.

The Southern Railway, in an attempt to take grain shipment to the South away from the barge and trucking industries, developed a new freight car capable of more efficient and economical grain shipment. Upon delivery of the cars in 1961, the company announced reduced rates on grain shipments, which it claimed were justified by the technological superiority of the new cars. The barge operators filed a protest with the ICC and the litigation began. For more than two years, the Southern's efforts to cut rates were frustrated. When the Commission finally granted a rate reduction, it refused to let the Southern cut as much as costs appeared to warrant: "Given the long delay that can be expected and the risk of inadequate returns on initial equipment investment, the Southern case shows how the ICC can impede technological progress and create a climate hostile to experimentation. The Commission, in Congressional testimony, has made it perfectly plain that it does not look kindly upon cost-cutting innovations that disturb the transport balance; it believes in a far more deliberate approach to technological change, one which in practice is likely to assure little change and limited innovation."[93]

Anticompetitive Nature. Regulatory agencies in transportation have been accused of going far out of their way to shelter firms already in the field against new competition. This is an aspect of the preoccupation with status quo which is inherent in regulatory bodies, according to Professor Marvin Bernstein, a long-time student of regulatory practices, who writes:

It is impossible to avoid the conclusion that regulation of particular industries by independent commissions tends to destroy rather than promote competition. The historical tradition of commissions is anti-competitive. Their basic methods, especially their reliance upon the case by case approach, place small business firms at a disadvantage. The growing passivity of the commissions' approach and the inconvenience of dealing with a large number of firms strengthen the commissions' tendency to identify their view of the public interest with the position of the dominant regulated firms. In short, regulation of particular businesses stacks the cards against the small competitive firms and weakens the form of competition.[94]

Motor-carrier certification policies of the ICC are also anti-competitive in nature. The ICC repeatedly emphasizes that where existing motor carriers have expanded their energy and resources in developing new facilities to handle available traffic, they are entitled to protection against competition. Hence, the ICC denies operating permits to other motor carriers. "This is what might be called the 'going concern' theory of regulation, reluctance to subject existing firms—especially large firms—to competitive pressure."[95]

Misallocation of Resources through Value-of-Service Rate Structures. The ICC has tended to perpetuate value-of-service rate-making, which encourages a carrier to base his rates on the value of goods transported, rather than on the cost of transportation. Thus, a carrier will charge high rates to transport goods of a high value. The shipper will theoretically not object since transportation, in his case, represents a small percentage of total cost. Theoretically, the profits from the transportation of high-valued commodities allows the carrier to reduce rates on goods which are of lower value. For shippers of lower valued goods, transportation is a significant cost factor, and they generally feel compelled to seek alternate modes wherever transport cost savings are possible.

This policy misallocates resources not only in transportation but in the total national economy as well. Railroads have a definite cost advantage over other modes in long-haul transport, but the ICC has required that they maintain artifically high rates on long hauls in compliance with the value-of-service rate structure, a structure applied also to motor carriers and water carriers. The result often is to achieve rate parity among these modes despite their wide differences in cost of operations. By forcing compliance with this pricing technique, the ICC prevents low-cost forms of transportation from fully exploiting their competitive advantages. Trucks and barges are carrying goods for which railroads have the cost advantage, and vice versa.[96]

David Boies sees the misallocation decreasing the total demand for transportation services, or at least reducing interregional competition. Each region of the country will try to produce more of what it consumes and import less than it would if resources were optimally allocated, Boies argues. Generally, he adds, the higher the costs of transportation, the less interregional competition and the more intraregional competition there will be.[97]

Economist George Hilton has attempted to quantify the additional costs which stem from regulation. "No one has rigorously estimated the welfare loss on the economy due to the existence of the ICC," he states.

But that loss is clearly large. Deregulation of motor carrier movements of chicken and frozen foods by judicial decisions in the 1950's resulted in falls in rates averaging about twenty percent. Whether this can be taken as a valid sample would indicate that the ICC is responsible for an increase of the common carrier freight bill by four to five billion dollars per year. If this is an overstatement, it is unlikely that the actual figure is under half that, or two billion dollars.[98]

Other studies have attempted to estimate the economic cost of transport regulation. In a study prepared in 1960, *Rationale of Federal Transportation Policy*, Ernest W. Williams, Jr., and David W. Bluestone estimated that "the annual transport bill would be reduced by several billions of dollars on freight alone," if traffic were allocated among the modes according to the cost of transport service. Ann Friedlaender, in *The Dilemma of Freight Transport Regulation*, has estimated that $500 million is paid in higher freight rates as a consequence of the ICC refusal to allow competitive pricing between railroads and motor carriers.[99] The common conclusion from all sources is that present ICC policies are exceptionally costly to shippers and consumers.

Burdensome to Carriers. The regulatory procedures can extract important resources from a carrier. The clearest examples are the restrictions placed on motor carriers applying for certificates of operation. A study by the Bureau of Investigation and Research found that these restrictions "create huge amounts of unnecessary, empty, additional mileage over circuitous routes, and idle truck time."[100] A more recent study detailed the effects on motor carriers' incomes. The study taken in New England showed that 17.2 percent of total miles operated in 1954 were empty, and the average load was 60.5 percent of capacity in intercity operation. The great majority of the carriers maintained that their operations would be more efficient and profitable if their certificates were broadened to let them carry more goods greater distances.[101] The Senate Committee on Small Business discovered several cases of unthrifty operations that might have been avoided if alternate route applications or return-haul restrictions had been granted to permit increased competition.

The ICC invited comments from carriers and other parties on five proposals to relax restrictions on routes, gateways, and radial points. James C. Nelson summarized these comments:

A number of carriers replied that such restrictions caused poor service, wasteful additional mileage, empty mileage on return hauls and partial loads—all of which contributed to higher operating costs, and thus higher costs to the consumer. The Pacific Eastern Refrigerated Lines, Inc., of Mount Vernon, Washington, submitted a tabulation showing that from thirty-five to four hundred and seventy excess miles were required on each trip from midwestern cities to Seattle, San Francisco or Los Angeles because the ICC required the trucks to pass through Rapid City, South Dakota.[102]

Other costs of regulation include legal fees and costs for protective activities connected with regulation. These costs are especially burdensome to small firms.

Stifling of Managerial Efficiency. Regulation has also been attacked because it assumes many of the functions that management performs in nonregulated industries. Regulatory agencies control maximum and minimum pricing and leave management without any authority over its most potent competitive weapon.

The ICC is responsible for granting operating privileges to railroads, motor carriers, pipelines, and barge lines. Airline companies must seek permission from the CAB. Control over these operating rights assumes other managerial functions. The regulatory agency, in effect, tells management whom it must service, how, and in what quantity.

Regulatory agencies control the organization of the regulated transport sector. President Kennedy was warmly applauded when he said that "the management of the various modes of transportation is subjected to excessive, cumbersome, and time-consuming regulatory supervision that shackles and distorts managerial initiative."[103]

Proponents of regulation argue that regulatory bodies need all of this power in order to safeguard the public welfare, and critics respond that no other American industry carries the extensive regulatory burdens that are imposed on transportation.

President Kennedy, in his Transportation Message of 1962, called for deregulation, and described the present system in these words:

> . . . pressing problems are burdening our national transportation system, jeopardizing the progress and security on which we depend. A chaotic patchwork of inconsistent and often obsolete legislation and regulation has evolved from a history of specific actions addressed to specific problems of specific industries at specific times. The patchwork does not fully reflect either the dramatic changes in technology of the past half century or the parallel changes in the structure of competition . . . I am convinced that less federal regulation . . . is in the long run a prerequisite of a healthy intercity transportation network.[104]

Contradicting and Incomplete Guidelines. Critics often tend to lay more blame than is justified on the regulatory commissions themselves. Actually, these agencies operate on rules set down by Congress in various pieces of legislation, notably the Transportation Acts of 1920, 1940, and 1958. Unfortunately, they have not provided a consistently sound blueprint for regulatory commissions to follow. David Boies describes the definitional weakness of the preamble of the Transportation Act of 1940:

> The major weakness of the Transportation Act of 1940 as an effective guide is that it says either too little or too much; almost every conceivable objective of transportation regulation is included, but no priorities are established which could help the commission or the courts determine which of the two or more conflicting policies should be given precedence. The Act mentions "adequate and efficient service," "unfair and destructive competitive practices," and "unreasonable charges" without ever defining them.[105]

Congress did not improve the quality of its directives in later years. The Transportation Act of 1958 seemed to admonish the ICC and change its policy with respect to intermodal rate competition. The act stated: "Rates of a carrier shall not be held up to a particular level to protect the traffic of any other mode of transportation." This seems a clear enough expression of intent. However, the act goes on to say that the ICC should also give due consideration to the objectives of the national transportation policy (1940) in dealing with these situations. The Commission was again left without adequate instructions and the controversy mounted. Dudley Pegrum sums up the telling argument against Congress's transportation legislation:

> Congress must share much of the blame for the difficulties which have become apparent, and much of the criticism should be aimed at them. Commissions cannot be expected to function as independent and objectively oriented agencies when Congress continuously assigns to them such conflicting legislation that obedience to one part brings conflict and contradiction with another. . . . Congress should recognize the fact that it cannot evade ultimately its responsibility by constantly shifting it to the shoulders of a commission.[106]

The Case for Regulation

After showing the substantial problems of regulation, many experts strongly believe that regulation is essential. Some problems, they argue, can be solved by reform within the existing framework, and the others, for the most part, are outweighed by the benefits which accrue to society from regulation. Above all, government must insure the continuance of the public services which the transportation industry performs.

The first obligation imposed on a carrier is to serve all who need and want service. This has been interpreted to include the obligation to provide adequate service with reasonable dispatch, and with facilities in reasonably good condition. The carrier also has a duty to provide service without discrimination and to deliver goods in the condition in which they were received. It is essential to the economy that competitors be able to secure equal services at equal costs. While discriminatory treatment of customers could be dealt with under antitrust legislation, such action would occur after the fact; there could still be irreparable damage to the party that was discriminated against. Regulatory hearings on all proposed rate changes provide an opportunity to prevent discrimination before any damage is done.[107]

Nondestructive free competition is possible only when competing carriers serve similar markets and have similar costs. This situation does not exist in transportation. Some carriers enjoy broader markets than others—both as to suitable commodities and geographic positions. Some carriers exercise disproportionate financial power as compared with competitors.

These internal differences add up to a situation in which there seems no chance for unregulated competition to operate in the national interest. The carrier with the lowest variable costs can cut rates in the short run to drive out competition, with increasing volume holding up profit. When the company attains monopoly status, the rates go higher than before. Regulation, say its advocates, prevents this.[108]

Many economists contend that motor carriers do not require regulation because competition will give the shipper the most effective system desirable. Locklin vehemently disagrees, saying that

> the special conditions existing in the motor carrier industry have resulted in a tendency for overcapacity to develop and to persist, and that under these conditions competition does not function as the theorist assumes. The ruinous type of competition does develop; discrimination in rates does appear; the condition of overcapacity does not correct itself automatically; and the struggle for survival in the face of inadequate revenues leads to deterioration of safety standards, evasion of safety regulations, financial irresponsibility, and generally unsatisfactory service.[109]

The disadvantages of unregulated industries are exemplified in the exempt portions of the motor-carrier industry. The Doyle Report lists the following: increased highway hazards due to low safety standards, less financial responsibility (particularly in reference to cargo insurance), and less economic stability of participating carriers. In some instances, many rates fluctuate often and in an irregular manner, according to the supply of trucks and the volume of shipments to be moved in a given locality. There is discrimination among shippers with regard to rates, and a tendency to cut rates in the face of hard competition, significantly slashing the income of exempt carriers.[110]

The desire of private industry to maximize profits also seems to call for regulation. The profit motive, if unregulated, would encourage carriers to seek out only the most profitable traffic.[111] Small firms needing service would be left without transportation. Some proponents of deregulation respond that government should subsidize the carriers so that they will assume these services that they would otherwise be unwilling to provide; but subsidy, of course, is a form of regulation. Requiring regulated carriers to provide uneconomic service and forcing them to make up the losses on other traffic inflates the entire transportation bill for the economy and adds to the misallocation of resources, most experts agree.

That reform is needed within the present framework is not disputed by most who favor regulation, but recognize the seriousness of the problems which regulation supposedly has caused. For example, legislative reorientation of rate regulation in the direction of cost-based pricing would greatly reduce misallocation of resources caused by ICC-sanctioned value-of-service ratemaking. Mechanisms to speed up the regulatory process could cut the delay which is such a burden to management. Within the last few years, the ICC has taken steps to alleviate this situation by granting temporary rate changes until a final decision is made.[112] But above all, regulatory law should be flexible and should be reviewed often by Congress and other independent research agencies.

CHAPTER 4

GOVERNMENT ROLE—ITS UNITY AND DIVERSITY

The definition of government role and examples of government investment offered in this book are generally used in arguments for a diversified transportation network, for coordination of transportation investments by government at all levels. The objective of such variety is to maximize public benefit and to insure impartial treatment of all modes.

Often when making a transport investment, the federal government either caters to concerns other than transportation or focuses on a single mode to the detriment of the system. National defense is a prime objective of government investment, but one which cannot always be consistent with social and economic considerations or overall transport needs. When the government initiates military transportation programs, for example, it separates the existing system, mode by mode, into autonomous, unrelated projects such as highway construction or development of new aircraft.

When the government recognized that airlines were essential to national defense, aircraft technology was expanded rapidly and private airlines derived huge side benefits. But when government failed to relate this program to transportation in general, the other modes suffered. Their own research was paltry compared with the massive tax-supported airline programs; railroads lost much of their competitive force, plus their intercity passenger business. Air carriers replaced ocean liners in shipping troops and supplies.

Similarly, the Interstate Highway Program in 1956, although based perhaps on sound military strategy, has had grave effects on other forms of transportation. Already booming, the motor-carrier mode received even more emphasis and the position of the rails in passenger and freight operations was further undermined. The Interstate Highway Program established an enormous fund earmarked solely for highway use. While all other modes were crying for government help throughout the 1960s, the federal highway program generated yearly revenues in excess of $4 billion.

Besides disrupting the transport field, the military goals side-tracked government from anticipating and remedying specific social and economic upsets. The decline of the railroads, the plight of urban mass transit, the urban congestion, and the disrupted innercity neighborhoods have to some extent resulted from government's preoccupation with national defense.

When government decides to invest, agencies are created to guide the investment, but these agencies are rarely integrated with others, even in the same general field. Government action thus can be disunified, uncoordinated, and even conflicting. For one thing, contradictions between vague legislative terms hamper policy makers and administrators. References to competition, juxtaposed with references to coordination, present conflicts difficult, if not impossible, for transportation planners to reconcile.

Due to certain advances in technology, the most economical and efficient way to move goods may require a combination of modes. With such recent techniques as piggyback and containerization, goods can be transported faster and cheaper. But these innovations also require greater coordination among all modes. Many experts advocate policy changes which would allow carriers to invest freely in other modes. Under such a policy, railroads, for example, could invest in motor carriers or airlines to create an integrated transportation company. However, the Transportation Act of 1940 stresses the need for maintaining competition in cases involving intermodal ownership of railroads, and the Civil Aeronautics Act likewise underscores a need for competition in cases of airline ownership by other modes. Congress in 1940 could not have foreseen developments such as piggyback or containerization, and perhaps never intended to stifle integrated transportation companies. Nevertheless, the ICC and the CAB continue to interpret the laws as banning such companies, thereby restricting intermodal ownership to services which merely supplement a firm's major operations. Perhaps some of the conflicts between competition and coordination could be eased by a reevaluation of the 1940 act, but Congress seems satisfied to leave things as they are.

Other conflicts occur among the separate government agencies, which fail to cooperate, and even contradict one another, further undermining national transportation policy. For instance, while the ICC becomes increasingly flexible in allowing discontinuance of passenger trains, the CAB allows local or feeder airlines to serve areas where their service cannot possibly be profitable, but to make up for that with airmail subsidies. This lack of coordination probably aggravates the already-serious imbalance in the nation's transportation plant. An overall policy could decide whether providing local-service airlines at the government's expense is indeed an efficient solution to the problem of airline service in not-so-populated areas; it might also determine whether the rapid abandonment of railroads is best for the country's overall transportation system.

At the same time, coordination between the ICC and the Army Corps of Engineers might end the crippling confusion surrounding the nation's inland waterways. The Army Corps of Engineers promotes waterway construction and improvement while the ICC, as it does with all modes, has responsibility for fair and impartial regulation. The ICC may feel that water transportation is less economical than overland in some areas, but it seems helpless to curb the activities of the Army Engineers. Water carriers under the wing of the Army Engineers can usually count on ICC cooperation, even if that includes turning down justifiable rate reductions by the competing modes.

Often the execution or operation of government policy stimulates conflicts between government agencies. Congress has, through various legislation, sought to encourage the ICC in developing a common-carrier transportation service which would serve anyone on a nondiscriminatory basis. However, some agencies frankly stand in the way of this goal with directives such as one adopted by the Department of Defense for securing transportation services "from the non-regulated for-hire motor carriers owned and operated by the agricultural cooperatives whenever their rates are the lowest." This is but one example of a government agency working in direct opposition to another.

Theoretically, Congress is supposed to control the regulatory agencies by establishing rules and principles which the agencies in turn apply independently to specific cases. Difficulties arise when Congress legislates new rules. The ICC in recent years has tended to follow the new rules for a short time, only to revert back to its old, established ways, even though they may be contrary to congressional intention. Thus, the independent regulatory agencies may give only passing deference to policies which Congress may feel are in the best interests of the country as a whole.

Efficient transit of import goods between ports of arrival and destinations can be facilitated by means of what are known as through-rates, wherein a shipper receives one transport bill which covers destination-to-destination charges. However, the setting of such rates is hindered by the present regulatory structure. Maritime operators must seek approval for rate levels from the Federal Maritime Commission, while railroad and motor carriers must seek theirs from the Interstate Commerce Commission. The two agencies are authorized by Congress to hold common sessions to establish "joint rates" for intermodal shipments, but setting up such sessions is very complicated, and the few which do get set up are usually ineffective. Each agency seems primarily concerned with defending the mode(s) which it regulates, rather than in bringing about a simplification in rate structure which would be in the best interests of the country at large. This seems to add strength to the demand for a unified and coordinated national transportation policy.

Often assigned functions may conflict even within one federal agency. The CAB, for example, was established as both regulator and promoter of the airlines, roles which come into conflict as the CAB uses its regulatory powers to promote the development of the air industry. Restricting entry and allowing mergers to protect financially pressed carriers are seen as justifiable forms of promotion which greatly benefit the industry. But because they limit air service, these actions may prove hostile to the best interests of regulation—or public welfare.

Conflict and lack of cooperation in Washington have stalled and confused transportation investment policies at all levels of government. Federal, state, and local authorities have difficulty getting together to plan a transport system on which they can all agree. Overall national plans for efficient transportation are jeopardized by the multiplicity of state and local goals. Cities and states may want more and bigger ports and the commerce which these ports will attract, while the federal planners insist that the country already has more ports than modern technology can justify. Yet, the federal government makes no effort to co-ordinate the port development plans, for it apparently prefers not to stir up regional jealousies even though coordination of activities might benefit the country as a whole. Meanwhile, in-dividual localities continue to develop independent port plans, even though the resultant duplication and waste may oppose the national interest.

Local governments also push for advanced airport construc-tion to handle modern equipment and to alleviate congestion, although national planners have long recognized that giving all cities such facilities would be wasteful. The best strategy for transport development in a given area may not require improved airport construction at all, but improved ground transportation to alleviate crowding at the existing airport. Ignored in the eag-erness to build bigger and finer air terminals are the many rec-ommendations to achieve a better overall transport system, in-cluding alternatives which might stem proliferation of air traf-fic. Thus, while the Metropolitan Transportation Authority in New York considers possible locations for a proposed fourth airport, little attention is paid to suggestions for a broad inter-governmental program to develop alternative means of trans-portation along the Eastern Seaboard. These alternatives might be advantageous in many ways, but they seem doomed unless the government structures coordinate their strategies.

Our system of government gives certain groups the oppor-tunity to articulate their special interests by lobbying. The framers of the Constitution hoped that the legislators would balance the demands of special interest groups against the needs and considerations of other groups and the general public, but the system has not worked perfectly. Although special interest groups often make valuable contributions in our government, they can be detrimental if they confine legislators' thinking to narrow paths.

Powerful special interest groups affect government decision making in transportation. Highway groups do everything pos-sible to maintain their exclusive hold on the $4-billion-a-year Highway Trust Fund. The shipping industry in 1968 helped put through a new multi-year merchant marine bill. All modes have lobbies protecting their special interests and generally making themselves useful to government, but each is concerned with specific transport investment decisions. Overall transport considerations get lost and forgotten in the confusion.

When the Department of Transportation was established in 1966, it raised the hopes of those who believed that maximization of benefits from government participation could be achieved only by a federal agency controlling all government investment. In theory, the new department could consider all the implications and effects, direct and indirect, of each government dollar spent for transportation. For example, how would a proposed new highway affect other modes of transportation and, as a consequence, the system as a whole? What are the overall implications of a proposed new airport? In short, the framework of the department was to be intermodal, not narrowly concerned with airline or highway or water or rail, but broadly with the best ways to move goods and people. Without significant structural changes, however, the department seems doomed as a possible vehicle for effective intermodal planning. The Federal Maritime Administration, which controls the government's promotional activities with respect to the merchant marine fleet, has been kept outside the department through industry lobbying efforts. Meanwhile, the department itself is organized along modal lines which frustrate intermodal policy formulation. The department contains no subdivision to deal with intermodal movement of people in dense corridors, but it does have a Federal Highway Administration, a Federal Aviation Administration, and a Federal Railroad Administration, each within the well-defined traditional barriers which must be removed before the benefits from government investment can be fully realized.

While the executive branch of government has failed to make significant progress, the legislative lags even farther behind in developing a total approach to transportation. Separate legislative committees in both the House and the Senate handle appropriations and consider policy alternatives for each mode. A comprehensive congressional review of all government transportation policies at one time is unheard of. Thus, special-interest legislation, such as the ten-year maritime development proposal, although perhaps appropriate in a total transportation framework, is handled by Congress as an isolated entity.

Many regulatory problems also are blamed on congressional failure to provide clear, consistent agency guidelines. It may be that the kinds of hard choices which will hurt certain special interests in the short run but will result in the long run in an effective system cannot be made by a body subject to special-interest pressures. But, Congress has adopted overall policies in other fields and may well have the ability to take a similar view of government investment in transportation.

The need for a diversified and efficient transportation system places enormous demands on society. But the burden of a fragmented and outmoded transport system may prove much harder to bear.

Today's system needs improvement, modernization, and, in some ways, complete restructuring. But few doubt that wise planning and proper motivation can still give America an efficient, cohesive, and perhaps outstanding, transport network.

STATISTICAL APPENDIX

TABLE 1:

AIRWAYS

Expenditures for years	Federal	State and Local
1925 to 1947	$334,806,569	
1947	88,201,605	
1948	88,730,833	
1949	106,841,866	
1950	121,311,131	
1951	120,204,879	
1952	119,218,553	
1953	119,002,193	
1954	112,202,520	
1955	112,099,345	
1956	122,053,358	
1957	208,586,318	
1958	318,858,835	NONE
1959	385,029,244	
1960	461,727,000	
1961	557,741,000	
1962	573,506,000	
1963	634,258,000	
1964	669,779,000	
1965	711,039,000	
1966	739,595,000	
1967	808,437,000	
1968	812,011,000	
1969	883,460,000	
1970 (est.)	1,150,926,000	
1971 (est.)	1,540,769,000	
TOTAL	11,342,855,000	

Expenditures for establishment, administration, maintenance and operations of the Federal Airways System, including flight and medical standards programs, years 1925 to date. Also included in years 1958-1971 are expenditures of the FAA for an accelerated research and development program for improving the national system of aviation facilities, and for administrative expenditures for that program. Research expenditures for Civil Supersonic Aircraft development (SST) are figured in the 1962 and 1971 totals.

Figures do not include costs of military facilities and funds transferred to the Civil Aeronautics Administration, the amounts of which could not be obtained. Also not included are expenditures for construction of National Capital Airport operation and maintenance of National Capital Airport.

Sources: Annual Budgets of the U.S. Government, 1925 and 1926, from Annual Reports of the Postmaster General.

SUBTABLE 1:

SST—Funds Spent for Civil Supersonic Development

Year	Expenditures
1968	$ 99,673,000
1969	80,603,000
1970 (est.)	163,042,000
1971 (est.)	275,000,000
TOTAL	$618,318,000

TABLE 2: AIRPORTS

Expenditures for years	Federal Grants in aid	Federal Admin. and Research	State and Local	Total
Prior to 1947	$1,758,019,920	Not available	$1,546,721,615	$3,304,741,535
1947	3,041,906	$258,859	80,000,000	83,300,765
1948	25,490,758	268,859	80,000,000	105,759,220
1949	49,908,900	633,558	80,000,000	130,542,458
1950	44,049,461	808,386	90,000,000	134,857,847
1951	39,703,042	778,847	90,000,000	130,481,889
1952	19,538,231	778,055	90,000,000	110,316,286
1953	11,007,077	645,415	100,000,000	111,652,492
1954	(855,556)	2,233,770	113,000,000	114,378,214
1955	19,698,475	2,132,334	114,000,000	135,830,809
1956	17,794,280	2,680,190	171,000,000	191,474,470
1957	45,141,216	3,330,650	225,000,000	273,471,866
1958	70,325,745	4,012,191	254,000,000	328,337,936
1959	72,956,360	4,506,700	308,000,000	385,463,060
1960	82,202,876	5,842,000	342,000,000	430,044,876
1961	73,783,676	7,638,000	422,000,000	503,421,676
1962	46,381,321	10,743,000	373,000,000	430,124,321
1963	75,003,438	9,957,000	361,000,000	445,960,000
1964	65,247,000	8,232,000	359,000,000	432,479,000
1965	70,598,000	9,649,000	415,000,000	495,247,000
1966	53,989,000	10,569,000	424,000,000	488,558,000
1967	64,147,000	11,346,000	466,000,000	541,493,000
1968	74,701,000	11,933,000	516,000,000	602,634,000
1969	103,671,000	12,878,000	not available	116,549,000
1970 (est.)	90,000,000	14,385,000	not available	104,385,000
1971 (est.)	89,000,000	15,162,000	not available	104,162,000
TOTAL	3,064,538,000	151,404,000	7,019,722,000	10,235,554,000

205

Federal expenditures for civil airports prior to 1947 include a military contribution of $1 billion as estimated by Undersecretary of Commerce Rothschild in April 1958, and other federal expenditures for civil airports by federal agencies prior to the Federal Airport Act of 1946. Grant agreements under the act are shown for the years 1947 through 1968, except when none was made; some were canceled in 1954. Expenditures for development of Washington and Dulles International airports, revenue-producing federal facilities, are not included.

The President's Airport Commission in 1952 estimated the acquisition cost of all U.S. Civil Airports, with their ground establishments, to be in the vicinity of $4 billion. Deducting from this $4 billion total the federal, state and, local expenditures of $695,258,465 shown for the 1947 to 1952 period leaves $3,304,741,535 as expended prior to 1947. Annual state and local expenditures for years prior to 1954 not available, but estimated here.

Sources: *The National Airport Program*, Sen.Doc. 95, 83rd Cong., 2nd Sess., p. 34; Hearings before the Subcommittee of the Committee on Interstate and Foreign Commerce on bills to amend the Federal Airport Act, U.S. Senate, April 14-17, 1958, p. 6; *Amendments to the Federal Airport Act*, Report No. 446, U.S. Senate, 88th Cong., 1st Sess., p. 7; Budgets of the U.S. Government; and *The Airport and Its Neighbors*, President's Airport Committee, May 16, 1952, p. 95. State and local expenditures for years 1954-1968 are from *Governmental Finances,* published annually by the Bureau of the Census, Table 3, Washington, D.C., Government Printing Office 1968-1971, for 1st two columns—U.S. Budget, 1970.

TABLE 3:

CASH SUBSIDY TO DOMESTIC AIRLINES [1]

Expenditures for years	Federal	State and Local
1939 to 1947	$118,678,000	
1947	16,500,000	
1948	29,600,000	
1949	33,500,000	
1950	36,800,000	
1951	34,922,000	
1952	25,401,000	
1953	25,379,000	
1954	30,753,000	NONE
1955	28,085,000	
1956	28,716,000	
1957	33,802,000	
1958	39,404,000	
1959	42,512,000	
1960	56,738,000	
1961	72,690,000	
1962	81,493,000	
1963	84,179,000	
1964	84,122,000	
1965	80,423,000	
1966	74,622,000	
1967	62,322,000	
1968	54,999,000	
1969	43,924,000	
1970 (est.)	37,308,000	
1971 (est.)	31,291,000	
TOTAL	$1,116,709,000	

[1]Includes domestic trunk, local service, and helicopter airlines. Subsidy payments to domestic airlines, as distinguished from compensation for carrying mail, not available separately for years prior to 1951, and are estimated here by applying the subsidy ratios (59 percent), as determined by CAB for entire 1939-1950 period, to the total mail payments for each year from 1947 through 1950. Subsidy payments from years 1961 to date include Alaskan and Hawaiian operations.

Sources: 1939-1950, CAB, *Administrative Separation of Subsidy from Total Mail Payments to Domestic Air Carriers*, September 1951, p. 5; 1951-1953, CAB, *Service Mail Pay and Subsidy for United States Certificated Air Carriers*, February 1961, Table 2; 1954-1962, CAB, *Subsidy for United States Certificated Air Carriers*, January 1963, Appendix No. 1; 1963-1971, Budgets of U.S. Government.

TABLE 4:

WATERWAYS

Expenditures for Years	Federal[1]	State and Local[2]	Total
Prior to 1947	$2,570,100,000	Not Available	$2,570,100,000
1947	89,100,000	$125,000,000	214,100,000
1948	115,700,000	125,000,000	240,700,000
1949	160,500,000	125,000,000	285,500,000
1950	190,400,000	150,000,000	340,400,000
1951	204,700,000	150,000,000	354,700,000
1952	215,000,000	150,000,000	365,000,000
1953	271,300,000	175,000,000	446,300,000
1954	97,600,000	195,000,000	292,600,000
1955	110,100,000	154,000,000	264,100,000
1956	146,400,000	200,000,000	346,400,000
1957	198,200,000	229,000,000	427,200,000
1958	222,600,000	219,000,000	441,600,000
1959	271,000,000	241,000,000	512,000,000
1960	293,500,000	237,000,000	530,500,000
1961	300,400,000	293,000,000	593,400,000
1962	309,300,000	292,000,000	601,300,000
1963	314,600,000	287,000,000	601,600,000
1964	323,771,000	291,000,000	624,771,000
1965	391,107,000	276,000,000	667,107,000
1966	420,252,000	318,000,000	738,252,000
1967	395,425,000	319,000,000	714,426,000
1968	388,158,000	407,000,000	795,158,000
1969	361,473,000	not available	361,473,000
1970 (est.)	397,399,000	not available	397,399,000
1971 (est.)	453,680,000	not available	453,680,000
TOTAL	9,211,766,000	4,958,000,000	14,169,766,000

[1]Includes inland waterways, intracoastal waterways, Great-Lakes and coastal-harbors obligations for construction, operation, and maintainence of channels and harbors, locks and dams, alteration of bridges over navigable rivers, advanced engineering and design, and other minor costs related to navigation. Expenditures by the Corps of Engineers exclude the navigation portion of multiple-purpose projects. The table does not include construction and operating expenditures for navigation on the Tennessee River and the U.S. portion of construction costs for the St. Lawrence Seaway.

[2]State and local expenditures for years 1954-1966 are for water transport and terminal facilities. Expenditures not available prior to 1954 but are estimated here.

Sources: Federal expenditures from Annual Reports of the Chief of Engineers, U.S. Army, and Budgets of the U.S. Government. State and local expenditures for years 1954-1968 are from *Government Finances*, published annually by the Census Bureau, Table 3.

TABLE 5:

MERCHANT MARINE

Expenditures for Years	Federal[1]	State and Local
1916 to 1947	$16,843,000,000	
1947	(281,000,000)[2]	
1948	183,000,000	
1949	124,000,000	
1950	100,000,000	
1951	101,000,000	
1952	230,000,000	
1953	235,000,000	
1954	153,000,000	
1955	163,000,000	
1956	220,000,000	
1957	181,000,000	
1958	174,000,000	
1959	202,000,000	
1960	270,000,000	NONE
1961	282,000,000	
1962	358,000,000	
1963	365,000,000	
1964	306,850,000	
1965	337,000,000	
1966	303,000,000	
1967	284,000,000	
1968	314,000,000	
1969	322,000,000	
1970 (est.)	328,000,000	
1971 (est.)	341,000,000	
TOTAL	22,459,000,000	

[1] Expenditures for years 1916-1926 are those of the U.S. Shipping Board Emergency Fleet Corporation. Expenditures for years 1927-1932 are those of U.S. Shipping Board and Merchant Fleet Corporation whose functions were transferred to the Department of Commerce in June 1933. Expenditures for years 1933-1938 are those of the U.S. Shipping Board Bureau and the U.S. Maritime Commission (established 1936). Expenditures for years 1939-1954 are described as "Promotion of Merchant Fleet" (functional code 451) by the Bureau of the Budget, and exclude accounts charged to national defense. Expenditures for years 1955 to date also exclude defense functions and are described as "Promotion of Water Transportation-Maritime Activities" (functional code 511 through 1958, 510 through 1960, and 502 through 1968).
[2] Excess of repayments and collections over expenditures.

Sources: Budgets of the U.S. Government for years 1928, 1935, 1941, and 1956 through 1971.

SUBTABLE 5:

MARITIME FLEET

Expenditures for Years	Operation-Differential Subsidy	Construction-Differential Subsidy	Totals
1968	$200,130,000	$104,315,000	$304,445,000
1969	194,703,000	96,512,000	291,215,000
1970 (est.)	205,760,000	90,257,000	296,017,000
1971 (est.)	193,000,000	112,000,000	305,000,000
TOTAL	$793,595,000	$403,084,000	$1,196,677,000

TABLE 6:

COAST GUARD

Expenditures for Years	Federal[1]	State and Local
1921 to 1947	$2,443,000,000	
1947	142,000,000	
1948	106,000,000	
1949	132,000,000	
1950	149,000,000	
1951	162,000,000	
1952	205,000,000	
1953	230,000,000	
1954	222,000,000	
1955	190,000,000	
1956	189,000,000	NONE
1957	194,000,000	
1958	219,000,000	
1959	229,000,000	
1960	238,000,000	
1961	276,000,000	
1962	284,000,000	
1963	297,000,000	
1964	349,806,000	
1965	386,493,000	
1966	405,030,000	
1967	493,683,000	
1968	545,327,000	
1969	547,869,000	
1970 (est.)	593,448,000	
1971 (est.)	596,940,000	
TOTAL	9,828,596,000	

[1] Expenditures by the U.S. Treasury and U.S. Navy for the Coast Guard, described as "Provision of Navigation Aids and Facilities—Coast Guard" or "Promotion of Water Transportation—Coast Guard," which exclude those accounts charged to national defense by the Bureau of the Budget.

Sources: Budgets of the U.S. government for years 1935, 1941, 1943, and 1948 through 1971.

TABLE 7:

HIGHWAYS—CALENDAR YEARS

Expenditures for Years	Federal	State and Local	Total
1921 to 1947	$8,952,000,000	$44,409,000,000	$53,361,000,000
1947	325,000,000	2,780,000,000	3,105,000,000
1948	407,000,000	3,312,000,000	3,719,000,000
1949	513,000,000	3,685,000,000	4,198,000,000
1950	499,000,000	3,984,000,000	4,483,000,000
1951	497,000,000	4,429,000,000	4,926,000,000
1952	567,000,000	4,803,000,000	5,370,000,000
1953	655,000,000	5,328,000,000	5,983,000,000
1954	695,000,000	6,287,000,000	6,982,000,000
1955	790,000,000	6,592,000,000	7,382,000,000
1956	897,000,000	7,445,000,000	8,342,000,000
1957	1,470,000,000	7,894,000,000	9,364,000,000
1958	2,455,000,000	7,882,000,000	10,337,000,000
1959	3,237,000,000	7,649,000,000	10,886,000,000
1960	2,753,000,000	8,008,000,000	10,761,000,000
1961	2,941,000,000	8,551,000,000	11,492,000,000
1962	3,173,000,000	9,205,000,000	12,378,000,000
1963	3,650,000,000	9,263,000,000	12,913,000,000
TOTAL	34,476,000,000	151,506,000,000	185,982,000,000

Note: For 1964-1968 see "Fiscal Years" table on page 215.

Sources: U.S. Dept. of Commerce, Bureau of Public Roads, *Highway Statistics Summary to 1955,* Tables HF-201 and HF-202 for years through 1947; *Highway Finance,* 1948-57, April 1959, Tables HF-1 and HF-2 for year 1948; Bureau of Public Roads Releases of February 1960; January 6, 1961; January 7, 1962; January 13, 1963; Table HF-1 for years 1949-1963.

SUBTABLE 7:

HIGHWAYS—FISCAL YEARS

Expenditures for Years	Federal	State	Local	Total
1965	$ 4,124,000,000	$ 9,844,000,000	$ 9,844,000,000	$18,007,000,000
1966	4,078,000,000	10,349,000,000	4,178,000,000	18,605,000,000
1967	4,159,000,000	11,284,000,000	4,571,000,000	20,014,000,000
1968	4,464,000,000	11,884,000,000	4,713,000,000	21,061,000,000
TOTALS	$16,825,000,000	$43,361,000,000	$17,501,000,000	$77,687,000,000

Source: U.S. Bureau of Census, Governmental Finances, GF-67 and GF-68, No. 3, Table 6, U.S. Government Printing Office, Washington, D.C., 1967 and 1968.

Sources for Statistical Appendix: Government Expenditures for Construction, Operation and Maintenance of Transport Facilities by Air, Highway, and Waterway, Bureau of Railway Economics, Association of American Railroads, March 1964, reprinted in *Issues in Transportation Economics*, Karl M. Ruppenthal, ed., 1965, pp. 36-44. The figures given in the tables by the Association of American Railroads have been updated. The same sources employed by the association were utilized except where noted. All figures are for fiscal years.

Notes for General Transportation Study

Chapter 1: A Historical Overview

1. Frank H. Mossman and Newton Morton, *Principles of Transportation*, 1957, pp. 38-39.
2. R.J. Sampson and M.T. Farris, *Domestic Transportation*, 1966, p. 19.
3. Dudley F. Pegrum, *Transportation: Economics and Public Policy*, 1963, p. 50.
4. Ibid., p. 52.
5. Mossman and Morton, *Principles of Transportation*, p. 42.
6. Pegrum, *loc. cit.*
7. Ibid.
8. Mossman and Morton, *op. cit.*, p. 45.
9. Pegrum, *op. cit.*, p. 56.
10. Ibid., p. 55.
11. Mossman and Morton, *op. cit.*, p. 46-47.
12. Sampson and Farris, *Domestic Transportation*, p. 19.
13. Pegrum, *op. cit.*, p. 60.
14. Sampson and Farris, *op. cit.*, p. 29.
15. See George M. Smerk, *Urban Transportation: The Federal Role*, 1965, pp. 123-126; Pegrum, *op. cit.*, pp. 452-453; and D. Philip Locktin, *Economics of Transportation*, 1966, pp. 617-618.
16. Pegrum, *op. cit.*, p. 61.
17. R.J. Barber, "Technological Change in American Transportation: The Role of Government Action," *Virginia Law Review*, June 1964, pp. 837ff.
18. Pegrum, *op. cit.*, p. 62.
19. Sampson and Farris, *op. cit.*, pp. 32-34.
20. Roger Gilman, "Port Problems and Policies," *Conference on Public Transportation*, United Transportation Union, 1970, p. 323.
21. Moody's Transportation Manual, 1969, p. 11.
22. "Pipeline Transportation Technology," *Handling and Shipping*, January 1969, pp. 64-67.

[23] Frank H. Mossman, *Principles of Urban Transportation*, 1951, p. 1.
[24] Smerk, *op. cit.*, p. 18.
[25] Ibid.
[26] Mossman, *Principles of Urban Transportation*, p. 2.
[27] Ibid.
[28] Ibid., p. 3.
[29] Ibid. pp. 3-4.
[30] Smerk, *op. cit.*, p. 24.
[31] Mossman, *Principles of Urban Transportation*, p. 5.
[32] Smerk, *op. cit.*, p. 28.

Chapter 2: Urban Metropolitan Transportation

[1] Dr. George H. Brown, Director, Bureau of Census, Remarks delivered at the Audit Bureau of Circulations, 56th Annual Meeting, Chicago, Illinois, October 22, 1970.
[2] Wilfred Owen, *The Metropolitan Transportation Problem*, 1966, p. 1.
[3] Dr. Brown. Remarks delivered at Downtown Economics Club, New York, New York, October 7, 1970.
[4] U. S. Department of Commerce, Bureau of Census, Census Report, 1970.
[5] Charles D. Baker, Assistant Secretary for Policy and International Affairs, Department of Transportation, in a speech delivered on March 16, 1970.
[6] U. S. Department of Commerce, Bureau of Census, 1970 Census Report. (News release from the Bureau of Census.)
[7] "Census Data Listed for 3-State Region," *New York Times*, September 2, 1970, p. 27.
[8] Homer Hoyt, *Traffic Quarterly*, April 1963, p. 296. "Effect of the Automobile on Patterns of Urban Growth."
[9] Automobile Manufacturers Association, *Urban Transportation Issues and Trends*, June 1963, p. 11.
[10] John A. Volpe, U.S. Secretary of Transportation, *DOT News*, in a speech delivered on Dec. 2, 1969.
[11] Dr. Brown, Remarks delivered at Downtown Economists Club, New York, New York, October 7, 1970.
[12] George M. Smerk, *Urban Transportation: The Federal Role*, 1965, pp. 209-210.
[13] Automobile Manufacturers Association, *Urban Transportation Issues and Trends*, June 1963, p. 26.
[14] Port of New York Authority, *Metropolitan Transportation—1980*, 1963, p. 295.
[15] Lewis M. Schneider, *Marketing Urban Mass Transit*, 1965, p. 28.
[16] Carlton C. Robinson, "Freeways in the Urban Setting," *Traffic Quarterly*, July 1963, p. 433.
[18] Automobile Manufacturers Association, *Automobile Facts and Figures*, 1969, p. 4.
[19] Henry J. Schmandt and G. Ross Stephens, "Public Transportation

and the Worker," *Traffic Quarterly*, October 1963, p. 26.

20 Automobile Manufacturers Association, *Urban Transportation Issues and Trends*, June 1963, p. 14;

21 Francis C. Turner, Federal Highway Administration, *DOT News*, in a speech delivered on June 2, 1970.

22 Automobile Manufacturers Association, *Urban Transportation Issues and Trends*, p. 22.

23 John A. Volpe, U.S. Secretary of Transportation, *DOT News*, in a speech delivered on November 9, 1969.

24 Automobile Manufacturers Association, *Automobile Facts and Figures*, 1968.

25 Automobile Manufacturers Association, *Urban Transportation Issues and Trends*, pp. 20-21.

26 *Statistical Abstract of the United States*, 1970, p. 326.

27 Wilfred Owen, *The Metropolitan Transportation Problem*, 1966 p. 25.

28 Ibid.

29 U. S. Department of Transportation, Bureau of Public Roads, *Highway Statistics*, 1967, Table UM-1.

30 Automobile Manufacturers Association, *Urban Transportation Issues and Trends*, p. 20.

31 Automobile Manufacturers Association, *Automobile Facts and Figures, 1968*, p. 50; U. S. Department of Transportation, Bureau of Public Roads, *Highway Statistics*, 1967, Table UM-1.

32 Automobile Manufacturers Association, *Urban Transportation Issues and Trends*, p. 5.

33 Ibid., p. 9.

34 Helen Leavitt, *Superhighway—Superhoax*, 1970, p. 5.

35 Ibid., p. 38;

36 Owen, *op. cit.*, p. 33;

37 Webb S. Fiser, *Mastery of the Metropolis*, 1962, p. 29.

38 Committee for Economic Development, *Developing Metropolitan Transportation Policies*, 1965, p. 23.

39 Fiser, *op. cit.*, p. 29.

40 Leavitt, *op. cit.*, pp. 5-6.

41 Ibid., p. 6.

42 Owen, *op. cit.*, p. 41.

43 Leavitt, *op. cit.*, p. 7.

44 Ibid., p. 10.

45 M. Earl Campbell, "Highway Traffic Safety—Is It Possible?" *Traffic Quarterly*, July 1965, p. 333.

46 Owen, *op. cit.*, p. 3.

47 John A. Volpe, U. S. Secretary of Transportation, *DOT News*, in a speech delivered on November 9, 1969.

48 Leavitt, *op. cit.*, p. 13.

49 John A. Volpe, *DOT News*, in a speech delivered on September 9, 1969.

50 American Transportation Association, *Transit Fact Book (1968)*, p. 9.

51 Owen, *op. cit.*, p. 74.
52 John A. Volpe, *Dot News*, in a speech delivered on April 18, 1970.
53 *Transit Fact Book (1969-1970)*, p. 4.
54 Owen, *op. cit.*, p. 87.
55 *Transit Fact Book (1969-1970)*, p. 5.
56 Ibid., pp. 4, 11.
57 Schneider, *op. cit.*, pp. 24-25.
58 Volpe, *DOT News*, in a speech delivered on April 28, 1970.
59 Owen, op. cit., p. 129.
60 *Transit Fact Book (1968)*, p. 6.
61 Edmund K. Faltermeyer, "The Rail Route to a More Mobile America," *Fortune*, July, 1966, p. 108.
62 Smerk, *op. cit.*, p. 72.
63 Ibid., p. 71.
64 Joint Committee on Washington Metropolitan Problems, *Hearings on Report of Washington Mass Transportation Survey*, 86th Congress, 1st Session, 1959. Cited by Jean Gottman, *Megalopolis*, 1961, p. 681.
65 Owen, *op. cit.*, p. 124.
66 Smerk, *op. cit.*, p. 64.
67 Richard J. Levine, "Better Transportation Out of Ghettos Sought by U.S., Local Groups," *Wall Street Journal*, August 16, 1968, p. 1.
68 Eric Schenker and John Wilson, "The Use of Public Mass Transportation in the Major Metropolitan Areas of the United States," *Land Economics*, XLIII, August 1967, pp. 362-363.
69 John A. Volpe, *DOT News*, in a speech delivered on September 23, 1969.
70 Schneider, *op. cit.*, p. 27.
71 Committee for Economic Development, *op. cit.*, p. 27.
72 Owen, *op. cit.*, p. 81.
73 Smerk, *op. cit.*, pp. 154-155.
74 Schneider, *op. cit.*, p. 150.
75 Owen, *op. cit.*, p. 204.
76 "Volpe Ties Road Funds to Bus Preference," *The Cleveland Plain Dealer*, September 2, 1970.
77 Schneider, *op. cit.*, p. 177.
78 L. K. Edwards, "High-Speed Tube Transportation." *Scientific American*, August 1965, p. 31.
79 Owen, *op. cit.*, p. 139.

Chapter 3: Case Studies

San Francisco
1 "New Plan on Hudson Crossings: No Toll West, Double Toll East," *New York Times*, July 24, 1970, p. 50.
Los Angeles
2 "Staving Off Auto Paralysis," *Business Week*, February 28, 1970, p. 54.

[3] Webb S. Fiser, *Mastery of the Metropolis*, 1962, p. 29.
[4] Wilfred Owen, *The Metropolitan Transportation Problem*, 1966, p. 74

Chicago

[5] "The Story Behind the Commuter Crisis," *Business Week*, March 14, 1970, p. 65.
[6] "Skokie Gets Them Coming and Going," *Railway Age*, October 7, 1968, p. 18.
[7] "Skokie Swift Is a Success," *Railway Age*, September 6, 1965, p. 19.
[8] David Thaler, "Is There a Better Way to Get to the Airport?" *Railway Age*, March 9, 1970, pp. 24-25.

Cleveland

[9] Cleveland Transit System, *The 1969 Annual Report*, p. 2.
[10] Joe Asher, "One Line, Maybe More," *Railway Age*, September 2, 1968, pp. 25-27.

New York

[11] Peter Hall, *The World Cities*, 1966, p. 205.
[12] "Saving New York From Strangling," *Business Week*, March 9, 1968, p. 64.
[13] "Battle of the Bottleneck Rumbling On," *New York Times*, June 28, 1970, p. 66.

Baltimore

[14] "How Baltimore Tamed the Highway Monster," *Fortune*, February 1970, p. 129.

Toronto

[15] "Toronto's Total Approach to Transit," *Railway Age*, June 3, 1968, p. 18.
[16] "Toronto Opens New 8-Mile Subway Line," *Railway Age*, March 7, 1966, p. 24.

Stockholm

[17] Goran Sedenblach, "Stockholm, A Planned City," *Scientific American*, September 9, 1966, pp. 116-118.

London

[18] F. S. Lloyd, "Planning Bus Services in Congested Cities," *Institute of Transport Journal*, XXXII, January 1967, p. 57.
[19] Ibid.
[20] David McKenna, "Commuting in the 1970's," *Institute of Transport Journal*, XXXII, March 1967, p. 88.
[21] Ibid.

Tokyo

[22] "Traffic Casualties," *Tokyo Municipal News*, August, 1968, p. 1.
[23] "Japan's Secret Weapon?" *Forbes*, April 15, 1970, p. 9.

Chapter 4: Intercity Transportation

[1] Bureau of Census, *1967 Census of Transportation*, p. 21;
[2] Ibid.
[3] Association of American Railroads, *Yearbook of American Railroad Facts*, 1965, 1966, 1967, and 1970. J. Moody, *Moody's Transportation Manual*, 1970.

[4] R. J. Sampson and M. T. Farris, *Domestic Transportation,* 1966, p. 67.

[5] Federal Aviation Agency, *FAA Statistical Handbook of Aviation,* 1965, p. 151.

[6] Bureau of the Budget, *Budget for 1969.*

[7] "Three Big Airlines Bid to Cut Flights on Some Routes," *Wall Street Journal,* August 31, 1970.

[8] Interstate Commerce Commission, *Annual Report,* 1967, p. 81.

[9] Interstate Commerce Committee, *Transport Economics,* Bureau of Economics, July 1968, p. 84.

[10] Dudley F. Pegrum, *Transportation: Economics and Public Policy,* 1963, p. 446.

[11] Interstate Commerce Commission, *Transport Economics, Bureau of Economics,* June 1968, p. 7.

[12] Editorial, "U.S. Railroad Plan Is Not Enough," *Los Angeles Times,* December 3, 1970.

[13] Carl Dreher, "Is It Back to the Rails?" *Nation,* July 4, 1966.

[14] Interstate Commerce Commission, *Annual Report,* 1965, p. 83.

[15] Edmund K. Faltermayer, "The Rail Route to a More Mobile America," *Fortune,* July 1966, p. 108.

[16] U. S. Department of Commerce, *Statistical Abstract of the United States,* 1968, p. 565.

[17] Center for Study of Responsive Law, *Surface Transportation, The Public Interest, and the ICC,* 1970, Volume II, Chapter XI, 1970, p. 1.

[18] Ibid., Volume II, Chapter XI pp. 20-25.

[19] Ibid., Volume II Chapter XI, pp. 25 and 33.

[20] Ibid., Volume II, Chapter XI, pp. 11-12.

[21] "Railroad Mercy Killings," Editorial, *New York Times,* December 6, 1970, p. E-10.

[22] Harold Mayer, speech delivered at United Transportation Union Conference, April 25, 1970, p. 7.

[23] Clarence D. Martin, Jr., "The Northeast Corridor—Widening the Planning Range," *Traffic Quarterly,* (April 1965), p. 156.

[24] Subcommittee on Surface Transportation of the Senate Commerce Committee, *High-Speed Ground Transportation,* 1965, p. 124.

[25] "Airports Outgrown," *The Economist,* August 26, 1967, pp. 723-724.

[26] Ibid.

[27] Michael Yafee, "Aerospace Technology Filling Major Role in High Speed Ground Transport Programs," *Aviation Week and Space Technology,* September 30, 1968, p. 40.

[28] Reginald N. Whitman, *DOT News,* in a speech delivered on January 13, 1970.

[29] Center for Study of Responsive Law, *op. cit.,* Volume II, Chapter XI, p. 12.

[30] Whitman, *loc. cit.*

[31] Center for Study of Responsive Law, *loc. cit.*

[32] Ibid., p. 13.

Notes for
Government Role
in Transportation

Introduction

1. Edward L. Throm, *Popular Mechanics' Picture History of American Transportation*, 1952, p. 24.
2. Dudley F. Pegrum, *Transportation: Economics and Public Policy*, 1963, p. 50.
3. Throm, *op. cit.*, p. 77.
4. Ibid., p. 82
5. Franklin M. Reck, *The Romance of American Transportation*, 1962, p. 180.
6. Throm, *op. cit.*, p. 201.
7. Act quoted by D. Philip Locklin, *Economics of Transportation*, 1966, p. 250.
8. Pegrum, *op. cit.*, p. 26.
9. "GOP Party Platform," *New York Times*, August 5, 1968.
10. Locklin, *op. cit.*, p. 18.

Chapter 1: Investment

1. U.S. General Land Office, *Annual Report of the Commissioner*, June 30, 1943, table 76, quoted by Robert S. Henry, "The Railroad Land Grant Legend in American History Texts," *The Mississippi Valley Historical Review*, XXXII, September 1945, p. 172.
2. The extent and value of government land grants is a moot question. Mr. Henry represents a conservative point of view. For a detailed discussion, both favorable and adverse, of his conclusions and methods see "Comments on 'The Railroad Land Grant Legend in American History Texts," *Mississippi Valley Historical Review*, XXXII, 1946, pp. 557-576. This article is a collection of letters written to the editors of the journal in response to Mr. Henry's article. See also Fred Shannon, *The Farmer's Last Frontier*, Vol. V of *The Economic History of the United States*, edited by Henry David et al, 1951, pp. 51-75.
3. David Ellis, "Comments on 'The Railroad Land Grant Legend in

American History Texts,' " *op. cit.,* pp. 561-563.
4 *1968 National Highway Needs Report,* Report to the Committee on Public works, 90th Cong., 1st sess., p. 165.
5 D. Philip Locklin, *Economics of Transportation,* 1966, pp. 72-77.
6 See Table 4.
7 Locklin, *op. cit.,* pp. 95-98.
8 Ibid., p. 764.
9 See Table 2.
10 George Rogers Taylor, *The Transportation Revolution, 1815-1860,* Vol. IV of *The Economic History of the United States,* edited by Henry David et. al., p. 50.
11 Carter Goodrich, *Government Promotion of American Canals and Railroads 1800-1890,* 1960, p. 274.
12 Robert William Fogel, *The Union Pacific Railroad: A Case in Premature Enterprise,* 1960, p. 72.
13 Goodrich, *op. cit.,* pp. 138-139, 211-212, 141-149.
14 "Saving New York from Strangling," *Business Week,* March 9, 1968, p. 64.
15 George Krambles, "Government Involvement With Transit in Chicago," *1968 Conference on Public Transportation,* Brotherhood of Railroad Trainmen, p. 69.
16 Lawrence E. Davies, "Bay Area Transit Is Facing Delays," *New York Times,* August 18, 1968, p. 76. For more information on the Bay Area Rapid, consult "Bay Area Waits for the Train," *Business Week,* May 11, 1968, pp. 164-166; Alan S. Boyd, "The Transportation Dilemma," *Virginia Law Review,* LIV, April 1968, p. 431.
17 Taylor, *op. cit.,* p. 26.
18 Ibid. pp. 382-383.
19 Federal Coordinator of Transportation, *Public Aids to Transportation,* Vol. II, 1938, also cited by Locklin, *op. cit.,* p. 105.
20 Taylor, *op. cit.,* p. 92.
21 See, for example, Stephen Salisbury, *The State, the Investor and the Railroad: The Boston & Albany 1825-1867,* 1967, p. 32.
22 Charles L. Dearing and Wilfred Owen, *National Transportation Policy,* 1949, pp. 84-90; Locklin, *op. cit.,* pp. 721-722.
23 *National Transportation Policy* (Doyle Report), Preliminary Draft of a Report to the Senate Committee on Interstate and Foreign Commerce, 87th Cong., 1st sess., p. 576.
24 George M. Smerk, *Urban Transportation: The Federal Role,* 1965, pp. 150, 168-170, 176.
25 Joseph L. Sarisky, "Sea and Air Subsidies: A Comparative Study," *Fordham Law Review,* XXXVI, October 1967, p. 66.
26 *1968 National Highway Needs Report,* Report to the Committee on Public Works, 90th Cong. 2nd sess., pp. 5; 54.
27 Ibid., p. 55.
28 D. Philip Locklin, *op. cit.,* p. 621. Smerk, *Urban Transportation: The Federal Role,* describes the nature of the rural protest, p. 120.
"The financial security of farmers was threatened by the poor highway system in the United States in the late nineteenth century. Trav-

el and shipment to points of any great distance from the railroads were slow, difficult and generally costly. Farmers and rural people in towns not served by rail were typically at a great disadvantage, and rural living standards had not generally kept pace with those in urban areas. Much of the rural population, in short, lived on the bleak and remote rim of the national society."

[29] Smerk, op. cit., p. 121. The only major federal assistance before the passage of the 1916 act was the improvement of the Cumberland Road undertaken by the federal government between 1806 and 1844. Consult the Doyle Report, op. cit., p. 165.

[30] Ibid., p. 123

[31] See Statistical Table 2.

[32] Locklin, op. cit., p. 768.

[33] See Table 3. Congress authorized the Civil Aeronautics Board to determine and pay subsidies to the airlines by provisions of the Civil Aeronautics Act. The following subsidy criteria were established:
"The need of each such air carrier for the compensation for the transportation of mail sufficient to insure the performance of such service, and, together with all other revenues of the air carrier, to enable such air carrier under honest, economical and efficient management, to maintain and continue the development of air transportation to the extent and of the character and quality required for the commerce of the United States, the Postal Service, and the National Defense."
See also statue quoted in Sarisky, op. cit., p. 70. For history of airmail subsidies before 1938, see Dearing and Owen, op. cit., pp. 44-58; Locklin, op. cit., pp. 762-764.

[34] See Table 3.

[35] Sarisky, op. cit., p. 81 ftn., explains the "use it or lose it" policy:
"The policy relates to the services offered by the subsidized local air carriers and is codified at 14 C.F.R. 399.11 (1966). Para. (b) states that 'under this "use it or lose it" policy, the Board will require each city to originate an average of five or more passengers per day during the 12-month period following the initial six months of operations. If a city is certificated on more than one segment, the five-passenger standard will be applied to each segment. If a city fails to meet this minimum traffic standard, the Board will, in the absence of unusual or compelling circumstances, institute a formal investigation to determine whether this service should be suspended or terminated.' "

[36] Ibid., pp. 62-63. Joint determination of subsidy rates by the Postmaster General and the U.S. Shipping Board was abolished by the Merchant Marine Act of 1928. The Act returned to the general plan of defining the rate of compensation for ocean mail carriage to various classes of vessels. See Doyle Report, op. cit., p. 169.

[37] Ibid., p. 66 ftn.
"The U.S. Maritime Commission was abolished by Reorganization Plan No. 21 of 1950, and the Commission's functions transferred to the Federal Maritime Board in the Department of Commerce and to the Secretary of Commerce. Reorganization Plan No. 7 of 1961 transferred the Federal Maritime Board's subsidy award function and

abolished the Board. By Department of Commerce order No. 117-A and 117-B, the Secretary of Commerce delegated all maritime subsidy functions to the Maritime Subsidy Board."

[38] Ibid., p. 67

[39] See Table 5.

[40] *National Transportation Policy* (Doyle Report), Preliminary Draft of a Report to the Senate Committee in Interstate and Foreign Commerce, 87th Cong., 1st sess., p. 569.

[41] Smerk, *op. cit.,* pp. 143-144.

[42] Preamble to Public Law 88-365, 88th Cong., 2nd sess., p. 1, as quoted by Smerk, *op. cit.,* p. 173.

[43] Ibid., p. 174.

[44] D.O.T., *Third Annual Report,* Fiscal Year 1969, pp. 178, 179, 183.

[45] Lawrence E. Davies, *op. cit.,* p. 76. See also David G. Hammond, "Governments in Transit," *1968 Conference on Public Transportation,* Brotherhood of Railroad Trainmen pp. 213-226.

[46] Figures on taxes paid and rate of assessment, except where noted, were taken from the Doyle Report, *op. cit.,* pp. 445-465.

[47] John F. Belt, "The Tax Handicap to Commuter Operations," *1968 Conference on Public Transportation,* Brotherhood of Railroad Trainmen, p. 171.

[48] Doyle Report, *op. cit.,* p. 567.

[49] Belt, *op. cit.,* p. 173.

[50] Thomas C. Cochran, "Land Grants and Railroad Entrepreneurship," *Journal of Economic History,* X, 1950, p. 60.

[51] Alfred D. Chandler, "Patterns of American Railroad Finance, 1830-1850," *Business History Review,* XXVIII, September 1954, p. 250.

[52] Milton S. Heath, *Constructive Liberalism, The Role of the State in Economic Development in Georgia to 1860,* 1954, pp. 201-202.

[53] M. Cecil Mackey, "The Federal Role in Transportation Research," *1968 Conference on Public Transportation,* Brotherhood of Railroad Trainmen, p. 317.

[54] Ibid.

[55] "President Signs Highway Aid Measure," *Traffic World,* August 31, 1968, p. 16.

[56] Housing and Home Finance Agency, Office of Transportation, *Urban Transportation: Fact Sheet on the Federal Aids Available to Localities on Problems of Urban Mass Transportation,* p. 3, as quoted by Smerk, *op. cit.,* p. 152.

Chapter 2: Promotion

[1] Carter Goodrich, *Government Promotion of American Canals and Railroads, 1800-1890,* 1960, p. 33.

[2] Ibid.

[3] *1968 National Highway Needs Report,* Report to the Committee on Public Works, 90th Cong., 2nd sess., p. 4.

[4] George M. Smerk, *Urban Transportation: The Federal Role,* 1966

p. 171.

5 Harold M. Mayer, "Some Geographic Aspects of Transport and Regional Planning," *Conference on Mass Transportation*, 1970, United Transportation Union, p. 201.

6 Joseph Goldberg, "Containerization As a Force for Change on the Waterfront," *Monthly Labor Review*, January 1968, p. 8.

7 See Table 5.

8 Report No. 91-1080 of the Senate Commerce Committee on Commerce on Merchant Marine Act of 1970, August 10, 1970.

9 Ibid. See also James J. Broz, "National Defense Needs a New Transportation Policy," *1970 Conference on Mass Transportation*, United Transportation Union, pp. 109-111.

10 Report of the Senate Commerce Committee, *op. cit.*

11 Joseph L. Sarisky, "Sea and Air Subsidies: A Comparative Study," *Fordham Law Review*, XXXVI, October 1967, p. 90.

12 Public Law 91-469.

13 "Luxury Liner Cruise Passengers Getting U.S. Bonus," *New York Times*, August 16, 1970, p. 78.

14 Mayer, *op. cit.*, pp. 196-197.

15 Charles E. Landon, "Technological Progress in Transportation on the Mississippi River System," *Journal of Business*, XXXIII, January 1960, p. 44.

16 Ibid.

17 *Annual Budget of the U.S. Government*, 1968-1969.

18 Stephen Salisbury, *The State, the Investor, and the Railroad: The Boston & Albany, 1825-1867*, 1967, p. 32.

19 Ibid.

20 Ibid.

21 Albert Fishlow, *American Railroads and the Transformation of the Ante-Bellum Economy*, 1965, p. 190.

22 Milton S. Heath, *Constructive Liberalism: The Role of the State in Economic Development in Georgia to 1860*, 1954, p. 281.

23 Fishlow, *op. cit.*, p. 191.

24 Arthur M. Johnson and Barry E. Supple, *Boston Capitalists and Western Railroads*, 1967, p. 253.

25 Interstate Commerce Commission, *Operating Revenues and Operating Expenses of Class I Railroads in U.S.*, Statement Q-100.

26 "Gavel Pounding, Congressional Shouting Highlight Hearing on Railroad Loan Guarantees," *Daily Traffic World*, June 24, 1970, p. 1.

27 Robert W. Harbeson, "Some Allocational Problems in Highway Finance," *Transportation Economics*, Bureau of Economic Research, 1965, p. 155.

28 *1968 National Highway Needs Report, op. cit.*, p. 5, Alan S. Boyd, "The Transportation Dilemma," *Virginia Law Review*, LIV, April 1968, p. 429, discusses the over-allocation of highway funds to rural roads:

"Our Federal Highway Administration reports that fifty percent of our motor vehicle travel was on urban streets, which represent only fourteen percent of the total road mileage in the United States. Local rural roads accounted for only fifteen percent of the travel but made up seventy-two percent of the total road mileage."

29 Ronald G. Shafer, "Efforts Grow to Ease Disruption from Roads Through Urban Areas," *Wall Street Journal,* June 27, 1968, p. 1. See also Richard J. Levine, "Better Transportation Out of Ghettos Sought by U.S., Local Groups," *Wall Street Journal,* August 16, 1968, pp. 1, 12; Harold M. Rose, "The Transportation System and the Negro Ghetto," *1967 Conference on Mass Transportation,* Brotherhood of Railroad Trainmen, pp. 155-162.

30 D. Philip Locklin, *Economics of Transportation,* 1966, p. 603.

31 Andrew M. De Voursney, "The Short-Haul Trip: Who Should Pay," *1970 Conference on Mass Transportation,* United Transportation Union, p. 215.

32 Lindsey, Robert, "Small Towns Left Isolated as Airlines Cut Service," *New York Times,* September 20, 1970, p. 1. All figures concerning CAB subsidies to regional carriers come from this source.

33 Harbeson, *op. cit.,* p. 140

34 All information concerning the new trust fund approach is taken from Paul J.C. Friedlander, "That New Air Fare Tax—It's Sly," *New York Times,* July 5, 1970, Travel Section.

35 Ronald Sullivan, "Cahill Drafts Plan on Transportation," *New York Times,* October 2, 1970, p. 63.

36 Richard J. Barber, "Technological Change in American Transportation: The Role of Government Action," *Virginia Law Review,* L, 1964, p. 824-889.

Chapter 3: Regulation

1 George W. Hilton, "Toward a Unified Transport Policy," *1970 Conference on Mass Transportation,* United Transportation Union, p. 67.

2 Major General John Doyle, "Regulation of Transportation—Too Much? Too Little?—Is it Needed?" *1966 Conference on Mass Transportation,* Brotherhood of Railroad Trainmen, p. 180.

3 James C. Nelson, "The Effects of Entry Control on Surface Transportation," in *Transportation Economics,* National Bureau of Economic Research, 1965, p. 383.

4 A natural monopoly is created by a decline in unit costs as sales increase, enabling one firm to serve a given market at lower costs than two or more firms. See John R. Meyer et al., *The Economics of Competition in the Transportation Industry,* 1959, p. 4. Natural monopoly characteristics are also discussed by Dudley F. Pegrum, *Transportation: Economics and Public Policy,* 1963, pp. 140-143.

5 Meyer et al., *op. cit.,* p. 5.

6 Many economists have recently disagreed with this statement, pointing out that railroads today have fewer fixed costs. See, for example, D. Philip Locklin, *Economics of Transportation,* 1966, pp. 154-156, and Pegrum, *op. cit.,* pp. 158-163.

7 Meyer et al., *op. cit.,* p. 6.

8 Ibid., p. 7.

9 For a discussion of state regulatory commissions which preceded federal regulation, see Clyde B. Aitchison, "The Evolution of the Interstate Commerce Act: 1887-1937," *George Washington Law Review,* V, March 1937, pp. 290-296; George H. Miller, "Origins of the Iowa Granger Law," in *United States Economic History,* edited by Harry N. Scheiber, 1964, pp. 310-329.

10 That government had the power to regulate commerce has never been forcefully questioned. However, the issue of which level of government acts in a certain circumstance was debated until the early twentieth century. The issue, as settled by the *Wabash Case* of 1886 and later by the *Minnesota and Shreveport Rate Cases* of 1913 and 1914 respectively, gives the federal government exclusive power over interstate commerce, the state government exclusive power over some areas of intrastate commerce, the other areas of intrastate commerce having "concurrent" power. "Concurrent" power means that either level of government may act; but if both legislate on the same subject matter, the federal law supersedes the state law. Only in the absence of federal legislation can the state act in this area of "concurrent" power. See Locklin, *op. cit.,* pp. 263-269; William C. Coleman, "The Evolution of Federal Regulation of Intrastate Rates: The Shreveport Rate Cases," *Harvard Law Review,* XXVIII, November 1914, pp. 34-81.

11 U.S. Senate, Select Committee on Interstate Commerce; Senate Report no. 46; cited by Gabriel Kolko, *Railroads and Regulations, 1877-1916.* Princeton, New Jersey: Princeton University Press, 1965.

12 Kolko, *op. cit.,* pp. 232-237.

13 "The fact that commodity discrimination was approved was made explicit by the Mann-Elkins Act of 1910 which made it the duty of regulated carriers to establish, observe and enforce just and reasonable classifications. This recognition of the classification principle amounts to recognition of the practice of class rate discrimination." Robert A. Nelson and William R. Greiner, "The Relevance of the Common Carrier Under Modern Economic Conditions," in *Transportation Economics,* National Bureau of Economic Research, 1965, p. 355.

14 Quoted in *Surface Transportation, the Public Interest, and the ICC,* Center for Study of Responsive Law, 1970, p. 4.

15 David Boies, Jr., "Experiment in Mercantilism: Minimum Rate Regulation by the ICC," *Columbia Law Review,* LXVIII, April, 1968, pp. 601-602.

16 Kolko, *op. cit.,* p. 56.

17 Ibid., pp. 81-83.

18 Ibid., pp. 81-82.

19 "Social Circle Case"—Cincinnati, New Orleans & Texas Pacific Railway Co., 162 U.S. 196.
"Maximum Freight Rate Case"—Interstate Commerce Commission v. Cincinnati, New Orleans & Texas Pacific Railway Co., 167 U.S. 479.
See Locklin, *op. cit.,* p. 216.

20 Kolko, *op. cit.,* p. 81.

21 See Boies, *op. cit.,* pp. 603, 608.

22 Kolko, *op. cit.,* p. 83.
23 Interstate Commerce Commission, *Statistics of Railways in the United States,* 1916, (Washington, 1918), p. 325. Cited by Kolko, *op. cit.,* p. 233.
24 For a complete discussion of the provisions of the Transportation Act of 1920, see Pegrum, *op. cit.,* pp. 311-316.
25 In applying this rate-schema, the ICC stayed within the bounds set out in the historic *Symth v. Ames* Supreme Court decision of 1898. The Supreme Court said:

> We hold that the basis of all calculations as to the reasonableness of rates to be charged by a corporation maintaining a highway under legislative sanction must be the fair value of the property being used by it for the convenience of the public. . . . What the company is entitled to is a fair return upon the value of that which it employs for the public convenience. On the other hand, what the public is entitled to demand is that no more be exacted from it for the use of a public highway than the services rendered by it are reasonably worth.

The case is cited in Locklin, *op. cit.,* p. 328. This has remained the standard for the determination of rate levels since that time.
26 Congress passed the Hoch-Smith Resolution in 1925 which directed the ICC to keep rates low on agricultural goods. The resolution stated:

> In view of the existing depression in agriculture, the Commission is hereby directed to effect with the least practicable delay such lawful changes in the rate structure of the country as will promote the freedom of movement by common carriers of the products of agriculture affected by that depression, including livestock, at the lowest possible lawful rates compatible with the maintenance of adequate transportation service.

Cited by Nelson and Greiner, *op. cit.,* p. 360.
27 Ibid., p. 363.
28 For a full discussion of the provisions of the Motor Carrier Act of 1935, see Pegrum, *op. cit.,* pp. 333-341.
29 The federal regulation of motor carriers like the railroads was based upon state regulatory commissions set up in the 1920s. Following the precedence set by the *Wabash Case* the Supreme Court prohibited the states from regulating the rates of motor carriers involved in interstate commerce. For a discussion of the state commissions, see Irwin S. Rosenbaum and David E. Lilienthal, "Motor Carrier Regulation: Federal, State and Municipal," *Columbia Law Review,* XXVI, December 1926, pp. 954-987; Val Sanford, "Motor Carrier Regulation—An Adventure in Federalism," *Vanderbilt Law Review,* XI, October 1958, pp. 987-1005; and Merrill J. Roberts, "The Motor Transportation Revolution," *Business History Review,* XXX, March 1956, pp. 57-95.
30 Boies, *op. cit.,* pp. 613-614; see also Dudley F. Pegrum, "The Economic Basis of Public Policy for Motor Transport," *Land Economics,* XXVIII, August 1952, pp. 244-263; Meyer et al., *op. cit.,* p. 216; Walter Adams, "The Role of Competition in the Regulated Indus-

tries," *American Economic Association Papers and Proceedings,* XLVII, May 1958, pp. 527-543; Merrill J. Roberts, "Some Aspects of Motor Carrier Costs: Firm Size, Efficiency and Financial Health," *Land Economics,* XXXII, August 1956, pp. 230-236.

31 Nelson and Greiner, *op. cit.,* p. 364.

32 Dr. E.W. Williams, Jr., *The Regulation of Rail-Motor Rate Competition,* 1958, pp. 210-211.

33 For a complete discussion of provisions of the Transportation Act of 1940, see Pegrum, *op. cit.,* pp. 321-324.

34 Boies, *op. cit.,* p. 618.

35 Williams, Jr., *op. cit.,* p. 214. For more discussion of the ICC's actions with respect to rate regulation during this period, see Robert W. Harbeson, "New Perspectives in Transport Regulation: The Cabinet Committee Report," *Northwestern Law Review,* LII September-October 1957, pp. 490-513; William J. Lavelle, "Our National Transportation Policy: The Need for Revision," *University of Pittsburgh Law Review,* XXVI June 1965, pp. 781-793; Howard W. Davis, "A Review of Federal Rate Regulation and Its Impact Upon the Railway Industry," *Land Economics,* XLIV, February 1968, pp. 1-10. Some specific cases cited by Boies, *op. cit.,* pp. 619-623, are Petroleum Products from Los Angeles to Arizona and New Mexico, 280 ICC 509 (1951); *Southwestern Tank Truck Carriers v. Abilene & Southern Ry.,* 284 ICC 75 (1952).

36 Boies, *op. cit.,* pp. 140ff.

37 Locklin, *op. cit.,* p. 796. For a complete discussion of the Civil Aeronautics Act, see Pegrum, *op. cit.,* p. 356.

38 Boies, *op. cit.,* pp. 624-625.

39 Cited by Pegrum, *op. cit.,* p. 326. The provisions of the Transportation Act of 1958 are discussed by Locklin, *op. cit.,* pp. 254-258.

40 Robert W. Harbeson, "The Regulation of Interagency Rate Competition Under the Transportation Act of 1958," *ICC Practitioners' Journal,* XXX, December 1962, pp. 287-305; see also Harvey A. Levine, "The Railroad Industry's Experience Under Section 15a(3) of the Transportation Act of 1958," *ICC's Practitioners' Journal* XXXV, January-February 1968, pp. 254-257.

41 Boies, *op. cit.,* p. 628.

42 The exact Supreme Court ruling citation has been taken from Boies, *op. cit.,* p. 628.

43 Ibid., p. 630.

44 The "Ingot Molds" Decision by the Supreme Court, June 1968, quoted in *Traffic World,* June 22, 1968, p. 70, defines fully distributed and out-of-pocket costs.

"Fully distributed costs are defined broadly by the ICC as the 'out-of-pocket costs plus a revenue ton and revenue ton-mile distribution of the constant costs, including deficits, (that) indicate the revenue necessary to a fair return on the traffic, disregarding any ability to pay.' New Automobiles in Interstate Commerce, 259 ICC 475, 513 (1945)."

"The long-term out-of-pocket costs were computed under an ICC sponsored formula which generally holds that 80 percent of rail operating expenses, rents and taxes are out-of-pocket in that they will vary with traffic. To this is added a return element of 4 percent on a portion of the investment (all of the equipment and 50 percent of the road property), which is apportioned to all traffic on a proportional basis."

[45] If the particular competing carrier is not regulated by ICC, then the railroad often is allowed to lower its rate below fully distributed costs.

[46] For support of this position, see Boies, *op. cit.*, pp. 628-634; and Levine, *op. cit.* For a history of the cases during this period, see Robert W. Harbeson, "Recent Trends in Regulation of Intermodal Rate Competition in Transportation," *Land Economics*, XLII August 1966, pp. 315-327; Bernard J. McCarney, "ICC Rate Regulation and Rail-Motor Carrier Pricing Behavior: A Reappraisal," *ICC Practitioners' Journal*, XXV July-August 1968, p. 716.

[47] See "Supreme Court Upholds ICC's Decision in 'Ingot Molds' Railroad Rate Case," *Traffic World*, June 22, 1968, pp. 69-74.

[48] ICC decision quoted by Eugene D. Anderson et al., "Ex Parte 230: The ICC 'Piggyback' Rulemaking Case," *ICC Practitioners' Journal*, XXXV, May-June, 1968, p. 616.

[49] Ibid., p. 620.

[50] Locklin, *op. cit.*, p. 749. See also *National Transportation Policy* (Doyle Report), Preliminary Draft of a Report to the Senate, Committee on Interstate and Foreign Commerce, 87th Cong., 1st Sess., pp. 529-533.

[51] James C. Nelson, *op. cit.* p. 399. For a complete discussion of the agricultural exemptions, see Doyle Report, *op. cit.*, pp. 516-529; Thomas G. Campbell, "Agricultural Exemptions from Motor Carrier Regulation," *Land Economics*, XXXVI, February 1960, pp. 14-25.

[52] Locklin, *op. cit.*, p. 610.

[53] The *Doyle Report*, *op. cit.*, p. 243.

[54] The Center for Responsive Law, Robert Fellmeth, Director, 1970, *Surface Transportation, the Public Interest, and the ICC*, Sec. III, p. 25.

[55] Cited in the Doyle Report, *op. cit.*, p. 240.

[56] *Review of ICC Practices and Policies*, Hearings before the Subcommittee on Surface Transportation, 91st Cong., 1st sess., June 24-25, 1969, p. 99. These hearings are commonly referred to as the "Oversight Hearings."

[57] Ibid., p. 99.

[58] Ibid., p. 98.

[59] New York Central and the Pennsylvania Railroad Merger Case, 327 ICC 491 (1966).

[60] Ibid., 327 ICC 683 (1966).

[61] *Western Railroad Mergers*, Department of Transportation, January, 1969, pp. 19-20. Staff study by the Office of the Assistant Secretary for Policy Development and the Federal Railroad Administration.

[62] Kent Healy, *The Effects of Scale in the Railroad Industry*, Yale University Press, 1961, cited in *Western Railroad Mergers, op. cit.*, p. 12.

[63] For a discussion of Penn Central's managerial woes and inefficient

service, see "High Cost of Money Hurts the Penn Central," *Business Week*, June 6, 1970, pp. 106-107; "The Penn Central's Troubles Branch Out," *Business Week*, June 20, 1970, pp. 92-94; "After Penn Central, Who Next?" *Newsweek*, July 6, 1970; "Uncle Sam, Can You Spare Millions?" *Time*, June 22, 1970, pp. 74-76; Stephen M. Aug, "3 Penn Central Chiefs Fired Over Debt Crisis," *Washington Star*, June 9, 1970.

[64] The Center for Responsive Law, *op. cit.*, p. 64

[65] Robert E. Gallamore, *Railroad Mergers: Costs, Competition, and the Future Organization of the American Railroad Industry*, unpublished Ph.D. dissertation, Harvard University, Cambridge, Massachusetts, 1968. Cited by *Western Railroad Mergers, op. cit.*, p. 110.

[66] The Center for Responsive Law, *op. cit.*, pp. 48-49.

[67] 386 US 425, 430 (1967).

[68] Locklin, *op. cit.*, p. 797.

[69] Richard J. Barber, "Airline Mergers, Monopoly, and the CAB," *Journal of Air Law and Commerce*, XXVIII, Summer 1961, p. 201.

[70] For example, see Michael E. Levine's "Is Regulation Necessary? California Air Transportation and National Regulatory Policy," *Yale Law Journal*, LXXIV, July 1965, pp. 1416-1447.

[71] "Airlines v. CAB," *New York Times*, November 1, 1970, p. 2.

[72] Martin L. Lindahl, "The Antitrust Laws and Transportation," *The Antitrust Bulletin*, XI, January-April 1966, pp. 77-87.

[73] Locklin, *op. cit.*, p. 811.

[74] James C. Nelson, "The Effects of Entry Control on Surface Transportation," in *Transportation Economics*, National Bureau of Economic Research, 1965, p. 383.

[75] Ibid., p. 386.

[76] Ibid., p. 387.

[77] James C. Nelson, "Toward an Efficient Role for Transport Regulation," *1970 Conference on Mass Transportation*, United Transportation Union, pp. 282-283.

[78] Locklin, *op. cit.*, p. 699.

[79] James C. Nelson, "Toward an Efficient Role for Transport Regulation," *op. cit.*, p. 284.

[80] James C. Nelson, "The Effects of Entry Control on Surface Transportation," *op. cit.*, pp. 388-389.

[81] Locklin, *op. cit.*, p. 755

[82] For further discussion of this case and ICC policy, see Michael Dorazio, "Common Ownership of Intermodal Transportation: An Appraisal," *University of Pittsburgh Law Review*, XXVII, October 1965, pp. 85-101; Herbert Burstein, "Railroads and Motor Carriers—Competition or Coordination," *Villanova Law Review*, VII, Summer 1962, pp. 563-586.

[83] Dorazio, *op. cit.*, pp. 91-92.

[84] Civil Aeronautics Act, Section 408 (b), cited by D. Philip Locklin, *op. cit.*, p. 801.

[85] Alfred Perlman, the twentieth Annual Salzberg Memorial Lecture at Syracuse University Transportation Conference, November, 1968,

cited by Peter S. Douglas, "The Economic Irrelevance of 'Common Ownership,' " *ICC Practitioners' Journal,* July-August, 1969, p. 1795.

[86] Stuart Saunders, *Journal of Commerce,* February 21, 1969, p. 4, cited by Peter S. Douglas, *op. cit.,* p. 1796.

[87] Merrill J. Roberts and Associates, Graduate School of Business, University of Pittsburgh, "Intermodal Freight Transportation Coordination: Problems and Potential," a study prepared in 1966 for the Under Secretary of Transportation, U.S. Department of Commerce, cited Peter S. Douglas, *op. cit.,* p. 1797.

[88] See Jim Hanscom, "Flight From Railroading," *The Exchange,* August 1968, pp. 8-13, "The Railway Conglomerates," *The Magazine of Wall Street,* April 13, 1968, pp. 9-12; and *Moody's Transportation Manual* 1969.

[89] See Colin Barrett, "Diversification—or Scatteration," *ICC Practitioners Journal,* pp. 198-208.

[90] Interstate Commerce Commission, Finance Docket No. 24743.

[91] See Stephen Aug, "Financial Maneuvers Drain Railroads, ICC Study Says," *Washington Star,* June 26, 1970, p. 1; "U.S. is Studying Effect on Rails of Holding Firms," *Wall Street Journal,* June 29, 1970, p. 4; and Robert Samuelson, "Diversion of Assets by Rails is Probed," *Washington Post,* June 27, 1970, p. 1.

[92] See Frank C. Porter, "A Penn Central Director's View: 'Poor and Inept Management'," *Washington Post,* June 26, 1970, p. 11, Robert E. Bedingfield, "Pennsy: Bad Management or Ailing Industry Debated," *New York Times,* June 28, 1970, Financial Section, Joseph Egehof, "Why Penn Fell: Perlman," *Chicago Tribune,* June 28, 1970, p. 1.

[93] Example drawn from Richard J. Barber, "Technological Change in American Transportation: The Role of Government Action," *Virginia Law Review,* L, 1964, pp. 824-889.

[94] Mervin Burnstein, Testimony in the Report of the Antitrust Subcommittee on the Judiciary, House of Representatives, 84th Cong. 1st sess., Airlines, p. 4 cited by Meyer et al., *op. cit.,* p. 11.

[95] Walter Adams, "The Role of Competition in the Regulated Industries," *American Economic Association Papers and Proceedings,* XLVII, May 1958, p. 529.

[96] For a complete discussion of this misallocation, see Barber, *op. cit.,* pp. 857-860; Meyer et al., *op. cit.,* pp. 10-15.

[97] Boies, *op. cit.,* p. 647.

[98] George W. Hilton, "Competitive Transportation: The Law of the Jungle—Or Is It?" Brotherhood of Railroad Trainmen, *1968 Conference on Mass Transportation,* p. 131.

[99] James C. Nelson, "Toward an Efficient Role of Transport Regulation," United Transportation Union, *1970 Conference on Mass Transportation,* p. 285.

[100] The Board of Investigation and Research study is quoted by James C. Nelson, "The Effects of Entry Control in Surface Transportation," *Transportation Economics,* National Bureau of Economic Research, 1965, p. 408. Board of Investigation and Research, *Feder-*

al Regulatory Restrictions Upon Motor and Water Carriers, S. Doc. 78, 79th Cong., 1st sess., 1945.

[101] Robert A. Nelson, "The Economic Structure of the Highway Carrier Industry in New England," in *Public Transportation for New England,* The New England Governors' Conference, November 1957, pp. 31-32, cited by Nelson, *op. cit.,* p. 408; and *ICC Administration of the Motor Carrier Act,* Hearings before the Senate Select Committee on Small Business, 84th Cong., 1st sess., November 30-December 2, 1955, pp. 3-9 and 30, cited by Nelson, *op. cit.,* p. 408.

[102] Statement filed by John S. Wallace, Office Manager, April 10, 1959, cited by Nelson, *op. cit.,* p. 409.

[103] Message from the President of the United States, House of Representatives, Document No. 384, 87th Cong., 2d sess., April 5, 1962.

[104] Ibid.

[105] Boies, *op. cit.,* p. 617.

[106] Dudley F. Pegrum, *Transportation: Economics and Public Policy,* 1963, pp. 274-275.

[107] Major General John Doyle, "Regulation of Transportation Too Much?—Too Little?—Is It Needed?," Brotherhood of Railroad Trainmen Conference, pp. 182-189.

[108] Doyle Report, *op. cit.,* pp. 156-157.

[109] Locklin, *op. cit.,* pp. 665-666.

[110] Doyle Report, *op. cit.,* pp. 522.

[111] Major General John Doyle, "Regulation of Transportation Too Much?—Too Little?—Is It Needed?," 1968 Brotherhood of Railroad Trainmen Conference, pp. 182-189.

[112] For example, see "ICC Delays Rail Rate Rises, Sets 3% Interim Boost," *Wall Street Journal,* June 20, 1968, p. 3.

Bibliography for Suggested Reading

General Transportation Study

Texts

American Transportation Association. *Transit Fact Book (1968)*.

Association of American Railroads. *A Review of Railroad Operations in 1965*, Special Series No. 100.

Association of American Railroads, *Yearbook of American Railroad Facts*, 1965, 1966, 1967, 1970.

Automobile Manufacturers Association. *Automobile Facts and Figures*, Automobile Manufacturers Association, Detroit, Michigan. (Annual publication.)

Automobile Manufacturers Association. *Urban Transportation Issues and Trends*, June 1963, Automobile Manufacturers Association, Detroit 2, Michigan.

Bebout, J. E., and Grele, R. J. *Where Cities Meet: The Urbanization of New Jersey*, Princeton, New Jersey: D. Van Nostrand Co., Inc., 1964.

Brotherhood of Railroad Trainmen. *Conference on Mass Transportation*, Cleveland, Ohio. (There are three volumes to the series: 1966, 1967, and 1968.)

Bureau of the Budget, *Budget for 1969*.

Bureau of the Census. *1967 Census of Transportation*, June, 1969.

Center for Study of Responsive Law. *Surface Transportation, The Public Interest, and the ICC*, Preliminary Draft, 1970.

Changing Tokyo, Supplement to the *Tokyo Municipal News*, 1967.

Cleveland/Seven County Transportation Land/Use Study. *A Framework for Action*, 1969.

Cleveland Transit System. *The 1969 Annual Report*, Cleveland, Ohio.

Committee for Economic Development. *Developing Metropolitan Transportation Policies*, New York, 1965.

Connecticut: Choices for Action, Transportation, 1966, State House, Hartford, Connecticut, 1966.

Danielson, Michael N. *Federal-Metropolitan Politics and the Commuter Crisis*, New York: Columbia University Press, 1965.

Dearing, Charles L., and Owen, Wilfred. *National Transportation Policy*, Wash., D.C.: Brookings Institute, 1949.

Federal Aviation Agency. *FAA Statistical Handbook of Aviation*. (Annual publication.)

Fiser, Webb S. *Mastery of the Metropolis*, Englewood Cliffs, N.J.: Prentice-Hall, Inc., 1962.

Fitch, Lyle C., and Associates. *Urban Transportation and Public Policy*, San Francisco: Chandler Publishing Co., 1964.

Fortune Market Research Department. *Fortune Airline Study*, Chicago: Time, Inc., 1962.

Frazier, Charles H. *Transportation: Lubricant to Our Region's Progress*, Philadelphia: PENJERDEL (Penn-New Jersey-Delaware Metropolitan Project, Inc.) November, 1962.

Fromm, Gary, ed. *Transportation Investment and Economic Development*, Wash., D.C.: Brookings Institute, 1965.

Futterman, Robert A. *The Future of Our Cities*, Garden City, New York: Doubleday & Co., Inc., 1961.

Goodrich, Carter. *Government Promotion of American Canals and Railroads: 1800-1890*, New York: Columbia University Press, 1960.

Gottmann, Jean. *Megalopolis*, Cambridge, Massachusetts: The M.I.T. Press, 1961.

Greer, Scott. *The Emerging City*, New York: The Free Press, 1962.

Hall, Peter. *The World Cities*, New York: McGraw-Hill Book Co., 1966.

Interstate Commerce Commission. *Annual Report*. (This is an annual publication.)

Interstate Commerce Commission. *Transport Economics*, Bureau of Economics. (This is a monthly publication.)

Kimmel, T., and Kaiser, W. *Focus: The Changing City*, New York: Friendship Press, 1963.

Lang, A. S., and Soberman, R. M. *Urban Rail Transit*, Cambridge, Massachusetts: The M.I.T. Press, 1964.

Leavitt, Helen. *Superhighway—Superhoax*, Garden City, New York: Doubleday & Co., 1970.

Locklin, D. Philip. *Economic of Transportation*, Homewood, Illinois: Richard D. Irwin, Inc., 1966.

MacAvoy, P. W. *The Economic Effects of Legislation*, Cambridge, Massachusetts: The M.I.T. Press, 1965.

Martin, B. V., Memmott, F. W., and Bone, A. J. *Principles and Techniques of Predicting Future Demand for Urban Area Transportation*, Cambridge, Massachusetts: The M.I.T. Press, 1961.

Message from the President of the United States. *Budget Message of the President, 1965*, H.R. Doc. No. 265, 88th Cong., 2nd Sess., 110 Cong. Rec. 704 (1964).

Message from the President of the United States. *Transportation Systems of Our Nation*, House Document No. 384, 87th Cong., 2nd Sess., April 5, 1962.

Meyer, J. R., Peck, M. J., Stenason, J., and Zwick, C. *The Economics of Competition in the Transportation Industry*, Cambridge, Massachusetts: Harvard University Press, 1959.

Mossman, Frank H. *Principles of Urban Transportation*, Cleveland, Ohio: The Press of Western Reserve University, 1951.

_____ and Morton, N. *Principles of Transportation*, New York: Ronald Press Co., 1957.

Mumford, Lewis. *The Highway and the City*, New York: Harcourt, Brace and World, Inc., 1963.

Mushkin, S. J. *Transportation Outlays of States and Localities: Projections to 1970*, Chicago, Council of State Government, 1965.

National Academy of Sciences. *U. S. Transportation*, Washington, D.C.: National Academy of Sciences, 1961.

National Bureau of Economic Research. *Transportation Economics*, New York: Columbia University Press, 1965.

North, Douglass C. *Growth and Welfare in the American Past*, Englewood Cliffs, New Jersey: Prentice-Hall, Inc., 1966.

Norton, Hugh S. *Modern Transportation Economics*, Columbus, Ohio: Charles E. Merrill Books, Inc., 1963.

Oi, W. Y. and Shuldiner, P. W. *An Analysis of Urban Travel Demands*, Evanston, Illinois: Northwestern University Press, 1962.

Osborn, F., and Whittick, A. *The New Towns*, New York: Mc-Graw-Hill Book Co., 1963.

Owen, Wilfred. *The Metropolitan Transportation Problem*, Garden City, New York: Doubleday & Co., 1966.

Pegrum, Dudley F. *Transportation: Economics and Public Policy*, Homewood, Illinois: Richard D. Irwin, Inc., 1963.

Port of New York Authority. *Metropolitan Transportation— 1980*, New York: Comprehensive Planning Office of the Port of New York Authority, 1963.

Rodwin, Lloyd, ed. *The Future Metropolis*, New York: George Braziller, 1961.

Ruppenthal, Karl M., ed. *Challenge to Transportation*, Stanford, California: Graduate School of Business, Stanford University, 1964.

ed. *Issues in Transportation Economics*, Columbus, Ohio: Charles E. Merrill Books, Inc., 1965.

ed. *Perspectives in Transportation*, Stanford, California: Graduate School of Business, Stanford University, 1963.

ed. *Revolution in Transportation*, Stanford, California: Graduate School of Business, Stanford University, 1960.

ed. *Transportation Frontiers*, Stanford, California: Graduate School of Business, Stanford University, 1962.

Transportation Progress, Stanford, California: Graduate School of Business, Stanford University, 1964.

Sampson, R. J., and Farris, M. T. *Domestic Transportation: Practice, Theory and Policy*, Boston: Houghton Mifflin Co., 1966.

Schneider, Lewis M. *Marketing Urban Mass Transit*, Boston: Graduate School of Business Administration, Harvard University, 1965.

Sites, James N. *Quest for Crisis*, New York: Simmons-Boardman Publishing Corp., 1963.

Smerk, George M. *Urban Transportation: The Federal Role*, Bloomington, Indiana: Indiana Univ. Press, 1965.

Subcommittee on Surface Transportation of the Senate Commerce Committee. *High-Speed Ground Transportation*, Washington, D.C.: Government Printing Office, 1965.

Transportation Research Forum. *Papers—Sixth Annual Meeting*, Oxford, Indiana: Richard B. Cross, Co., 1965.

U. S. Dept. of Commerce. *Statistical Abstract of the United States*, Washington, D.C.: Government Printing Office, 1970 (91st Edition).

U. S. Department of Housing and Urban Development. *Tomorrow's Transportation: New Systems for the Future*, Washington, D.C.: Office of Metropolitan Development, Urban Transportation Administration, 1968.

United Transportation Union Conference, 1970. Conference on Public Transportation.

Vernon, Raymond. *Metropolis 1985*, Garden City, New York: Doubleday & Co., Inc., 1963.

Warner, Stanley L. *Stochastic Choice of Mode in Urban Travel*, Evanston, Illinois: Northwestern University Press, 1962.

Weaver, Robert C. *The Urban Complex*, Garden City, New York: Doubleday & Co., Inc., 1964.

Wingo, Lowdon, ed. *Cities and Space*, Baltimore, Maryland: Johns Hopkins Press, 1963.

Transportation and Urban Land, Washington, D.C.: Resources for the Future, Inc., 1961.

Periodicals

"A Billion-dollar Boost for Transit," (interview with W. J Ronan), *Railway Age*, April 3, 1967, pp. 21-24, 52ff.

"ACI Goes to Work on Chicago Transit Line," *Railway Age*. April 13, 1970, p. 64.

"Airport Access: the Role of Transit," *Railway Age*, July 3-10, 1967, pp. 42-43, p. 67.

"Airports Outgrown," *The Economist*, August 26, 1967, pp. 723-724.

"BART Begets a Building Boom," *Railway Age*, March 6, 1967, pp. 24-25.

"Bay Area Waits for the Train," *Business Week*, May 11, 1968, pp. 164-166.

"Biggest Snarl on City Highways," *Business Week*, October 18, 1969, p. 144.

"Budd Finishes First of High-Speed Cars," *Railway Age*, August 7, 1969, pp. 18-20.

"Burgeoning Traffic Clogs Airport Roads," *Aviation Week*, November 14, 1966, pp. 167-169.

"C & O and B & O's Blueprint for Applied Research," *Railway Age*, September 19, 1966, pp. 24-32.

"Car Population Rate Turns Upward," *Ward's Automotive Reports*, March 17, 1969, p. 1.

"Changing Tokyo: Metropolitan Freeways," *Tokyo Municipal News*, XVIII (April 1968), p. 1.

"Changing Tokyo: Subway Construction," *Tokyo Municipal News*, XVII (December 1967), p. 2.

"Chicago Getting Two More Median-Strip Transit Lines," *Railway Age*, December 4, 1967, pp. 28-30.

"Chicago Plans New Rail-to-Rail Links," *Railway Age*, November 3, 1969, p. 22.

"Chicago's Lucky Train Riders," *Railway Age*, September 6, 1965, p. 38.

"Chicago's Median Course," *Railway Age*, December 2, 1968, pp. 28-29.

"Clear Track Ahead for Airporters?" *Railway Age*, December 2, 1968, pp. 28-29.

"Cleveland: CTS Is Set to Go," *Railway Age*, Aug. 1, 1966, pp. 15-16.

"Competing Modes Will Get Tougher," *Railway Age*, February 13, 1967, pp. 36-37.

"Comprehensive Appraisal of Research Needs in the Search for Greater Rail Transport Efficiency," *Railway Age*, September 21, 1966, pp. 32-35.

"Corridor Cars Get Ready for 150 m.p.h. Tests," *Railway Age*, November 14, 1966, pp. 15-17.

"Do Fast Trains Have a Real Future?" *Business Week*, January 25, 1969, pp. 92-98.

" 'Extracar' Drive Boosts Riders, Revenues for L.A. Transit District," October 10, 1966, p. 92.

"Freeway Congestion," *Engineering News Record*, November 20, 1969, p. 34.

"Free Transit: A Way Out of Traffic Jams," *Business Horizons*, Spring, 1965.

"Future of Mass Transportation," *Dun's Review and Modern Industry*, June 2, 1965, pp. 158A-158C.

"Gearing Rails for Modern Passenger Transportation," *Commercial and Financial Chronicle*, August 18, 1966, p. 595.

"Golden Gate Bridge Agency in the Transit Business," *Engineering News Record*, November 20, 1969, p. 44.

"High-Speed Rail Link Mapped in Pennsylvania," *Railway Age*, May 1, 1967, pp. 18-20.

"High-Speed Transit for Megalopolis," *Public Utilities Fortnightly*, August 19, 1965, pp. 54-56.

"Highways in a Broader Context," *Engineering News*, March 23, 1967, p. 31.

"How Baltimore Tamed the Highway Monster," *Fortune*, February, 1970, p. 129.

"How CTA Halted a Decline," *Railway Age*, September 6, 1965, pp. 15-19.

"How Ivan Gets Home," *Business Week*, August 15, 1964, pp. 98-100.

"How Leading Authorities View Outlook for Railroad Industry," *Commercial and Financial Chronicle*, August 18, 1966, p. 593.

"I.C. Proposes Bi-travel Electric M-U's," *Railway Age*, August 5, 1968, p. 19.

"Japan Sets a Rapid Pace," *Railway Age*, May 11, 1970, p. 38.

"Japan's Secret Weapon?" *Forbes*, April 15, 1970, p. 9.

"Los Angeles Works to Ease Road Jams," *Aviation Week*, November 14, 1966, p. 55.

"Long Island Rail Road Begins Test of Budd Turbine," *Railway Age*, October 3, 1966, p. 34.

"More Traffic in Towns," *Economist*, December 10, 1966, p. 1119.

"New Car Registrations Crash 9.4 Million Barrier in 1968," *Ward's Automotive Reports*, February 24, 1969, p. 1.

"New England's Future Geared to Transport," *Railway Age*, December 20-27, p. 33.

"New York's Rail Bus," *Science Digest*, January, 1970, pp. 88-89.

"Northeast Corridor: Cars Are a Big Factor," *Railway Age*, July 18, 1966, p. 20.

"Northeast Corridor Test Results Will be Crucial," *Railway Age*, June 27, 1966, p. 668.

"Northwest Passage Will Speed Travel for Chicago Commuters," *Railway Age*, November 7, 1966, p. 21.

"Pace of Activity Rises Steadily: Transit at Midyear," *Railway Age*, July 3-10, 1967, pp. 37-38.

"Penn-Central Gets Most Sophisticated Commuter Cars," *Railway Age*, October 7, 1968, p. 21.

"Philadelphia Gets Set for Added Transit Lines," *Railway Age*, May 6, 1968, pp. 21-22.

"Rails Accrue 'Incremental' Passenger Train 'Profit'; Data Held Not True Measure," *Traffic World*, October 5, 1968, p. 92.

"Rail Transit: Another Year of Breakthroughs," *Railway Age*, July 4, 1966, pp. 30-31.

"Railway Age Weekly," *Railway Age*, May 16, 1966, p. 37.

"Research: Key to Superior Railroads," *Railway Age*, October 3, 1966, pp. 84-85.

"Role of Railroads in High-Speed and Mass Transportation," *Public Utilities Fortnightly*, September 15, 1966, pp. 82-85.

"San Francisco: Transportation Needs Found Close to Home," *Engineering News Record*, May 12, 1966, p. 26.

"Saving New York from Strangling," *Business Week*, March 9, 1968, p. 64.

"Skokie Gets Them Coming and Going," *Railway Age*, October 7, 1968, pp. 18-19, 24.

"Skokie Swift Is a Success," *Railway Age*, September 6, 1965, pp. 19, 22.

"Staving Off Auto Paralysis," *Business Week*, February 28, 1970, p. 54.

"South Jersey Transit Cars Designed for New Service," *Railway Age*, May 6, 1968, pp. 19-20.

"Stockholm Transit Accents Design," *Railway Age*, February 6, 1967, p. 21.

"Systems Approach Is Vital for Future," *Railway Age*, May 8, 1967, pp. 30-31.

"The Story Behind the Commuter Crisis," *Business Week*, March 14, 1970, p. 60.

"Tide Turns for Transit," *Business Week*, October 20, 1962, p. 76.

"Tokyo-Yokohama Freeway," *Tokyo Municipal News*, XVIII (October 1968), p. 1.

"Toronto Experiments with 6 Transit Cars," *Railway Age*, February 18, 1970, p. 56.

"Toronto Opens New 8-Mile Subway Line," *Railway Age*, March 7, 1966, pp. 23-24.

"Toronto's Total Approach to Transit," *Railway Age*, June 3, 1968, pp. 17-19.

"Toronto Transit: New from the Word GO," *Railway Age*, May 1, 1967, pp. 24-25.

"Traffic Casualties," *Tokyo Municipal News*, XVIII (August 1968), p. 1.

"Transit: Dirt Will Fly in 1969," *Railway Age*, January 6-13, 1969, pp. 22-23, 26.

"Transit Line Gets on Track in Philadelphia," *Business Week*, September 28, 1968, pp. 162-168.

"Transit Turns a Corner in 1967," *Railway Age*, January 2/9, 1967, pp. 39, 44.

"Transport on and off the Road," *The Economist*, December 3, 1966, pp. 1025-1026.

"Transportation 1967: Special Report," *Modern Industry*, April 1967, pp. 1-124.

"Transportation Planning Questioned by CED," *Public Utilities Fortnightly*, May 27, 1965, pp. 59-60.

"Transportation Research Booms," *Engineering News Record*, May 12, 1966, pp. 21-23.

"Transportation Research Receives Mellon Grant," *Engineering News*, April 13, 1967, pp. 36-37.

"Transportation: Techniques and Trends," *Engineering News*, January 26, 1967, pp. 74-76.

"Transportation: Techniques and Trends," *Engineering News Record*, May 12, 1966, pp. 82-90.

"Transportation: The Cities Can Be Beautiful," *Engineering News*, October 27, 1966, pp. 18-19.

"Trends in Transportation," *Modern Industry*, February 1967, pp. 113-115.

"Tri-state Comes Up With Transport Plan," *Railway Age*, May 30, 1966, p. 112.

"Turbo Train and the Metroliner: On the Right Track?" *Railway Age*, May 20, 1968, pp. 26-31.

"Turbo Trains Set for Boston Service," *Railway Age*, November 4, 1968, p. 16.

"Uneasy Riders," *Newsweek*, February 9, 1970, p. 59.

"Urban Transit Picks Up Some Speed," *Business Week*, September 22, 1969, p. 60.

"Where Commuting by Train Is a Pleasure," *Business Week*, January 3, 1970, p. 53.

"Whys and Hows of Transit Get a Going-Over at Boston Meeting," *Railway Age*, July 4, 1966, p. 32.

"Year of the Carrier," *Dun's Review and Modern Industry*, May 2, 1966, pp. 102-103.

Asher, Joe. "Bart's Growing Pains," *Railway Age*, March 7, 1966.

"Boston: Lots of Plans—But Also Lots of Action," *Railway Age*, November 4, 1968, pp. 14-15.

"One Line—Maybe More," *Railway Age*, September 2, 1968, pp. 25-27.

"Transit Gets on the Ballot—Cautiously," *Railway Age*, August 5, 1968, pp. 25-26.

Barber, R. J. "Technological Change in American Transportation—The Role of Government Action," *Virginia Law Review*, L (June, 1964), pp. 824-889.

Bartley, Robert. "Illinois-Central Proposes Bi-Level Electric M-U's," *Railway Age*, August 5, 1968, pp. 16-19.

Blaine, J.C.D. "Problems of Coordination and Harmonization of Transport in the Common Market," *American Business Law Journal*, III (Winter 1965), p. 45ff.

"The Role of the ICC in the Administration of National Transportation Policy," *North Carolina Law Review*, XLIV (1965), pp. 357-379.

Bretey, Pierre R. "The Railroad Renaissance: Cyclical or Fundamental?" *Journal of Financial Analysts*, XXII (May-June 1966), pp. 35-38.

Buck, H. W. "Evaluation of Alternative Transportation Proposals: The Northeast Corridor," *American Institute of Planners Journal*, XXXII (November 1966), pp. 332-333.

Campbell, M. Earl. "Highway Traffic Safety—Is It Possible?" *Traffic Quarterly*, July 1965, pp. 333-354.

Dreher, Carl. "Is It Back to the Rails?" *Nation*, Vol. 203, No. 1 (July 4, 1966), pp. 11-15.

Edwards, L. K. "High-Speed Tube Transportation," *Scientific American*, CCXIII (August, 1965), pp. 30-40.

Faltermayer, Edmund K. "The Rail Route to a More Mobile America," *Fortune*, July, 1966, pp. 107-109ff.

Farmer, Richard N. "Whatever Happened to the Jitney?" *Traffic Quarterly*, April 1965, pp. 263-279.

First National City Bank, N.Y. "From Metropolis to Megalopolis," *Monthly Economic Letter*, June 1965, pp. 63-66.

Galton, Lawrence. "Commuting at 1,000 m.p.h.," *New York Times Magazine*, October 24, 1965, pp. 76-77 ff.

Gilliland, W. "CAB Coordination of Unlike Modes of Transportation," *Public Utilities Fortnightly*, September 2, 1965, pp. 15-28.

Gormley, W. P. "Urban Redevelopment to Further Aesthetic Conditions," *Law and Contemporary Problems*, XXX (Winter 1965), pp. 2ff.

Gottfield, Gunther M. "Rapid Transit Expansion in Stockholm, Sweden," *Traffic Quarterly*, October 1964, pp. 576-588.

Gunzburg, M. L. "Transportation Problems of the Megapolitan," *UCLA Law Review*, XII (March 1965), p. 800 ff.

Hendrix, Frank. "Federal Transport Statistics: An Analysis," *Transportation Journal*, V (Fall 1965), pp. 5-15.

Houser, F. N. "Metropolitans: $130 Million for 620 Commuter Coaches," *Railway Age*, December 2, 1968, pp. 19-20, 22.

"Turbotrain: Can It Put Profit in Passengers?" *Railway Age*, June 19, 1967, pp. 25-28.

Hoyt, Homer. "Effect of the Automobile on Patterns of Urban Growth," *Traffic Quarterly*, April 1963, pp. 293-301.

Kagayama, Tomoo. "Commuter Traffic in Tokyo and Osaka," *Traffic Quarterly*, October 1965, pp. 609-622.

McKenna, David. "Commuting in the 1970's," *Institute of Transport Journal*, XXXII (March 1967), pp. 87-93.

Martin, Clarence D., Jr. "The Northeast Corridor—Widening the Planning Range," *Traffic Quarterly*, April 1965, pp. 155-163.

Lewis, R. G. "New Tokaido Line: Japan's Billion-Dollar Gamble Pays Off," *Railway Age*, January 23, 1967, pp. 24-26.

Lloyd, F. S., "Planning Bus Services in Congested Cities," *Institute of Transport Journal*, XXXII (January 1967), pp. 52-57.

Mayer, Harold M. "Some Observations on the Future of Cities and Urban Areas," *Traffic Quarterly*, July 1964, pp. 371-382.

Nelson, Robert A. "Railroad Mergers and Public Policy," *Land Economics*, XLI (1965), pp. 183-188.

"Remarks at Case Institute of Technology, Cleveland, Ohio," Presented at BRT Conference on Mass Transit, Chicago, 1966.

Norton, H. S. "Survival of the Common Carrier," *Public Utilities Fortnightly*, LXXVI (September 2, 1965), pp. 29-42.

Owen, W. "Transportation and the City," *Transportation Journal*, VI (Winter 1966), pp. 24-32.

Ray, Ron. "Where Do We Go from Here?" *Distribution Manager*, April 1967, pp. 41-44.

Regional Planning Association, Inc. *Population—1954-1975 in the New York-New Jersey-Connecticut Metropolitan Region*, Bulletin #85.

Reuss, Henry S. "A Breakthrough in New Urban Transport Systems," *Traffic Quarterly*, January 1, 1966, pp. 21-30.

Robinson, Charlton C. "Freeways in the Urban Setting," *Traffic Quarterly*, July 1963, pp. 432-438.

Rose, A. "Decade of Metropolitan Government in Toronto," *Buffalo Law Review*, XIII (Spring 1964), pp. 539ff.

Rose, J. R. "Regulation of Rates and Intermodal Transport Competition," *ICC Practitioners Journal*, XXXIII (October 1965), p. 11ff.

Schenker, Eric, and Wilson, John. "The Use of Public Mass Transportation in the Major Metropolitan Areas of the United States," *Land Economics*, XLIII (August, 1967), p. 362.

Schramm, F. B. "Inventions, Anyone?" *Distribution Manager*, April 1967, pp. 24-31.

Schmandt, J., and Ross, Stephen G. "Public Transportation and the Worker," *Traffic Quarterly*, October 1963, pp. 573-583.

Shaw, R. B. "At Last—A New Rapid Transit Program for Cities and Suburban Areas," *Magazine of Wall Street*, July 10, 1965, pp. 400-403.

Singer, Russell E. "Future Role of the Automobile in Urban Transportation," *Traffic Quarterly*, April 1964, pp. 156-168.

Smerk, George M. "Demand Considerations in Urban Transportation," *Traffic Quarterly*, July 1964, pp. 421-422.

         "Federal Urban Transport Policy," *Traffic Quarterly*, January, 1967, pp. 29-52.

Smith, R. D. "Reshaping London's Bus Services," *Institute of Transport Journal*, XXXII (September 1968), pp. 450-455.

Thaler, David. "Is There a Better Way to Get to the Airport?" *Railway Age*, March 9, 1970, pp. 24-25

Vuchic, Vukan R. "Role of Transportation in Hamburg, Germany," *Traffic Quarterly*, January 1964, pp. 118-140.

Ward, Barbara. "Cities for 3,000 Million People," *The Economist*, July 8, 1967, pp. 112-121.

Wilson, George W. "The I.C.C. Profit Criteria—Rail vs. Truck," *Transportation Journal*, VI (Fall 1966), pp. 17-19.

Yafee, Michael. "Aerospace Technology Filling Major Role in High-speed Ground Transport Programs," *Aviation Week and Space Technology*, September 30, 1968, pp. 40-66.

Newspapers

"An Economy Wave Stalls Transport," *New York Times*, August 6, 1967, p. 14.

"Battle of the Bottleneck Rumbling On," *New York Times*, June 28, 1970, p. 5.

"Bergen to Oslo by Rail," *New York Times*, August 20, 1967. Section 10, p. 1.

"High-speed Train Motor Is in Works," *Los Angeles Times*, Wire Service, August 21, 1967.

"Nassau Presents Broad Program for Improving Transportation," *New York Times*, August 7, 1967.

"New Plan on Hudson Crossings: No Toll West, Double Toll East," *New York Times*, July 24, 1970, p. 50.

"Pennsy Hopes High-Speed Test Will Transform Trains from Work to Show Horses," *New York Times*, August 28, 1967, p. 25.

"Rail Passenger Income Led Costs in 1954-1966, ICC Study Asserts," *Wall Street Journal*, October 2, 1968, p. 12.

"Rapid Shows Slight Rise," *Cleveland Plain Dealer*, July 17, 1966.

"Text of the Message on Transportation Sent to Congress by President Johnson," *New York Times*, March 3, 1966, p. 20C

"Three Big Airlines Bid to Cut Flights on Some Routes," *Wall Street Journal*, August 31, 1970.

"Three Cities Will Vote on Rapid Transit," *New York Times*, October 20, 1968, p. 84.

"270 Modern Cars Ordered by L.I.R.R. to Speed Service," *New York Times*, August 28, 1967, p. 24.

"U.S. Railroad Plan Is Not Enough," *Los Angeles Times*, December, 1970.

"Washington's Too-Limited Flyer," *Cleveland Plain Dealer*, August 29, 1967.

Bartley, Robert. "San Francisco Area Sets Transit Pace," *Wall Street Journal*, May 20, 1966, p. 14.

Bedingfield, Robert. "High-Speed Train to Capitol Due this Year," *New York Times*, October 11, 1968, pp. 45, 75.

Chapin, Emerson. "Japan Expanding Modern Rail Net," *New York Times*, August 18, 1968, p. 9.

Levine, Richard J. "Better Transportation Out of Ghettos Sought by U.S. Local Groups," *Wall Street Journal*, August 16, 1968, p. 1.

Lissner, William. "Regional Plan Official Assails Transit Programs As Inadequate," *New York Times*, March 9, 1968, p. 21.

McAllister, William. "San Francisco's Hopes in Transit Skill Riding on the Streetcar," *Wall Street Journal*, March 30, 1970, p. 4.

Mlachak, Norman. "Freeways Alone Cannot Solve All Problems of Mass Transit," *Cleveland Press*, April 5, 1965, p. A4.

———. "Hyde Suggests Transfer of Transit System to the County," *Cleveland Press*, April 7, 1966, p. 1.

———. "Thousands More Need Way Downtown," *Cleveland Press*, April 4, 1966.

Sabath, Donald. "Subway is Key to Toronto Spurt," *Cleveland Plain Dealer*, July 10, 1966.

Schanberg, Sydney. "Ronan Lays Transit Crisis to a 30-year Lag in City," *New York Times*, August 25, 1968, p. 1.

Treon, William C. "Rapid: Blessing or Hokum?" *Cleveland Plain Dealer*, July 17, 1964, p. 1.

Government Role in Transportation

Texts

Board of Investigation and Research. *Federal Regulatory Restrictions Upon Motor and Water Carriers*. S. Doc. 78, 79th Cong., 1st Sess., 1945.

Black, Robert C., III. *Railroads of the Confederacy*, Chapel Hill: The University of North Caroline Press, 1952.

Brotherhood of Railroad Trainmen. *1966 Conference on Mass Transportation*. Cleveland, Ohio, 1967.

———. *1967 Conference on Mass Transportation*, Cleveland, Ohio, 1968.

———. *1968 Conference on Public Transportation*, Cleveland, Ohio, 1968.

Conant, Michael. *Railroad Mergers and Abandonments*, Berkeley and Los Angeles: University of California Press, 1964.

Dearing, Charles L., and Owen, Wilfred. *National Transportation Policy*, Washington, D.C.: Brookings Institution, 1949.

Department of Transportation. *Third Annual Report/1969. Western Railroad Mergers*. Office of the Assistant Secretary for Policy Development and the Federal Railroad Administration. Washington, D.C.: U.S. Government Printing Office, 1969.

Dixon, Frank H. *Railroads and Government*, New York: Charles Scribner's Sons, 1922.

Federal Aviation Administration. *Statistical Handbook*, 1967. Washington, D.C.: U.S. Government Printing Office.

Federal Coordinator of Transportation. *Public Aids to Transportation*, Vol. II, Washington D.C.: U.S. Government Printing Office, 1938.

Fishlow, Albert. *American Railroads and the Transformation of the Ante-Bellum Economy*, Cambridge, Massachusetts: Harvard University Press, 1965.

Fogel, Robert William. *Railroads and American Economic Growth: Essays in Econometric History*, Baltimore, Maryland: The Johns Hopkins Press, 1964.

————. *The Union Pacific Railroad: A Case in Premature Enterprise*, Baltimore, Maryland: The Johns Hopkins Press, 1960.

Friedlaender, Ann F. *The Dilemma of Freight Transport Regulation*, Washington, D.C.: Brookings Institution, 1969.

Fromm, Gary, ed. *Transport Investment and Economic Development*, Washington, D.C.: Brookings Institution, 1965.

Goodrich, Carter. *Government Promotion of American Canals and Railroads 1800-1890*, New York: Columbia University Press, 1960.

Heath, Milton S. *Constructive Liberalism, The Role of the State in Economic Development in Georgia to 1860*, Cambridge, Massachusetts: Harvard University Press, 1954.

ICC Administration of the Motor Carrier Act. Hearings before the Senate Select Committee on Small Business. 84th Cong., 1st Sess., November 30-December 2, 1955.

Interstate Commerce Commission. *81st Annual Report of the ICC*, 1967.

Johnson, Arthur M., and Supple, Barry E. *Boston Capitalists and Western Railroads*, Cambridge, Massachusetts: Harvard University Press, 1967.

Locklin, D. Philip. *Economics of Transportation*, Sixth Edition, Homewood, Illinois: Richard D. Irwin, Inc., 1966.

Long-Range Maritime Program. Hearings before the Subcommittee on Merchant Marine of the Committee on Merchant Marine and Fisheries, 90th Cong., 2nd Sess., Washington, D.C.: U.S. Government Printing Office, 1968.

Lyon, Peter. *To Hell in a Day Coach*. Philadelphia: J. B. Lippincott Company, 1968.

MacGill, Caroline E., et al. *History of Transportation in the United States Before 1860*, Peter Smith, 1948, Murray Printing Co., Cambridge, Mass.

Message from the President of the United States. *Transportation System of Our Nation*, House Document No. 384, 87th Cong., 2nd Sess., April 5, 1962.

Meyer, John R., et al. *The Economics of Competition in the Transportation Industry*, Cambridge, Massachusetts: Harvard University Press, 1959.

National Bureau of Economic Research. *Transportation Economics*, New York: Columbia University Press, 1965.

National Transportation Policy (Doyle Report). Preliminary Draft of a Report to the Senate Committee on Interstate and Foreign Commerce, 87th Cong., 1st Sess., Washington, D.C.: U.S. Government Printing Office, 1961.

Nelson, James C. *Railroad Transportation and Public Policy*, Homewood, Illinois: Richard D. Irwin, Inc., 1963.

1968 National Highway Needs Report. Report to the Committee on Public Works, 90th Cong., 2nd Sess., Washington, D.C.: U.S. Government Printing Office, February 1968.

Pegrum, Dudley F. *Transportation: Economics and Public Policy*, Homewood, Illinois: Richard D. Irwin, Inc., 1963.

Problems of the Railroads (Smathers Report). Report of Subcommittee on Surface Transportation, Commission on Interstate and Foreign Commerce, U.S. Senate, 85th Cong., 2nd Sess., Washington, D.C.: U.S. Government Printing Office.

Reck, Franklin M. *The Romance of American Transportation*, New York: Crowell, 1962.

Report on Regulatory Agencies to President-Elect (Landis Report). Senate Committee on the Judiciary, 86th Cong., 2nd Sess., Washington, D.C.: U.S. Government Printing Office, December, 1960.

Review of ICC Practices and Policies. Hearings before the Subcommittee on Surface Transportation of the Committee on Commerce, U.S. Senate, 91st Cong., 1st Sess., on review of Interstate Commerce Commission Policies and Practices, Washington, D.C.: U.S. Government Printing Office, 1969.

Revision of Federal Transport Policy (Weeks Report). Report of Presidential Advisory Committee on Transport Policy and Organization, Washington, D.C.: U.S. Government Printing Office, 1955.

Ruppenthal, Karl M., ed. *Issues in Transportation Economics*, Columbus, Ohio: Charles E. Merrill Books, Inc., 1965.

Salisbury, Stephen. *The State, the Investor, and the Railroad: The Boston & Albany, 1825-1867*, Cambridge, Massachusetts: Harvard University Press, 1967.

Sampson, Roy J., and Farris, Martin T. *Domestic Transportation: Practice, Theory and Policy*, Boston: Houghton Mifflin Company, 1966.

Scheiber, Harry N., ed. *United States Economic History*, New York: Alfred A. Knopf, 1964.

Shannon, Fred. *The Farmer's Last Frontier*, Vol. V. of *The Economic History of the United States*, Edited by Henry David et al., 9 Vols., New York: Rinehart & Company, Inc., 1951.

Sharfman, I. L. *The Interstate Commerce Commission*, 4 Vols., New York: The Commonwealth Fund, 1931-1937.

Smerk, George M. *Urban Transportation: The Federal Role*, Bloomington: Indiana University Press, 1965.

Stover, John F. *The Railroads of the South, 1865-1900*, Chapel Hill: University of North Carolina Press, 1955.

Taylor, George Rogers, and Neu, Irene D. *The American Railroad Network, 1861-1890*, Cambridge, Massachusetts: Harvard University Press, 1956.

Taylor, George Rogers. *The Transportation Revolution, 1815-1860. Vol. IV of The Economic History of the United States,* Edited by Henry David et al., 9 Vols., New York: Rinehart & Company, Inc., 1951.

Throm, Edward L. *Popular Mechanics' Picture History of American Transportation*, New York: Simon and Schuster, 1952.

U.S. Bureau of the Census, *Annual Budget of the U.S.*

U.S. Department of Commerce. *Federal Transportation Policy and Program* (Mueller Report), Washington, D.C.: U.S. Government Printing Office, March 1960.

United Transportation Union, *1970 Conference on Mass Transportation*, Cleveland, Ohio, 1970.

Williams, Dr. E. W., Jr. *Regulation of Rail-Motor Rate Competition*, New York: Harper and Brothers, 1958.

Winther, Oscar. *The Transportation Frontier: Trans-Mississippi West 1865-1890*, New York: Holt, Rinehart and Winston, 1964.

Periodicals
"After Penn Central, Who Next?" *Newsweek,* July 6, 1970.

"L.A. Airport Expansion Bond Sale Approved," *Aviation Week and Space Technology*, August 5, 1968, p. 47.

"Bay Area Waits for the Train," *Business Week*, May 11, 1968, pp. 164-166.

"Can Marriage Save the Erie Lack?" *Business Week*, March 30, 1968, pp. 138-140.

"Crisis Facing Air Travel," *U.S. News and World Report*, August 5, 1968, pp. 27-29.

"Gavel Pounding, Congressional Shouting Highlights Hearing on Railroad Loan Guarantees," *Daily Traffic World*, June 24, 1970, p. 1.

"Gremlins Slow High-Speed Trains," *Business Week*, August 3, 1968, pp. 104-105.

"High Cost of Money Hurts the Penn Central," *Business Week*, June 6, 1970, pp. 106-107.

"House Clears Maritime Program Bill," *Daily Traffic World*, May 26, 1970, p. 1.

"Is the Passenger Train Riding Into History?" *Business Week*, July 13, 1968, pp. 128-129.

"Lockheed Rolls Out Its Jumbo Jet," *Business Week*, March 2, 1968, pp. 78-84.

"Penn-Central, the Merger That Misfired," *U.T.U. News*, July 18, 1970, pp. 4-5.

"President Signs Highway Aid Measure," *Traffic World*, August 31, 1968, pp. 15-16.

"Saving New York from Strangling," *Business Week*, March 9, 1968, p. 64.

"STOL Runway Open at La Guardia Airport," *Aviation Week and Space Technology*, August 12, 1968, p. 44.

"The Penn Central's Troubles Branch Out," *Business Week*, June 20, 1970, pp. 92-94.

"The Railway Conglomerates," *The Magazine of Wall Street*, April 13, 1968, pp. 9-12.

"Transit Programs Get a New Driver," *Business Week*, June 29, 1968, p. 116.

"Uncle Sam, Can You Spare Millions?" *Time*, June 22, 1970, pp. 74-76.

"Webb Raps Value-of-Service Rates," *Traffic World*, March 10, 1962, pp. 16-19, 52.

Abend, Richard A. "Federal Aid to Municipal Transportation: Salvation or Pandora's Box?" *Business History Review*, XXXVI (Fall 1966), pp. 265-279.

Abrams, Richard A. "Brandeis and the New Haven-Boston & Maine Merger Battle Revisited," *Business History Review*, XXXVI (Winter 1962), pp. 408-430.

Adams, Walter. "The Role of Competition in the Regulated Industries," *American Economic Association Papers and Proceedings*, XLVII (May 1958), pp. 527-543.

Aitchison, Clyde B. "The Evolution of the Interstate Commerce Act: 1887-1937," *George Washington Law Review*, V (March 1937), pp. 289-403.

Allen, William H. "Section 408 of the Federal Aviation Act: A Study in Agency Law-Making," *Virginia Law Review*, XLV (November 1959), pp. 1073-1103.

Anderson, Eugene D.; Borghesani, Paul D.; and Towle, William H. "Ex Parte 230: The ICC 'Piggyback' Rulemaking Case," *ICC Practitioners' Journal*, XXXV (May-June 1968), pp. 616-651.

Aug, Stephen M. "3 Penn Central Chiefs Fired Over Debt Crisis," *Washington Star*, June 9, 1970.

Barber, Richard J. "Airline Mergers, Monopoly, and the CAB," *Journal of Air Law and Commerce*, XXVIII (Summer 1961), pp. 189-236.

Bard, Robert L. "The Challenge of Rail Passenger Service: Free Enterprise, Regulation, and Subsidy." *The University of Chicago Law Review*, XXXIV (Winter 1967), pp. 301-340.

Barnes, Donald K. "State Taxation of Interstate Commerce: Chaos and New Hopes," *Western Reserve Law Review*, XVI (June 1965), pp. 859-892.

———. "State Taxation of Interstate Commerce: Nexus and Apportionment." *Marquette Law Review*, XLVIII (Fall 1964), pp. 218-227.

Barrett, Colin. "Diversification or Scatteration," *ICC Practitioners' Journal*, XXXVII (January-February, 1970)..

Beard, Charles H. "Government Activities in Transportation," *ICC Practitioners' Journal*, XIX (May, 1952), pp. 796-804.

Beardsley, Peter T. "Restrictions Against Rail Entry into Other Transportation Fields," *Law and Contemporary Problems*, XXVII (Autumn 1959), pp. 643-652.

Beatty, Marion. "Railroad Regulation From 533 A.D. to 1958," *The Journal of the Bar Association of the State of Kansas*, XXVII (November 1958), pp. 186-193.

Behling, Burton N. "The Role of Cost in the Minimum Pricing of Railroad Services," *Journal of Business*, XXXV (October 1962), pp. 357-366.

Beverly, Phil C. "Railroad Mergers: The Forces of Intermodal Competition," *American Bar Association Journal*, L (July 1964), pp. 641-645.

Boies, David, Jr. "Experiment in Mercantilism: Minimum Rate Regulation by the Interstate Commerce Commission," *Columbia Law Review*, LXVIII (April 1968), pp. 599-663.

Boyd, Alan S. "The Promotion of Civil Aeronautics and the CAB." *Journal of Air Law and Commerce*, XXXI (Spring 1965), pp. 126-132.

———. "The Transportation Dilemma." *Virginia Law Review*, LIV (April 1968), pp. 428-434.

———. "The United States Department of Transportation," *Journal of Air Law and Commerce*, XXXIII (Spring 1967), pp. 225-233.

Boyd, Harper W., Jr. "Industrial Self-Regulation and the Public Interest," *Michigan Law Review*, LXIV (May 1966), pp. 1239-1254.

Braden, Charles W. "The Story of the Historical Development of the Economic Regulation of Transportation," *ICC Practioners' Journal*, XVIII (April 1952), pp. 659-690.

Brown, David A. "New York Congestion Spurs Defensive Response by Midwest Controllers," *Aviation Week and Space Technology*, August 12, 1968, pp. 41-42.

Brownlee, O.H., and Heller, W. W. "Highway Development and Financing," *American Economic Association Papers and Proceedings*, XLVI (May 1956), pp. 232-250.

Bunke, Harvey C. "A Critical Analysis of Some Aspects of Interstate Commerce Commission Rate Policy," *Land Economics*, XXXII (May 1956), pp. 134-143.

———. "The Status of Rate-Making," *Land Economics*, XXXVI (May 1960), pp. 129-141.

Burstein, Herbert. "Railroads and Motor Carriers—Competition or Coordination," *Villanova Law Review*, VII (Summer 1962), pp. 563-586.

Bush, John W. "Reflections on Competitive Rate-Making—1967," *ICC Practioners' Journal*, XXXV (March-April 1968), pp. 429-435.

Calkins, G. Nathan, Jr. "Federal-State Regulation of Aviation," *Virginia Law Review*, L (December 1964), pp. 1386-1402.

Campbell, Thomas C. "Agricultural Exemptions from Motor Carrier Regulation," *Land Economics*, XXXVI (February 1960), pp. 14-25.

Chandler, Alfred D. "Patterns of American Railroad Finance 1830-1850," *Business History Review*, XXVIII (September 1954), pp. 248-263.

Clarke, Owen, "State Federal Cooperative Regulation of Motor Carriers," *ICC Practitioners' Journal,* XXII (December 1954), pp. 197-202.

Cochran, Thomas C. "The Executive Mind: The Role of Railroad Leaders, 1845-1890," *Business History Review*, XXV (December 1951), pp. 230-241.

————. "Land Grants and Railroad Entrepreneurship," *Journal of Economic History*, I (1950), pp. 53-67.

————. "Nineteenth-Century Railroad Entrepreneurs: Competition and Cooperation," *Explorations in Entrepreneurial History*, III (October 1950), pp. 20-23.

Cohn, Eugene L. "Regulating the Trucking Industry," *Illinois Bar Journal*, XLVII (September 1959), pp. 9-17.

Coleman, William C. "The Evolution of Federal Regulation of Intrastate Rates: The Shreveport Rate Cases," *Harvard Law Review*, XXVIII (November 1914), pp. 34-81.

Cook, John Wesley. "State Net Income Taxation of Interstate Commerce," *Taxes*, XLII (August 1964), pp. 512-529.

Coyle, John J. "A Reconsideration of Value of Service Pricing," *Land Economics*, XLI (May 1965), pp. 193-199.

Craig, Peter S. "A New Look at Section 416 (b) of the Civil Aeronautics Act." *Journal of Air Law and Commerce*, XXI (Spring 1954), pp. 127-158.

Cramton, Roger C. "Diversification of Ownership in the Regulated Industries—The Folklore of Regulation." *American Bar Association Section of Antitrust Law Proceedings*, XIX (August 1961), pp. 362-373.

Dane, John, Jr. "A Solution to the Problem of State Taxation of Interstate Commerce," *Villanova Law Review*, XII (Spring 1967), pp. 507-534.

Davis, Howard W. "A Review of Federal Rate Regulation and Its Impact Upon the Railway Industry," *Land Economics*, XLIV (February 1968), pp. 1-10.

Dearing, Charles L. "Toll Road Rates and Highway Pricing," *American Economic Papers and Proceedings*, XLVII (May 1957), pp. 441-452.

————, and Owen, Wilfred. "The Reorganization of Transport Regulation." *American Economic Papers and Proceedings*, XL (May 1950), pp. 261-270.

Dodge, William. "Common Goals of Common Carriers—A Blueprint for Intermodal Coordination." *ICC Practioners' Journal*, XXXI (October 1963), pp. 15-27.

Dorazio, Michael. "Common Ownership of Intermodal Transportation: An Appraisal." *University of Pittsburgh Law Review*, XXVII (October 1965), pp. 85-101.

Doster, James F. "The Conflict Over Railroad Regulation in Alabama," *Business History Review*, XXVII (December 1954), pp. 329-342.

————. "Vicissitudes of the South Carolina Railroad, 1865-1878: A Case Study in Reconstruction and Regional Traffic Development," *Business History Review*, XXX (June 1956), pp. 175-196.

Douglas, Peter S. "The Economic Irrelevance of 'Common Ownership'," *ICC Practitioners' Journal*, July-August, 1969, p. 1795.

Ellis, David. "Comments on the Railroad Land Grant Legend in American History Texts," *The Mississippi Valley Historical Review*, XXXII (1945), pp. 557-563.

Farmer, Richard N. "Common Goals of Common Carriers—A Blueprint for Inter-Modal Coordination," *ICC Practitioners' Journal*, XXXI (November 1963), pp. 149-156.

Fields, Gordon B. "Constitutional Law-Taxation-Congressional Power to Regulate State Taxation of Interstate Commerce," *Oregon Law Review*, XLIV (February 1965), pp. 140-148.

Freas, Howard. "Aspects of Transportation Based on Regulatory Experience in the United States," *ICC Practioners' Journal*, Pt. I-II: XXVI (December 1958), pp. 273-291; XXVI (January 1959), pp. 385-423.

———. "Ratemaking Powers of the Interstate Commerce Commission," *The George Washington Law Review*, XXXI (October 1962), pp. 54-84.

Friendly, Henry J. "The Federal Administrative Agencies: The Need for Better Definitions of Standards," *Harvard Law Review*, LXXV (April 1962), pp. 1072-1091.

Fubrman, Fredrick E., and Buland, George L. "Integrated Ownership: The Case for Removing Existing Restrictions on Common Ownership of the Several Forms of Transportation," *The George Washington Law Review*, XXXI (October 1962), pp. 156-185.

Fulda, Carl H. "The Regulation of Aviation," *American Bar Association Section of Antitrust Law Proceedings*, XIX (August 1961), pp. 377-381.

Gates, Paul W. "The Homestead Law in an Incongruous Land System," *The American Historical Review*, XLI (July 1936), pp. 652-681.

———. "The Role of the Land Speculator in Western Development," *The Pennsylvania Magazine of History and Biography*, LXVI (July 1942), pp. 314-333.

Gelder, John W. "Air Law—The Federal Aviation Act of 1948," *Michigan Law Review*, LVII (June 1959), pp. 1214-1227.

Goldberg, Joseph. "Containerization as a Force for Change on the Waterfront," *Monthly Labor Review*, January, 1968, pp. 4-11.

Green, Fletcher M. "Origins of the Credit Mobilier of America," *The Mississippi Valley Historical Review*, XLVI (September 1959), pp. 238-251.

Hale, G. E., and Hale, Rosemary D. "Competition or Control: The Chaos in the Cases," *University of Pennsylvania Law Review*, CVI (March 1958), pp. 641-683.

———. "Competition or Control: Motor Carriers," *University of Pennsylvania Law Review*, CVII (April 1960), pp. 775-831.

———. "Competition or Control: Air Carriers," *University of Pennsylvania Law Review*, CIX (January 1961), pp. 311-360.

Hanscom, Jim. "Flight From Railroading," *The Exchange*, August, 1968, pp. 8-13.

Harbeson, Robert W. "New Perspectives in Transport Regulation: The Cabinet Committee Report," *Northwestern Law Review*, LII (September-October 1957), pp. 490-513.

———. "Recent Trends in Regulation of Intermodal Rate Competition in Transportation," *Land Economics*, XLII (August 1966), pp. 315-327.

———. "Some Allocational Problems in Highway Finance," *Transportation Economics*, Bureau of Economic Research, 1965, p. 155.

———. "Some Public Policy Issues in Regulated Industries: Commentary," *Land Economics*, XLI (May 1965), pp. 159-160.

———. "The Regulation of Interagency Rate Competition Under the Transportation Act of 1958," *ICC Practitioners' Journal*, XXX (December 1962), pp. 287-305.

———. "The Transportation Act of 1958," *Land Economics*, XXXV (May 1959), pp. 156-171.

Harris, Owen. "Introduction: Symposium on the Interstate Commerce Commission," *The George Washington Law Review*, XXXI (October 1962), pp. 1-28.

Hartman, Paul J. "State Taxation of Interstate Commerce: A Survey and an Appraisal," *Virginia Law Review*, XLVI (October 1960), pp. 1051-1120.

Healy, Kent T. "Discriminatory and Cost-Based Railroad Pricing," *American Economic Review Papers and Proceedings*, XLVII (May 1957), pp. 430-440.

————. "The Merger Movement in Transportation," *American Economic Papers and Proceedings*, LII (May 1962), pp. 436-444.

Hedges, James B. "Promotion of Immigration to the Pacific Northwest by the Railroads," *The Mississippi Valley Historical Review*, XV (September 1928), pp. 183-203.

Henry, Robert S. "The Railroad Land Grant Legend in American History Texts," *The Mississippi Valley Historical Review*, XXXII (September 1945), pp. 171-194.

Hilton, George. "The Decline of Railroad Commutation." *Business History Review*, XXXVI (Summer 1962), pp. 171-187.

Johnson, Joseph H., Jr. "The Proposed Federal Interstate Taxation Act," *The Alabama Lawyer*, XXXVII (July 1966), pp. 225-230.

Hutchins, J.G.B. "One Hundred and Fifty Years of American Navigation Policy," *Quarterly Journal of Economics*, LIII (February 1939), pp. 238-260.

Hutchinson, Everett. "Regulation-Stimulus or Stumbling Block." *ICC Practioners' Journal*, XXVII (September 1960), pp. 1069-1073.

Jones, William K. "Antitrust and Specific Economic Regulation: An Introduction to Comparative Analysis," *American Bar Association Section of Antitrust Law Proceedings*, XIX (August 1961), pp. 261-278.

———. "Interstate Trucking and the Legislative History of the Motor Carrier Act of 1935." *American Bar Association Section of Antitrust Law Proceedings*, XIX (August 1961), pp. 279-299.

Kennedy, C. J. "The Early Business of Four Massachusetts Railroads," *Business History Review*, Pt. I-IV (March 1951), pp. 52-72; XXV (June 1951), pp. 84-98; XXV (September 1951), pp. 188-203; XXV (December 1951), pp. 207-229.

Keyes, Lucille Sheppard. "The Protective Functions of Commission Regulation," *American Economic Association Papers and Proceedings*, XLVII (May 1958), pp. 544-552.

———. "A Reconsideration of Federal Control of Entry Into Air Transportation," *Journal of Air Law and Commerce*, XXII (Spring 1955), pp. 192-202.

Klein, Maury, and Yamamura, Kozo. "The Growth Strategies of Southern Railroads, 1865-1893," *Business History Review*, XLI (Winter 1967), pp. 358-377.

Landon, Charles E. "Technological Progress in Transportation on the Mississippi River System," *Journal of Business*, XXXIII (January 1960), pp. 43-62.

Lavelle, William J. "Our National Transportation Policy: The Need for Revision," *University of Pittsburgh Law Review*, XXVI (June 1965), pp. 781-793.

LeBaron, A.D. "The New Haven Decision and Interstate Commerce Commission Rate Prescription," *Land Economics*, XL (August 1964), pp. 324-331.

LeBaron, A.D. "The 'Theory' of Highway Finance: Roots, Aims, and Accomplishments," *National Tax Journal*, XVI (September 1963), pp. 307-319.

Leonard, W. N. "Discussion of Railroad Mergers and Public Policy," *Land Economics*, XLI (May 1965), pp. 189-192.

Levin, David R. "Federal Aspects of the Interstate Highway Program," *Nebraska Law Review*, XXXVIII (March 1959), pp. 377-406.

Levine, Harvey A. "The Railroad Industry's Experience Under Section 15a(3) of the Transportation Act of 1958," *ICC Practitioners' Journal*, XXXV (January-February 1968), pp. 252-267.

Levine, Michael E. "Is Regulation Necessary? California Air Transportation and National Regulatory Policy," *Yale Law Journal*, LXXIV (July 1965), pp. 1416-1447.

Liipfert, Eugene T. "Consolidation and Competition in Transportation: The Need for an Effective and Consistent Policy," *The George Washington Law Review*, XXXI (October 1962), pp. 106-135.

Lindahl, Martin L. "The Antitrust Laws and Transportation," *The Antitrust Bulletin*, XI (January-April 1966), pp. 37-90.

McCarney, Bernard J. "ICC Rate Regulation and Rail-Motor Carrier Pricing Behavior: A Reappraisal," *ICC Practitioners' Journal*, XXXV (July-August 1968), pp. 707-719.

McGehee, R. Bruce. "The Inherent Advantages of Carrier Modes Under The National Transportation Policy," *ICC Practioners' Journal*, XXXIV (July-August 1967), pp. 722-735.

McKean, Edwin L. R. "State Taxation of Interstate Commerce: The National Interest," *University of Pittsburgh Law Review*, XXVI (March 1965), pp. 579-592.

Mackie, David I. "Governmental Responsibilities in the Field of Local Burdens on Railroad Facilities," *Law and Contemporary Problems*, XXIV (Autumn 1959), pp. 653-669.

———— "The Necessity for a Federal Department of Transportation," *Journal of Public Law*, VIII (Spring 1959), pp. 1-46.

Maclay, Hardy K., and Burt, William C. "Entry of New Carriers into Domestic Trunkline Air Transportation," *Journal of Air Law and Commerce*, XXII (Spring 1955), pp. 131-156.

Magnuson, Warren G. "Motor Carrier Act of 1935: A Legislator Looks at the Law," *The George Washington Law Review*, XXXI (October 1962), pp. 37-53.

Martin, James W., and Pardue, Beulah Lea. "Comparative Tax Loads on Railroads in Nine Southern States," *National Tax Journal*, I (March 1948), pp. 25-30.

Maxwell, W. David. "The Regulation of Motor Carrier Rates by the Interstate Commerce Commission," *Land Economics*, XXXVI (February 1960), pp. 79-91.

Melton, Lee J., Jr. "Transport Coordination and Regulatory Philosophy," *Law and Contemporary Problems*, XXIV (Autumn 1959), pp. 622-642.

Meyer, John R. "Competition, Market Structure, and Regulatory Institutions in Transportation," *Virginia Law Review*, L (March 1964), pp. 212-230.

Morgan, Charles S. "Evaluation of Public Regulation: Discussion," *American Economic Association Papers and Proceedings*, XLVIII (May 1958), pp. 562-564.

Nelson, James C. "Effects of Public Regulation on Railroad Performance," *American Economic Association Papers and Proceedings*, L (May 1960), pp. 495-505.

————. "Highway Development, the Railroads, and National Transport Policy," *American Economic Association Papers and Proceedings*, XLI (May 1951), pp. 495-505.

————. "Policy Issues and Economic Effects of Public Aids to Domestic Transport," *Law and Contemporary Problems*, XXIV (Autumn 1959), pp. 531-556.

———. "The Pricing of Highway, Waterway and Airway Facilities," *American Economic Association Papers and Proceedings*, LII (May 1962), pp. 426-535.

Nelson, Robert A. "Railroad Mergers and Public Policy," *Land Economics*, XLI (May 1965), pp. 183-189.

———. "Rate-Making in Transportation—Congressional Intent," *Duke Law Journal*, MCMLX (Spring 1960), pp. 221-238.

O'Mahoney, Joseph S. "Legislative History of the Right of Entry in Air Transportation Under the Civil Aeronautics Act of 1938," *Journal of Air Law and Commerce*, XX (Summer 1953), pp. 330-350.

Owen, Charles L., and Plant, Albin M. "Merger in the Domestic Air Transport Industry," *Virginia Law Review*, XLVII (December 1962), pp. 1428-1466.

Pegrum, Dudley F. "The Economic Basis of Public Policy for Motor Transport," *Land Economics*, XXVIII (August 1952), pp. 244-263.

———. "Investment in the Railroad and Other Transportation Industries Under Regulation," *American Economic Association Papers and Proceedings*, XLVII (May 1957), pp. 416-429.

———. "Transportation Problems in the American Economy: A Discussion," *American Economic Association Papers and Proceedings*, LII (May 1962), pp. 447-449.

Phillips, Charles F. "Railroad Mergers: Competition, Monopoly, and Antitrust," *Washington and Lee Law Review*, I (Spring 1962).

Roberts, Merrill J. "The Motor Transportation Revolution," *Business History Review*, XXX (March 1956), pp. 57-95.

———. "Some Aspects of Motor Carrier Costs: Firm Size, Efficiency and Financial Health." *Land Economics*, XXXII (August 1956), pp. 228-238.

Rosenbaum, Irwin S., and Lilienthal, David E. "Motor Carrier Regulation: Federal, State and Municipal," *Columbia Law Review*, XXVI (December 1926), pp. 954-987.

Sabine, James E. "Constitutional and Statutory Limits on the Power to Tax," *Hastings Law Journal*, XII (August 1960), pp. 23-41.

Sanford, Val. "Motor Carrier Regulation—An Adventure in Federalism," *Vanderbilt Law Review*, XI (October 1958), pp. 987-1005.

Sarisky, Joseph L. "Sea and Air Subsidies: A Comparative Study," *Fordham Law Review*, XXXVI (October 1967), pp. 59-93.

———. "Transport Regulation and the Railroad Problem," *Southern Economic Journal*, XXXII (January 1957), pp. 256-271.

Sawyer, Charles. "The Government's Role in Transportation," *ICC Practioners' Journal*, XIX (May 1952), pp. 787-795.

Schary, Philip B. "The Civil Aeronautics Board and the All-Cargo Airlines: The Early Years," *Business History Review*, XLI (Autumn 1967), pp. 272-284.

———. "Competition, Regulation and the Air Freight Industry," *Journal of Air Law and Commerce*, XXX (Winter 1964), pp. 62-71.

Schoffer, Walter F. "State and Federal Power Over Vehicles in Interstate Commerce," *Oklahoma Law Review*, XII (August 1959), pp. 331-340.

Smerk, George M. "Subsidies for Urban Mass Transportation," *Land Economics*, XLI (February 1965), pp. 62-65.

Stern, Robert L. "The Commerce Clause and the National Economy, 1933-1946," *Harvard Law Review*, Pt. I-II; LIX (May 1946), pp. 646-693; LIX (July 1946), pp. 883-947.

Sutton, Robert M. "The Origins of American Land-Grant Railroad Rates," *Business History Review*, XL (Spring 1966), pp. 66-76.

Taylor, Benjamin B. "The Commission and Innovations in Ratemaking," *ICC Practioners' Journal*, XXXII (June 1965), pp. 776-781.

————. "Willis Report on Interstate Taxation: New Laws to Make Sweeping Changes," *The Journal of Taxation*, XXIII (December 1965), pp. 374-378.

Tierney, Paul J. "Can Transport Regulation Be Maintained Apart from Promotion?" *ICC Practioners' Journal*, XXXV (March-April 1968), pp. 400-406.

Tippy, Roger. "Review of Route Selections for Federal and State Highway Systems," *Montana Law Review*, XXVII (Spring 1966), pp. 131-150.

Tipton, Stuart G., and Gewirtz, Stanley. "The Effect of Regulated Competition on the Air Transport Industry," *Journal of Air Law and Commerce*, XXII (Spring 1955), pp. 157-191.

Watkins, Harold D. "Traffic Jam Defies Easy Solution," *Aviation Week and Space Technology*, August 12, 1968, pp. 40-41.

Webb, Charles A. "Changing Concepts and New Ideas in Ratemaking," *ICC Practioners' Journal*, XXXI (September 1964), pp. 1102-1106.

Wilson, George W. "Effects of Value-of-Service Pricing Upon Motor Common Carriers," *The Journal of Political Economy*, LXIII (August 1955), pp. 337-344.

————. "Nature of Competition in the Motor Transport Industry," *Land Economics*, XXXVI (November 1960), pp. 387-391.

Williams, Ernest W., Jr. "An Evaluation of Public Policy Toward the Railway Industry," *American Economic Association Papers and Proceedings*, XLI (May 1951), pp. 506-518.

———. "Some Aspects of the Problems of Intercarrier Competition," *Vanderbilt Law Review*, XI (October 1958), pp. 971-985.

Wheeler, James O. "Work Trip Length and the Ghetto," *Land Economics*, XLIV (February 1968), pp. 107-112.

Zook, Paul D. "Recasting the Air Route Pattern by Airline Consolidations and Mergers," *Journal of Air Law and Commerce*, XXI (Summer 1954), pp. 293-311.

Zimmerman, Edwin. "Carrier Mergers and the Relevance of Antitrust," *ICC Practitioners' Journal*, XXXIV (September-October 1967), pp. 958-963.

Newspapers

"Airlines V. CAB." *New York Times*, November 1, 1970, p. 2.

"Alleghany-Lake Central Merger Passed by CAB," *Wall Street Journal*, June 25, 1968, p. 2.

"B & M Board Will Urge Holders to Spurn Plan to Merge With N & W," *Wall Street Journal*, June 20, 1968, p. 3.

"ICC Delays Rail Rate Rises, Sets 3% Interim Boost," *Wall Street Journal*, June 20, 1968, p. 3.

"ICC Report Calls for Congressional Study of Rail Passenger Service, Tougher Laws," *Wall Street Journal*, June 27, 1968, p. 5.

"GOP Party Platform," *New York Times*, August 5, 1968.

"Great Western Road Sets Special Dividend of $7.3818 on Common," *Wall Street Journal*, June 20, 1968, p. 26.

"Luxury Liner Cruise Passengers Getting U.S. Bonus," *New York Times*, August 16, 1970, p. 78.

"Milwaukee Road Urges Court to Allow Merger of the Northern Lines," *Wall Street Journal*, June 25, 1968, p. 14.

"L & N Monon Railroads' Boards Vote Merger," *Wall Street Journal*, June 21, 1968, p. 11.

"N & W and C & O Roads Accept Justice Unit's Conditions for Merger," *Wall Street Journal*, July 9, 1968, p. 13.

"Penn Central's Chief Bids Shippers Accept a Freight Rate Boost," *Wall Street Journal*, July 9, 1968, p. 15.

"Penn Central to Spend More in 1968 to Improve Facilities for Freight," *Wall Street Journal*, July 3, 1968, p. 6.

"Senate Approves One Billion Dollars for Merchant Fleet," *New York Times*, September 20, 1970, p. 85.

"Supreme Court Upholds ICC's Decision in 'Ingot Molds' Railroad Rate Case," *Traffic World*, June 22, 1968, pp. 69-74.

"U.S. Is Studying Effect on Rails of Holding Firms," *Wall Street Journal*, June 29, 1970, p. 4.

Barber, Richard. "Technological Change in American Transportation: The Role of Government Action," *Virginia Law Review*, L, 1964, pp. 824-889.

Bedingfield, Robert E. "Pennsy: Bad Management or Ailing Industry Debated," *New York Times*, June 1970, Financial Section.
————"Railroad Orphan: Passenger Runs," *New York Times*, July 14, 1968, Sec. 3, p. 1.

Davies, Lawrence E. "Bay Area Transit Is Facing Delays," *New York Times*, August 18, 1968, p. 76.

Egehof, Joseph. "Why Penn Fell: Perlman," *Chicago Tribune*, June 28, 1970, p. 1.

Fandell, Todd E. "North Western-Great Western Train Rolls in First Step of Heineman's Master Plan," *Wall Street Journal*, July 1, 1968, p. 26.

Friedlander, Paul J.C. "That New Air Fare Tax—It's Sly," *New York Times*, July 5, 1970, Travel Section.

Levine, Richard J. "Better Transportation Out of Ghettos Sought by U.S. Local Groups," *Wall Street Journal,* August 16, 1968, p. 1.

Lindsey, Robert. "Small Towns Left Isolated As Airlines Cut Service," *New York Times,* September 20, 1970, p. 1.

Porter, Frank C. "A Penn Central Director's View: 'Poor and Inept Management'," *Washington Post,* June 26, 1970, p. 1.

Samuelson, Robert. "Diversion of Assets by Bails Is Probed," *Washington Post,* June 27, 1970, p. 1.

Shafer, Ronald G. "Efforts Grow to Ease Disruption from Roads Through Urban Areas," *Wall Street Journal,* June 27, 1968, p. 1.

Sullivan, Ronald. "Cahill Drafts Plan on Transportation," *New York Times,* October 2, 1970, p. 63.

INDEX

PLEASE TURN PAGE FOR SPECIAL OFFER

For four years, our union has sponsored Transportation Conferences at the University of Chicago. Papers and seminar reports of these Conferences have become classic references in the transportation field. The UTU Conference Reports containing session summaries and papers written by leading thinkers in the field, have always been sent free to a select list of libraries, educators, planners, and others. But the request for "extra copies" invariably followed, and in too many cases UTU had to answer, "Sorry—we're out." With the cooperation of Popular Library, we are reprinting the Conference series, plus a new "Handbook" of U.S. transportation, as a 5-volume paperback set—and offering them, with the publisher's permission, at cost before they go on regular retail at a price at least twice that of this special offer.

Charles Luna, President of UTU

NOW AVAILABLE AT $2.25

THE UTU TRANSPORTATION LIBRARY

● Full reports, including papers, of the 1966 (Overview), 1967 (Urban Transportation), 1968 (Government Role) and 1970 (U.S. Transportation Policy Needs) Conferences on Mass Transportation.

● The new "Handbook of Transportation in America," including history of American Transportation and a survey of government role.

Transportation Books
Popular Library Inc.
355 Lexington Avenue
New York, N.Y. 10017

Please send me_____sets of the UTU Transportation Library. I enclose $2.25 for each set ordered. After 10 days, if not completely satisfied, I may return the set for a full refund.

NAME_____TITLE_____

COMPANY (or School)_____

STREET_____

CITY_____STATE_____ZIP CODE_____